1784439

D1141935

ON THOM...

ON... ...EEK LOAN

...before th... ...st d...

On Thomas Hardy

Late Essays and Earlier

Peter Widdowson

First published in Great Britain 1998 by
MACMILLAN PRESS LTD
Houndmills, Basingstoke, Hampshire RG21 6XS and London
Companies and representatives throughout the world

A catalogue record for this book is available from the British Library.

ISBN 0–333–67997–0 hardcover
ISBN 0–333–67998–9 paperback

First published in the United States of America 1998 by
ST. MARTIN'S PRESS, INC.,
Scholarly and Reference Division,
175 Fifth Avenue, New York, N.Y. 10010

ISBN 0–312–21078–7

Library of Congress Cataloging-in-Publication Data
Widdowson, Peter.
On Thomas Hardy : late essays and earlier / Peter Widdowson.
p.   cm.
Includes bibliographical references (p.   ) and index.
ISBN 0–312–21078–7 (cloth)
1. Hardy, Thomas, 1840–1928—Criticism and interpretation.
I. Title.
PR4754.W465 1998
823'.8—dc21   97–26677
                                                              CIP

This book is printed on paper suitable for recycling and made from fully managed and
sustained forest sources.

10   9   8   7   6   5   4   3   2   1
07   06   05   04   03   02   01   00   99   98

Printed in Malaysia

For Neville and Pat Shrimpton

'When We Were Young'

Contents

Acknowledgements

The author and publishers wish to thank the following for permission to use copyright material: Manchester University Press for Peter Widdowson, 'Hardy in History: A Case Study in the Sociology of Literature', *Literature in History* (1983); Northcote House Publishers Ltd for parts of Peter Widdowson, 'Arabella and the Satirical Discourse in *Jude the Obscure*', from *Thomas Hardy* (Writers and their Work Series, 1976); Everyman's Library for parts of Peter Widdowson, 'Hardy's "Quite Worthless" Novel: *A Laodicean*', Introduction to *A Laodicean* by Thomas Hardy (forthcoming).

Every effort has been made to trace the copyright holders, but if any have been inadvertently overlooked the publishers will be pleased to make the necessary arrangement at the first opportunity.

Abbreviations

All page references to Hardy's novels are to the Macmillan 'New Wessex' editions of 1974–75 (since reprinted, with some variations in pagination). Details of the volumes used are given below. All other notes and references are keyed to the References at the end of the book. The standard collected editions of Hardy's shorter poems are Gibson (ed.) (1976) and Hynes (ed.) (1982, 1984a, 1985); however, most of the poems referred to in the present volume are included in Widdowson (ed.) (1996a).

The following abbreviations are used throughout – usually once the full title has already been given.

Ds	*The Dynasts* (1902–07), ed. Harold Orel (Macmillan, 'New Wessex' edition, 1978)
DR	*Desperate Remedies* (1871), with intro. by C. J. P. Beatty (Macmillan, 1975)
FMC	*Far from the Madding Crowd* (1874), with intro. by James Gibson (Macmillan, 1974/5)
HE	*The Hand of Ethelberta* (1876), with intro. by Robert Gittings (Macmillan, 1975)
HS	*Human Shows, Far Phantasies, Songs and Trifles* (1925)
Jude	*Jude the Obscure* (1896), with intro. by Terry Eagleton (Macmillan, 1974)
Laod.	*A Laodicean* (1881), with intro. by Barbara Hardy (Macmillan, 1975)
The Life	Florence Emily Hardy, *The Life of Thomas Hardy 1840–1928* (Macmillan, 1962, paperback edition 1975) (see note in References)
LLE	*Late Lyrics and Earlier with Many Other Verses* (1922)

MC   *The Mayor of Casterbridge* (1886), with intro. by F. B.
            Pinion (Macmillan, 1974/5)
MV   *Moments of Vision and Miscellaneous Verses* (1917)
PBE   *A Pair of Blue Eyes* (1873), with intro. by Ronald Blythe
            (Macmillan, 1975)
PPP   *Poems of the Past and the Present* (1901)
RN   *The Return of the Native* (1878), with intro. by J. C. S.
            Tremblett-Wood (Macmillan, 1974/5)
SC   *Satires of Circumstance, Lyrics and Reveries with
            Miscellaneous Pieces* (1914)
Tess   *Tess of the d'Urbervilles* (1891), with intro. by James
            Gibson (Macmillan, 1974/5)
TL   *Time's Laughingstocks and Other Verses* (1909)
T-M   *The Trumpet-Major* (1880), with intro. by Ray Evans
            (Macmillan, 1974/5)
TT   *Two on a Tower* (1882), with intro. by F. B. Pinion
            (Macmillan, 1975)
UGT   *Under the Greenwood Tree* (1872), with intro. by
            Geoffrey Grigson (Macmillan, 1974)
Ws   *The Woodlanders* (1887), with intro. by F. B. Pinion
            (Macmillan, 1974/5)
W-B   *The Well-Beloved* (1897), with intro. by J. Hillis Miller
            (Macmillan, 1975)
WP   *Wessex Poems and Other Verses* (1898)
WW   *Winter Words in Various Moods and Metres* (1928)

Introduction

One thing is clear: when asked as a youth what I wanted to be when I grew up, I did not answer 'a Hardy specialist'. And yet, so it seems, I have become one. That life is governed by fortuity has struck me forcibly – perhaps through spending too much time in the company of Thomas Hardy – while preparing the present volume. If I hadn't gone to Sweden in 1968 to take up my first lecturing post – never having read a word of Hardy – and hadn't met an English colleague who was teaching *Tess of the d'Urbervilles* (as I was also to do) to large groups of bemused Swedish students for whom fatalistic tragedy in rural Dorset was not a burning issue in their lives just then, who knows what I might have done and become? But my friend was obsessed by the questions of determinism and free will he saw *Tess* as principally raising, and on my very first evening in northern Sweden, I was introduced to *that* burning issue without more ado. So I read *Tess*; tried to explain what 'a blighted star' and 'the ache of modernism' might mean to young people whose own blights and aches had more to do with the consumption of *brenvin* and the pursuit of sex than with savouring *fin-de-siècle* angst; and discussed, deep into the long winter nights, how far Tess was a victim of, or instrumental in, her own 'Fate': did she jump or was she pushed? We never solved it – which perhaps helps to explain why I became 'a Hardy specialist'.

For Hardy remains a mystery to me in all sorts of ways, as will become clearer below; and if you find yourself spending large chunks of your professional life teaching and writing about one writer in particular, then it certainly helps if that writer remains a mystery to you. Right from the start, wrestling with *Tess* in Sweden, I knew that I could not explain even to myself wherein lay the force of that work: whether it said something Hardy meant or whether it conveyed all sorts of things Hardy did not mean at all; what kinds of characters Tess, Alec and Angel were (whether they were 'credible' or not); whether the narrative voice was straight, ironic or variably both – and, if so, when it stopped being the one and became the other; whether my friend was right that the novel was 'about' free will and determinism or whether it was really

1

about class and gender (I wouldn't have put it quite like that at the time); why the prose was so dense, rich, mannered, awkward, unstable – I could not even decide on a word to describe it (now I would resort to saying 'all of them'). As I read more of Hardy's fiction (the poetry was to follow much later – I'm not even sure I knew he was also a poet at that stage), my awe increased as the mystery deepened, and the questions became insistent: what *is* going on here? if it is good, *why* is it good (something told me that it would be perfectly possible for others to regard it as often thoroughly bad)? This puzzlement was compounded when I discovered that, in addition to the eight or so 'major' 'Wessex Novels', there were six 'minor' ones which, at that point, were not in print and were regarded by the *cognoscenti* at best as Hardy's juvenilia or failed 'experiments', at worst as entirely worthless. When it further became clear that novels like *The Hand of Ethelberta*, *A Laodicean* and *The Well-Beloved* were, in fact, scattered throughout Hardy's writing career, and that they showed all the hallmarks of his 'major' fiction, if in rather more extreme form, then my anxieties about explaining and evaluating his work deepened. Reading Hardy's critics did not help, either: indeed, they seemed crucially instrumental in establishing 'Hardy the Novelist' as the great comic-tragic realist of Love, Life and Death in rural Wessex – as long as one ignored his manifest 'flaws' and suppressed those perverse 'minor novels'.

The plot thickened even further when I learnt that after the publication of *Jude the Obscure* in 1895, and the book version of *W-B* in 1897, Hardy – seemingly at the height of his powers and fame as an author – gave up writing fiction and turned his attention to poetry for the last 30 years of his life. Why did he do this, I asked myself – surely not just because late-Victorian Mrs Grundies thought *Tess* and *Jude* beyond the moral pale? Eight volumes of verse – some 950 individual poems – followed, with Hardy's sixth volume, *Late Lyrics and Earlier* appearing in the same year (1922) as T. S. Eliot's *The Waste Land* and James Joyce's *Ulysses*. But this was to leave out *The Dynasts*, Hardy's vast epic poetic-drama written because 1902 and 1907, his first major task after giving up the novel, 'unstageable' in its entirety, and commingling realistic historical scenes from the Napoleonic Wars with the gnomic visions of supernatural spirits looking down (in both senses) on the aspirations and folly of humankind. What on earth (or off it) was Hardy up to?

More and more deeply mired in the problematics of Hardy's career and *oeuvre*, and back in England, discussing such with long-suffering groups of students, I was fascinated to learn that the 'standard' biography, by his second wife, Florence Emily, *The Life of Thomas Hardy 1840–1928*, had, in fact, been composed by Hardy himself in the 1920s, but to be passed off – it is written in the third person – as by his wife after his death. This text, then, demanded to be read, in some sense, as his last fiction, and a close reading does indeed reveal the extraordinary strategies, suppressions, occlusions, half-truths and evasions Hardy deployed in this piece of defensive self-fashioning – not least that he had always regarded himself as *really* a poet and that the novels (on which he had laboured for 30 years with obsessive care) were 'mere journeywork' in the 'trade'[1] of fiction written to earn a living. In addition to – literally – 'writing his life' as he wished it to be read, his apparent self-valorization of his novels, by placing them in different categories in the General Preface to the 'Wessex Edition' of his works in 1912, had also to be taken into account. So too did his, to me now clearly ironic and obfuscatory, prefaces to the novels and volumes of poems, and the fact that during his lifetime he compiled selections of his own poems – including the pre-emptively titled *Chosen Poems*. Once again, academia and criticism confused rather than clarified things: by continually arguing about whether Hardy was primarily poet or novelist, whether he was properly seen as a Victorian novelist or a Modern poet, or whether – despite the chronology – it was vice versa; and solving such debates by casting him as unequivocally 'transitional'.

But leaving aside which course 'Hardy' might appear on in education syllabuses ('The 19th-Century Novel', 'Modern English Poetry', 'Victorian Literature', 'English Literature 1880–1930'), it was clearly apparent, as I pursued my arcane labours through the 1970s, 1980s and into the 1990s, that Hardy was actually still 'Our Contemporary'. 'Hardy's Wessex' is an inescapable tourist attraction and is a crucial component of the heritage industry; he remains widely popular, both as poet and novelist, amongst a large and diverse reading-public; scores of editions of his works are currently in print, invariably with attractive covers invoking a 'lost' rural world; sophisticated contemporary criticism, theorized by Marxism, feminism and poststructuralism, now insistently 're-reads' Hardy's work as postmodern textuality traversed by troubled discourses of class and gender; and a growing number of his fictional works have been adapted for television and film – from John Schlesinger's 1960s pastoral, *Far from the Madding Crowd*, through the BBC serial of *The Mayor of Casterbridge* and Polanski's *Tess*, to the recent television version of *The Return of the Native*, the film of *Jude*, and the as yet unreleased film of *The Woodlanders*. What makes Hardy so popular? What do people find in/make of either his own works or the visual reproductions of them? What cultural and ideological meanings and values are ascribed to them? *Why does* Hardy remain 'Our Contemporary'? The essays in this volume provide some of my tentative and equivocal answers to these questions.

Perhaps Hardy was a good (lucky?) choice of author after all for a critic of broadly materialist persuasion, interested at once in cultural history, in the nature and function of 'literary studies', and in the close analysis of literary texts. 'Good little Thomas Hardy'[2] has allowed my sequestered self (not quite as remote from late-20th-century hurly-burly as 'Wessex', but, compared to less privileged participants, nearly so) to explore each of these in relation to a sizeable body of work which, while still mystifying its interpreter, has allowed for an empirical focus in our contemporary theoretical and method-ological maze. The essays collected in this volume are witness to the opportunity Hardy so fortuitously gave me. It may seem an odd tribute, but I suppose I should thank Sweden for Thomas Hardy.

* * * * *

There is a nagging sense that to collect together and edit one's own essays smacks of presumption, pretension and self-preoccupation. My excuses for doing so, however, are as follows: that the essays here have appeared over a period of about 15 years in a variety of diverse publications; that some, in fact, are new and, until now, un-published; that they are all part of the same general project, and thus comprise a fairly coherent *book*, rather than a merely eclectic compi-lation of disparate pieces – hence their nomination here as 'chap-ters'; and that they represent my anticipated signing-off from Hardy criticism, at least for a while. As I have noted elsewhere,[3] there seems to be a limit to what one can find new to say in one lifetime about any individual writer (however mystifying); and so to recycle what I have already said in the present format helps to prevent me recycling it in some other guise as though it were brand-new.

From my own perspective, the earliest essay here, 'Hardy in History: A Case-Study in the Sociology of Literature', is the most significant for a number of reasons. It was given as a conference paper, and then published in the journal *Literature and History*, in 1982/3 – at a point, in other words, when the newly-felt effects of contemporary critical theory were radically destabilizing 'English Studies' wherever its dominion had ruled, and it reflects my own attempt to participate in that process. I wanted to combine theory with empirical practice in replacing the old 'English' with something less 'ideologically innocent',[4] and my baffling bedfellow – originator of the 'Hardy industry' – seemed the ideal focus for it. The essay was also part of the wider 'Literature and History' project: of finding ways of studying literature and history interdisciplinarily, beyond the older 'text and context' model. Most importantly for me, however, it was the sketch, maquette, blueprint and dummy-run for both the larger piece of work which eventually became the book, *Hardy in History: A Study in Literary Sociology* (1989), and, as it turns out, for all the cognate pieces of work which make up the present volume. Although it shows signs of its age (as indeed does its author), I retain a soft spot for it and have let it stand almost exactly as it was when first published – precisely because it speaks as something of a period-piece. Apropos of this, I should add that, although the essay (and the later book) seem to have had some subsequent effect on the study of literature, it was, at that point, no more than one among several instances of the more general recognition that if the canon were to be dismantled, then a writer like Hardy (among other celebrities even more 'canonic') was indeed for turning. By 1982, Raymond Williams, John Goode and Terry Eagleton had all published innovative materialist criticism on Hardy, as had Mary Jacobus, Elaine Showalter and Patricia Stubbs from within feminism, and Penny Boumelha's book, *Thomas Hardy and Women: Sexual Ideology and Narrative Form*, came out in the same year.[5]

The other chapters in the book fill out that original sketch in different ways, but they all relate to each other. (This, I now realize, is borne out rather less persuasively by the fact that some ideas, forms of words and quotations reappear with unnerving regularity from essay to essay – but not, I hope, to the detriment of my overall case.) The essays' most apparent common component is the following-through, in each case, of the implications of my notion – first outlined in the essay mentioned above and developed more fully in the book of similar title – of a 'critiography' (never a pretty word) as lying at the heart of any reconstructed and scrupulous study of literature. This proposes that the authors and texts which we read at any particular historical moment are, in effect, constituted by the critical and cultural inscription they carry with them: be it the received critical wisdom, the 'Introductions' and 'Explanatory Notes' which invariably accompany modern editions of them, the pictorial covers which front them, their reproduction in other cultural forms and locales (journalism, radio, television, film, tourism), their place and representation in education syllabuses, or the perception of them that people may reveal in ordinary social intercourse. Before we can read 'the text', in other words, we need to understand how it has been discursively constructed for us already, and, if necessary, to strip away its naturalized accretions. This is not to suggest that we can thus restore some essential 'text in itself' which we then read 'correctly': on the contrary, it is to recognize and accept that any reading will be partial, provisional and historically determined – will be held, so to speak, within the horizons of possible comprehension the cultural formation makes available at any given historical moment. Thus each essay seeks to locate Hardy's works within the critical/cultural matrix which has already shaped them – this is especially evident in those which deal with the 'minor novels' and the poetry – and then to re-read them against their naturalized graining. In doing so, each reading offers itself only as an alternative way of perceiving Hardy's works – one which seeks to release them from inherited constraint on behalf of a more libertarian cultural politics – and therefore acknowledges its own unavoidable partiality.

Picking up this acceptance of being 'partial' (in both senses), the opening chapter of the book offers a synoptic account of Hardy's life and career, structured around three determinate 'themes' in it – war, class and sex – in order to give some sense of the complex nature of the author we have in hand and to establish reference points for later readings. Chapter 2 is the originary essay for my general approach discussed above. The third, on *HE*, develops the theme of Hardy's acute class-consciousness – especially in relation to the fraught, unstable mobility of what he here calls 'the metamorphic classes of society'[6] (and of which he himself was a member) – and proposes that this novel, rather than Florence Emily

Hardy's official 'biography', represents the true 'Life'. At the same time, the essay offers a detailed recuperative reading of one of Hardy's most despised 'minor novels', suggesting that, rather than being a grotesque failure of fictional decorum (and perversely ignoring 'Wessex'), its performative and self-reflexive artifice presents both a strategic challenge to conventional realism and an exposure of the destructive 'fictions' fostered by a class society. Similarly, Chapter 4 on *Laod.* explores the way Hardy's other 'quite worthless' novel may, in fact, be seen as at once a sophisticated, self-conscious mockery of the misrepresentations implicit in a realism which purports to 'tell things as they really are', and a further satire on the artifice/iality of a class system in volatile transition. Both chapters propose that the effect of such re-readings of these 'minor novels' is to bring into bold relief the presence of similar issues and fictional strategies in *all* the novels – not least, the 'major' ones. Chapter 5 goes to the other end of the canonic scale in presenting Hardy's arguably most celebrated 'tragic' novel, *Tess*, as one also focused on the dangerous conjuncture of members of the 'metamorphic classes'. But in addition, it sees Tess herself as not so much a 'character' in the realist mode, but rather as a textual amalgam of society's (primarily male sexual) images of her. In this, and in the novel's mannered and disrupted/ive textuality, the essay once more finds in *Tess* a critique of a realism premised on essentialist notions of character, and hence a kind of postmodernist fiction before its time.

Chapter 6 switches to Hardy's poetry, and offers a 'critiographical' and recuperative reading of it, showing how it has been shaped, trimmed and domesticated by critics and editors over the last 50 years. In particular, it analyses in detail the reduction that has been effected – in the process of making 'Selections' of his work – of the huge poetic *oeuvre* to a core canon of about 80 'great' poems which represent the 'true', 'most characteristic' Hardy. On the analogy of the 'minor novels' in his fiction, the essay then brings back into view some of his most neglected poems; asks what critical and cultural determinants are at work in the discrimination of his 'finest' poetry from his 'bad'; and speculates on what happens to our perception of Hardy the Poet if the least familiar poems are restored to the canon cheek-by-jowl with the 'great' ones. The final substantive chapter of the book returns to the last of Hardy's major 'tragic' novels, *Jude*, approaching it by way of his own comments in *The*

Life on his first 'lost' novel, *The Poor Man and the Lady*. It argues that the most appropriate term to describe *Jude* – and indeed all Hardy's fiction – is neither 'comedy' nor 'tragedy', but *satire*. Close analysis of the discourses of absurdity in the novel – at once in plot, characterization and narrative style – is adduced in evidence, combined with a reading of Arabella as the novel's satiric focus. This repositions her, *contra* Jude and Sue, who are usually assumed to be the true protagonists, as a character whose presence and presentation demands more serious critical attention and explanation than it normally receives. The satire, I suggest, is once more directed at the injustices of a class society, at idealism and asceticism, at the presumptions of a realism which claims to depict the 'literal truth', and at readers who are seduced by the fictions constructed on behalf of a specious Christian/humanist society by its dominant cultural mode of representation: 'tragic realism'. It is as a reflex of this that the essay proposes the real reason for Hardy's abandoning of fiction for poetry and poetic drama to be that he had taken the novel-form available to him to the point of self-deconstruction.

A brief postscript is appended to the volume on the recent reproduction of *Jude the Obscure* as the film *Jude*. By way of this, it thus concludes in the appropriate recognition – with a postmodern millennium upon us – that Hardy is indeed still 'Our Contemporary', but that for the majority of people who now come to his work for the first time, it will be in the form of recycled images. And criticism, in future, will need to be equipped to engage with them. 'Thomas Hardy' as simulacrum is a notion Hardy himself may well have relished.

* * * * *

My involvement with Hardy, then, spans a long and eventful period in the chronicle of literary studies more generally and of Hardy studies in particular. It begins in those innocent days in the late 1960s – right on the cusp of the shift from old-style 'Lit. Crit.' to the radical *événements* incident on the arrival of the 'Moment of Theory' – and arrives at a situation now in which 'good little Thomas Hardy' of rural Wessex has become the *enfant terrible* of 19th-century fiction and the poet whose 'linguistic moment' refuses any ontologically stable 'grand narratives' of self, history or language for the 20th century.[7] My Swedish Thomas Hardy in 1968, still susceptible to passionate debate about the place of 'Fate' in his work, and to painstaking exegesis of his 'unifying' patterns of symbolism and imagery, is today transmogrified into a Deconstructionist *avant la lettre* (it's interesting that French automatically offers itself as the appropriate language in which to articulate such matters). His work is now a terrain of riven textuality whose major landmarks are fault-lines which expose the substrata of cultural politics, class, sexuality and gender beneath – discourses themselves striated by the unstable language of which they are composed. My latest essay on Hardy, 'Thomas Hardy and Critical Theory', for the forthcoming *Cambridge Companion to Thomas Hardy*[8] but unavailable for inclusion in the present volume, offers a synoptic account of the history, dominant features and effects of this process.

Suffice to say here, that both Hardy and Hardy studies have been changed out of all recognition in the course of the theorization of criticism, and so too has the nature of the mystification in which he nevertheless continues to envelop me. The fundamental question this new figure poses for me (but perhaps, after all, it is the one the old Hardy always already posed) is still disconcertingly seldom asked even by his most sophisticated contemporary critics, and it is this: is Hardy *in control* of his text? Does he *intend* his effects and tropes – whatever we may read them to signify? Are they *strategic*, or is his writing merely protean textuality which is made to enunciate – in its decoding by contemporary criticism – the tacit ideological complexities and contradictions of both its moment of production and its moment of reproduction? Is it Hardy the *writer* or the Hardy *reader* who ultimately determines the 'meaning' of his work? Such a question cannot, of course, ever anticipate a certain answer, but it is telling, I think, that it should be the infinitely enigmatic Thomas Hardy – of all the writers I am familiar with – who forces the overwhelming question upon my attention so pointedly and unremittingly. And on that note – of a man who clearly submits – I wish the spectator well in observing my wrestlings with one of the slipperiest practitioners in the game.

1

Thomas Hardy: A Partial Portrait

It is a commonplace of literary criticism that 'major author X' was a 'transitional' writer who lived and worked in a 'transitional' period. This does not get us very far, however, since all periods are, in the nature of historical process, transitional; and all major writers, by dint of their perceived majority, will also be transitional in that they modify by innovation the literary culture of which they are a part. As Thomas Hardy has so often been awarded the 'transitional' accolade, we may ask: is it any more illuminating in relation to him than it is to anyone else?

Born a stonemason's son in a small Dorset village on 2 June 1840, Hardy died 88 years later on 11 January 1928, an internationally eminent novelist and poet. It is difficult to imagine how a period so long and eventful – beginning some 14 years before the Charge of the Light Brigade, when Tennyson and Dickens were in their prime, and ending ten years after World War I, when Hardy's literary contemporaries included Eliot, Joyce and Woolf – could be anything but 'transitional'.[1] Nor is it conceivable that Hardy's own work in two genres would not have been inscribed by the macro and micro social and cultural processes shaping that long life; nor again, that his *oeuvre* did not help to shape and inscribe the cultural theme-park in which he still remains so large an attraction. What this initial essay aims to do, therefore, is block in those aspects of Hardy's life and work which, it will propose, are most germane in

This essay, with a couple of pages cut, is the Introduction to my edition, *Thomas Hardy: Selected Poetry and Non-Fictional Prose* (London: Macmillan, 1996).

establishing that to call Hardy a transitional writer is indeed to mean something.

Oddly enough, his long life was, compared with many writers, markedly uneventful. Furthermore, there are readily available several major biographies of him,[2] as well as Florence Emily Hardy's *The Life of Thomas Hardy 1840–1928* (albeit dictated in the third person to his second wife during the 1920s, with the clear intention that it should be passed off as a 'definitive' biography by her – and hence, in some senses, his last fiction[3]). It is not this chapter's business, then, to chart in miniature the slow diurnal un-ravelling of Hardy's life. Rather, it takes three themes in his bio-graphical narrative and uses each to construct a 'partial portrait', to set in place something of an historical context for it, and to bring into bold relief public and private issues which help to gloss Hardy's writing. The three themes are: war, class and sex – the second and third of which closely interrelate. Consideration will then be given to the fact that Hardy actually had *two* literary 'lives' in his lifetime – that of novelist, 'followed' (he claimed he was always *really* this) by that of poet.

* * * * * * * *

The choice of war as a motif in Hardy's life is, of course, in part a way of plotting its long chronology, and of indicating the huge transition between the social and cultural world he was born into and the one he died in. But war also fascinated and repelled Hardy, and was the subject of a sizeable proportion of his poetry. In addi-tion, it helps to account – especially in relation to World War I – for the bleakness of his vision (in common with so many of his Modernist contemporaries) in what he saw as the 'new Dark Age'[4] of the post-war period.

When Hardy was born in 1840, the Battle of Waterloo (1815) was only 25 years in the past; and the revolutionary wars with France, the spectre of Napoleon stalking Europe, and threat-of-in-vasion scares on the south coast of England, were still fresh in older peoples' memories (see the poem 'One We Knew' in *Time's Laughingstocks*). Hardy, of course, was to use that recent past as the context for *The Trumpet-Major* and as the subject of his huge 'epic-drama' *The Dynasts* (1902–07). As implied above, the Crimean War (in which the clash of traditional and modern modes of warfare became shockingly apparent) had begun when Hardy was 13; and the outbreak of the Franco-Prussian War (1870) co-incided with his courtship of his first wife, Emma – *The Life*[5] recording that they were reading Tennyson in the garden at St Juliot, Cornwall (see below, p. 21) 'on the day the bloody battle of Gravelotte was fought', and that Hardy, reminded of this occasion 'by a still bloodier war' in 1915, composed 'In Time of "The Breaking of Nations"' (*Moments of Vision*). The Boer War of 1899–1902 in South Africa – which coincided with the turn of the 19th century and signals British imperialism entering 20th-century crisis – involved Hardy more directly: the husband of his friend, Florence Henniker (see below, pp. 19–20), fought there, as did Hardy's nephew, and he produced a sequence of war poems prompted by it (in *Poems of the Past and the Present*). His response was characteristically ambiguous: although he and Emma were, like many English 'liberals', 'Pro-Boer',[6] and despite a life-long loathing of war as *realpolitik*, he was, nevertheless and self-confessedly, stirred and fascinated by matters military. He wrote to Mrs Henniker: 'It seems a justification of the extremist pessimism that at the end of the 19th Centy [sic] we settle an argument by the Sword, just as they wd have done in the 19th Centy B.C.'; and later: 'I constantly deplore the fact that "civilized" nations have not learnt some more excellent … way of settling disputes than the old & barbarous one, after all these centuries; but when I feel that it must be, few persons are more martial than I, or like better to write of war in prose or rhyme'.[7] In fact, however, none of Hardy's war poems, then or later, could be classed, in his own phrase, as 'Jingo or Imperial'.[8]

It is sometimes held that the 'real' end of the 19th century was in August 1914, with the outbreak of the so-called Great War – a watershed between the 'old' world and the 20th century heralded by an event which, in scale and nature, seemed to be symptomatic of what the 'new' world held in store. Certainly for Hardy, now 74, it was a profoundly shattering occurrence; and despite publishing the patriotic (if subdued) 'Men Who March Away' (*MV*) in *The Times* on 9 September 1914 and contributing to the war-effort in small ways,[9] it is to his credit that he abhorred the war from the start, when much of the nation was seized by wild patriotic fervour and other poets were producing works of 'heroic' banality. *The Life* (364–5) records his shock (he had not anticipated this 'convulsion of nations' so soon), and his fear that, rather than being 'over by

Christmas ... it might be a matter of years and untold disaster'. The following extract encapsulates both Hardy's horror at the war, and his cast of mind after it:

> A long study of the European wars of a century earlier had made it appear to him that common sense had taken the place of bluster in men's minds; and he felt this so strongly that ... as long before as 1901 he composed a poem called 'The Sick Battle-God', which assumed that zest for slaughter was dying out. It was seldom he had felt so heavy at heart as in seeing his old view of the gradual bettering of human nature ... completely shattered by the events of 1914 and onwards. War, he had supposed, had grown too coldly scientific to kindle again for long all the ardent romance which had characterized it down to Napoleonic times, when the most intense battles were over in a day, and the most exciting tactics and strategy led to the death of comparatively few combatants. Hence nobody was more amazed than he at the German incursion into Belgium, and the contemplation of it led him to despair of the world's history thenceforward. He had not reckoned on the power still retained there by the governing castes whose interests were not the people's. (365–6).

A letter of 28 August 1914 to a friend also confirms what the likely effect on his poetry was to be:

> the recognition that we are living in a more brutal age than that, say, of Elizabeth ... does not inspire one to write hopeful poetry ... but simply to sit still in apathy, and watch the clock spinning backwards, with a mild wonder if, when it gets back to the Dark Ages, and the sack of Rome, it will ever move forward again to a new Renascence, and a new literature.[10]

And a note to the poet Henry Newbolt, shortly after the war ended in 1918, sums up Hardy's feelings by then: 'I confess that I take a smaller interest in the human race since this outburst than I did before.'[11]

Hardy was to live for another ten years; and the notion of a return to the 'Dark Ages' is repeated and developed in the long prefatory 'Apology' to *Late Lyrics and Earlier* in 1922, with late poems also, especially in the posthumously published *Winter Words*, conveying this state of mind. By this time, as noted earlier, he was now the contemporary of the Modernist writers (*LLE* was published in the same year as *The Waste Land*). The poet born two years after an upbeat Victorian Tennyson, in 'Locksley Hall', wrote:

> Forward, forward let us range,
> Let the great world spin for ever down the ringing grooves of change.

> Thro' the shadow of the globe we sweep into the younger day:
> Better fifty years of Europe than a cycle of Cathay.

– could now ponder, if he chose, T. S. Eliot's cultural despair: 'These fragments I have shored against my ruins.' Ezra Pound sent a presentation copy of *Hugh Selwyn Mauberley* and famously recognized Hardy as a fellow modern poet;[12] the contemporary of George Eliot (reviewers thought *Far from the Madding Crowd* was by her[13]) was now the contemporary of Virginia Woolf (who wrote perceptively that Hardy always seems to hover on 'the margin of the unexpressed'[14]); the novelist who was recommending Thackeray's *Vanity Fair* (1848) as 'one of [his] best' to his sister in 1863[15] could now have recommended *Ulysses* (also 1922), had he been so minded and she not long-dead; the D. H. Lawrence who had written so acutely on Hardy's fiction in his *Study of Thomas Hardy* of 1914[16] had already published *The Rainbow* and *Women in Love* years before and, by 1928, had completed (and had banned) *Lady Chatterley's Lover*.

The writer whose family, in his youth, had played the violins in the gallery 'quire' of Stinsford parish church now listened to Big Ben ring in the New Year (1924/5) on the 'wireless';[17] he who was born only six years after the Tolpuddle Martyrs (six Dorset farmworkers) were sentenced to transportation for forming a trade-union branch now lived through the General Strike of 1926; he who had grown up in the world of Palmerston, Disraeli, Gladstone, Garibaldi and Bismarck now grew old in that of Ramsay MacDonald, Stalin, Hitler and Mussolini.

How far, and in what ways, Hardy's poetry may in itself register any of this is an open question, but that it is a poetry 'of transition' cannot be doubted. And it is apposite again here to recall that a central aspect of Hardy as 'transitional' writer is that in 1896, after the publication of *Jude the Obscure*, he effectively ceased writing prose fiction, thereafter devoting himself exclusively to poetry for the next 30 years. In other words, while Hardy may be seen chronologically as a 19th-century novelist, or at least as a transitional novelist poised on the brink of Modernism who never quite took the plunge (see below, p. 25), as a poet he belongs almost entirely to the 20th century – although whether his *poetry* is better seen as 'Victorian' rather than 'Modern' is a problem most secondary and tertiary education syllabuses invariably wrestle with, as they also do, in fact, with his fiction: the ultimate index, perhaps, of 'transitional' status.

* * * * * * * *

Hardy was born into what Raymond and Merryn Williams have called the 'intermediate class'[18] within 19th-century rural society. Neither labourers nor landowners, its members were usually copyholders or lifeholders (about whom Hardy wrote sympathetically and bitterly in *Tess of the d'Urbervilles* and in the essay, 'The Dorsetshire Labourer' (1883)) who supplied most of the skills which the rural community then needed. For Hardy, it was this, his own class, which was most comprehensively dispossessed and deracinated by developments in the rural economy in the second half of the 19th century – 'migration' to the large towns being only the most common and visible symptom of this. However, another characteristic of this group – less crudely economically determined – was the tendency of its members to be meritocratically upwardly mobile, and, by way of education in particular, to 'migrate' to both physical and *other class* locations. This is clearly true for Hardy himself (but also, in an equally significant way, for his cousin Tryphena Sparks, who attended a teacher-training college in London and then became an elementary school headteacher until she married). Hardy acquired a considerable basic education (he left school at 16 – late, for one of his social group), and then became an architect's 'pupil'. He went to London in the same business in the 1860s; read voraciously, visited theatres, art galleries and museums, and became a (self-)educated young man – up to a point. However, he did not receive the advanced formal (classical) education he was acutely conscious some of his acquaintances had (such as his friend and mentor Horace Moule and his brothers – sons of the vicar of Fordington in Dorchester and Cambridge graduates – together with other young men he met in the architects' offices in Dorchester and London); there was never any real chance of his going up to Cambridge (despite *The Life's* implication that there was[19]) and, as it turned out, the 'native' returned from London to Dorset in 1867 with his career still to make.

That career, of course, was soon to be one of tyro-novelist, struggling to get his work placed in the literary market-place of publishers and periodicals – an experience, for the sharply class-sensitive Hardy, overdetermined by the fact that his earliest attempts at fiction were subjected (with luck, as it turned out) to the critical scrutiny of publishers and their readers from the Victorian *haut-bourgeois* intelligentsia (Alexander Macmillan, John Morley, Leslie Stephen, George Meredith). In the event, his rapid success as a novelist is a classic instance of a meritocratic 19th-century rise to fame and fortune by way of the metropolitan market-place of letters. But it should not be disregarded that, when successful, he nevertheless built a house, Max Gate, on the outskirts of Dorchester – and therefore lived most of his eminent professional life away from London (while visiting it extensively as a literary and social celebrity). For Hardy's 'true' class position,[20] and one aspect, then, of his 'transitional' character, is at once that of *déraciné* countryman and metropolitan man-of-letters who elects to live in Dorset – belonging neither to his class of origin, nor yet to the urban intelligentsia amongst whom his professional success positions him. The result was that Hardy was obsessed by class and class-relations, and preternaturally attuned to their minutiae (as in this symptomatic casual observation: 'The defects of a class are more perceptible to the class immediately below it than to itself'[21]). It is perhaps no surprise, therefore, that his first ('lost') novel was entitled *The Poor Man and the Lady* – 'a sweeping dramatic satire', *The Life* tells us, on, amongst other things, 'the squirearchy and nobility, London society, the vulgarity of the middle class ... the tendency of the writing being socialistic, not to say revolutionary' (61). Neither is it without point that, in old age, while composing *The Life*, Hardy should devote several sympathetic pages to this earliest and unpublished work, describing it as 'too soon for [its] date' (18), and explaining – pointedly in my context here – that it was suppressed because 'in genteel mid-Victorian 1869 it would no doubt have incurred ... severe strictures which might have handicapped a young writer for a long time' (62; for further discussion of his views on this novel, see Chapter 7, below). Class, compromise and chagrin indeed marked Hardy's career as a novelist throughout.

All his novels – but most overtly and significantly, perhaps, the strategically anti-realist *The Hand of Ethelberta* (in some ways a more revealing 'Life' than *The Life*; see also Chapter 3, below), and (the part-autobiographical) *Jude* – show the marks of this obsession. *The Life* itself, however, written when he had become the Grand Old Man of English Letters, constantly betrays the inverted snobbery of the insecure parvenu in its passing comments on Hardy's 'lack of social ambition' (15), his shrinking from 'the business of social advancement' (53), his dislike of 'the fashionable throng' (266) – all juxtaposed (despite the disclaimer that 'Hardy does not comment much on these society-gatherings, his thoughts running upon other subjects' (201)) with an exhaustive, tedious and unilluminating catalogue of his hob-nobbings, from the 1890s onwards, with the great and the good of English society. But despite 'the popularity of Hardy as an author now making him welcome anywhere' (253), the class insecurity is still clearly heard in this note of 1887: 'I spoke to a good many; was apparently unknown to a good many more I knew' (199). It is not without point either, as we shall see below, that Hardy continually claims 'an indifference to a popular novelist's fame' (57), and gives up writing fiction – having 'made it' in that (second-class) genre – for what he calls 'poetry and other forms of *pure* literature' (63; my emphasis). Furthermore, *The Life* is at pains to convey his studiedly 'balanced' and impartial political stance – he is 'quite outside politics' (169), 'not a bit of a politician' (268) – which is also likely to result from his anomalous class position. A revealing memorandum of 1880 suggests that the contradictions inherent in this produce a passive alternativism (typical of a 'superior', apolitical liberal-humanism) which may account for the deterministic philosophy and ironic quietism so often remarked in his writing:

> I find that my politics really are neither Tory nor Radical ... I am against privilege derived from accident of any kind, and am therefore equally opposed to aristocratic privilege and democratic privilege. (By the latter I mean the arrogant assumption that the only labour is hand-labour – a worse arrogance than that of the aristocrat, – the taxing of the worthy to help those masses of the population who will not help themselves when they might, etc.) Opportunity should be equal for all, but those who will not avail themselves of it should be cared for merely – not be a burden to, nor the rulers over, those who do avail themselves thereof. (204)

The confusion in the articulation of this passage is symptomatic of the confusion in Hardy's class allegiance, although it is interesting to perceive here that 'meritocracy' is his real theme. His rejection of politics would seem to result in his conception of a neutral and un-conscious power (the 'Immanent Will') governing the universe – a metaphysical displacement of his lack of a secure social and politi-cal philosophy. Irresolutely placed between belief in religion (a God-controlled universe) and materialism (a human-controlled history), the contradictions and ambiguities in Hardy's intellectual and class positions rendered him unable, on the one hand, to follow a 'socialistic' logic because of his newly acquired social status, or, on the other, to accept the conventional political, social and religious orthodoxies of the ruling class.

Hardy, then, is left occupying an apolitical space as 'writer', bol-stered by an eclectic and factitious deterministic myth of History. Much of his work – and certainly, as we shall see in Chapter 6, the critical 'shaping' of his poetry within the cultural arena of 20th-century Modernism – may well result from the consciousness of dis-placement, insecurity and disaffection in one who does not 'belong' to any of the constituent locales in which he is nevertheless situ-ated. And Hardy's consanguinity with the cultural pessimism of Anglo-American Modernism is, indeed, clearly traced in the follow-ing note of 1891:

> Democratic government may be justice to man, but it will probably merge in proletarian, and when these people ['crowds parading and traipsing round' the British Museum] are our masters it will lead to more of this contempt [for rare antiquities], and possibly be the utter ruin of art and literature.[22]

* * * * * * *

One inescapable manifestation of Hardy's insecurity – closely inter-related with his class-consciousness – is his preoccupation with women, sex and sexuality. It is notable that one of the earliest rem-iniscences in *The Life* (18–20) is of the very young Hardy's relation-ship with 'the lady of the manor' in Stinsford, who 'had grown passionately fond of Tommy almost from his infancy ... whom she had been accustomed to take into her lap and kiss until he was quite a big child. He quite reciprocated her fondness.' *The Life's* language here – at once precociously sexual and sharply conscious of the woman's rank – is striking: 'the *landowner's wife* to whom he had grown more attached than he cared to own. In fact, though he was only nine or ten and she must have been nearly forty, his feeling for her was almost that of a *lover*'; 'in spite of his *lover-like* promise of fidelity to *her ladyship*' (my emphases). From there on, the often dry and defensive pages of *The Life* nevertheless mention the many women Hardy observes or has some, more or less eroticized, passing contact with. A small sample would include: 'the bride, all in white, [who] kissed him in her intense pleasure at the dance', when the 12-year-old Thomas was playing the fiddle at her wedding (23); the 'pink and plump' dairymaid, four years older, who was the 15-year-old's Sunday-School companion – 'though she was by no means a model of virtue in her love-affairs' (25); 'that girl in the omnibus [with] one of those faces of marvellous beauty which are seen casually in the streets but never among one's friends.... Where do such women come from? Who marries them? Who knows them?' (220); a 'Cleopatra in the railway carriage ... a good-natured amative creature by her voice, and her heavy moist lips' (229); the girl of 'the streets' who thanks him for sharing his umbrella 'by holding on tight to my arm and bestowing on me many kisses' (265); and, perhaps most revealingly, the 'handsome girl: cruel small mouth: she's of the class of interesting women one would be afraid to marry' (212).

The phrase 'eroticized, passing contact' was used above for two reasons. First, as Hardy's biographers make clear, apart from his two marriages (see below, p. 21), he had a number of more or less unsatisfactory 'love-affairs' in the course of his life – from the 'pretty girl' the 14-year-old 'fell madly in love with', who was 'a total stranger' and soon 'disappeared for ever,[23] to the (non-)affairs with the younger and beautiful upper-class married women, Mrs Florence Henniker and Lady Agnes Grove, in the 1890s when his first marriage was in serious trouble and he appears to have been undergoing a mid-life crisis. There has also been much (unverified) speculation about a 'mystery girl' in London in the 1860s, from whose 'free' intellectual and sexual thinking and behaviour Hardy retreated back to Dorset in 1867;[24] and about the possible affair with/engagement to his cousin, Tryphena Sparks (see 'Thoughts of Phena', *Wessex Poems*) in the late 1860s – the result of which, it has been unreliably suggested, was an illegitimate son.[25] But, in addition, there are the many – literally – passing 'relationships' when Hardy simply *sees* a woman and reflects on her appearance, or fantasises some kind of more intimate involvement with her (see 'Faintheart in a Railway Train', *LLE*). This leads on to the second reason for my phrase above: Hardy very clearly eroticizes – i.e. invests with a gratuitous sexual charge – women and events otherwise innocent of erotic significance (note above, for example, 'the intense pleasure' the bride, 'all in white', finds in the dance). This is the origin of the notion of the 'male gaze', which has featured so prominently and properly in recent feminist, and otherwise gendered, criticism. It is everywhere apparent in Hardy's fiction (especially *Tess*), but it also informs a significant proportion of his poetry. At times, the longing 'gaze' is prurient; at others, pathetic. But scopophilia is a fundamental drive and discourse in his work, and cannot be ignored.

Two further points may be connected to this element in Hardy's writing. First, apropos of his class-consciousness, 'the-poor-man-and-the-lady' theme is very clearly a part of it. *The Life*, while parading his familiarity with society beauties and aristocratic ladies (a mark of his having 'arrived'), again iteratively indulges in a kind of inverted snobbery – presenting Hardy as disdaining such women (superficial, spoilt, 'beneath him' in all but rank), while often making pejorative comparisons with women of his own, or a lower, class. After a visit to a women's teacher-training college (both Tryphena Sparks and his sister Mary had attended one), he comments: 'how far nobler in its aspirations is the life here than the life of those I met at the crush [society event] two nights back' (235); and of 'Mrs T. and her great eyes' at such a crush: 'the most beautiful woman present.... But these women! If put into rough wrappers in a turnip-field, where would their beauty be?' (224). In the failure of his (wishful-thinking) affairs with Mrs Henniker and Lady Grove, Hardy's nose-against-the-window fascination with (elusive) sex is overdetermined by the class exclusion/alienation he feels in respect of the 'Ladies' he desires but cannot have. The second point relates: the majority of Hardy's 'love-affairs' were stillborn or came to nothing (as many of the poems 'about' them attest) – often, it would seem, because of his own diffidence, shyness, scopophilic preference, or lack of sexual drive. The women, then, become 'lost prizes' (the phrase is from 'Thoughts of Phena'), and the poems ones of regret, frustration, self-disdain. Fused with his class insecurity, this sense of sexual failure must surely be one of the matrices in which Hardy's work is formed, and may explain at once his celebration of women's robust sexuality and his prurient, vicarious fascination with their sexual misfortunes.

Hardy was married twice: first to Emma Gifford, who died in 1912, and then to Florence Emily Dugdale, whom he had known since 1905 when he was 72 and she 35. Little needs to be said here about the second marriage, but the first needs some comment. As an architect's draughtsman in 1870, Hardy was sent to St Juliot, near Boscastle in Cornwall, to make drawings for the local church's restoration. Emma was the daughter of the rector there; both she and Hardy were clearly ready to find a partner; and both represent[26] their meeting and courtship as intensely romantic – snatched, during Hardy's visits, in the wildly beautiful countryside of the north Cornish coast (around Tintagel). For extra measure, Emma's father did not think Hardy good enough for his daughter – so the class/sex nexus was also in play. Nevertheless, they were married, and the relationship initially appears to have been happy (although they were never to have children). As Hardy worked at becoming a novelist, they lived for a while in London, then Weymouth, then back near Hardy's birthplace, finally settling at Max Gate on the edge of Dorchester. Relations deteriorated as Hardy became successful, and by the 1890s, with the publication of *Tess* and then *Jude*, the already troubled marriage soured badly – Emma loathing Hardy's 'atheism' and jealous of his relationships with younger women, and Hardy embarrassed by her behaviour and resentful of her antipathy. They struggled on, however, even when his volumes of poetry began to appear and clearly contained love poems to other women than her. Emma's sudden – and to Hardy, apparently, unexpected – death in 1912 put an end, so it seemed, to a relationship which had begun as an intense (perhaps overcharged) love-affair and ended in bitterly alienated cohabitation. What happened, of course, is one of the central Hardy myths: overcome with remorse and guilt, and leaving his new second wife at home, he revisited the scenes of his and Emma's courtship; wrote, in a burst of creative energy, his famous 'Poems of 1912–13' (*Satires of Circumstance*) in which he 'rememoried' (to use Toni Morrison's word[27]) their love-affair in 1870; and created a sequence of love poems which revivifies the past, thus exorcizing and erasing the stricken years in between. The point here, in the context of Hardy's sexual mindset, is that these poems are, in a very clear sense, the quintessence of the 'lost prize' syndrome noted earlier – the sense of failure and loss paradoxically charged now with the eroticism which had drained from the relationship itself. Here, Hardy can, as it were, realize the promise of that intense sexual bonding which he and Emma at once experienced and failed to fulfill by reanimating it in the 'present' of his poetry. Florence Emily, with a perceptiveness perhaps honed by vexation, is reported as saying: 'all the poems about [Emma] are a fiction but fiction in which their author has now come to believe'.[28] Thus the 'Poems of 1912–13' are not so much of regret and nostalgia, but of the transposed reliving of a missed opportunity. Again, we may recognize in this a 'transitional' Modernist perception of 'reality' – for the artist if for no one else – where it lies, not so much in the material experience itself, but in the consciousness that registers it. 'The poetry of a scene', Hardy once reflected, 'varies with the minds of the perceivers. Indeed, it does not lie in the scene at all.'[29]

* * * * * * * *

To say that Hardy had 'two careers' – first novelist, then poet – is to misrepresent him, at least in his own estimation, since he presents himself as *always* primarily a poet. I noted earlier his disdain for novel-writing and his snobbish hankering to enter the realms of 'pure literature', but this is, in fact, a structuring theme of *The Life*, and is inflected there in a number of ways. Early on, when Hardy was first in London, and immediately prior to his starting *The Poor Man and the Lady*, it notes that he 'had begun to write verses, and by 1866 to send his productions to magazines' (47); that although unsuccessful, he did not 'by any means abandon verse which he wrote constantly, but kept private'; and that he read only poetry at this point (1866–67) since he believed that 'in verse was concentrated the essence of all imaginative and emotional literature' (48). Later, the primacy of his preference for poetry is kept regularly in our view: 'the poetic tendency had been his from the earliest' (384); '"I wanted to write poetry in the beginning. Now I can"' (401).

This strategic self-presentation is reinforced by one, surely disingenuous, aspect of the (auto)biography: the disrespect with which it treats his novel-writing career, despite the fact that for 30 years Hardy had laboured, with dedicated care for his craft, to produce serious fiction. Purely material factors are adduced as the impetus to start: 'he was committed by circumstances to novel-writing as a regular trade' (104); and the notion of Hardy as no more than a paid professional hack is reiterated throughout, despite some revealing slippages which suggest what a grotesque misrepresentation this is. In an early 'quoted' letter to Leslie Stephen, he expresses his willingness to court a popular readership at the expense of artistic integrity, and rejects, 'for the present circumstances', any 'higher aims' in favour of getting 'to be considered a good hand at a serial' (100). While commenting on the 'damage' Hardy had done to *The Mayor of Casterbridge* – '*as an artistic whole*' (my emphasis) – in the interests of newspaper serialization, *The Life* adds, nevertheless, that 'as he called his novel-writing "mere journeywork" he cared little about it as art' (179). After *The Woodlanders*, which, it is reported, 'he often said ... in some respects ... was his best novel' (185), and as Hardy was commencing the immense creative labour of writing *Tess* and *Jude*, we are told: 'He now went about the business mechanically' (182–3). Finally, after the publication of *Jude* and *The Well-Beloved* (1896, 1897), *The Life* neatly sums up its theme: 'and so, ended his prose contributions to literature ... which had ever been secondary to his interest in verse' (286), adding, in a shameless perjury, that 'if he wished to retain any shadow of self-respect', he must abandon fiction and 'resume openly that form of [literary art] which had always been instinctive with him .... the change, after all, [being] not so great as it seemed. It was not as if he had been a writer of novels proper' (291).

If we relate this extraordinary depreciation of his fiction to Hardy's over-wrought class-consciousness, then the sub-text of the narrative of his 'two careers' becomes apparent. For the 'character' of Hardy *The Life* wishes to depict is that of eminent man-of-letters; familiar of the noble and famous; above the pettiness of ambition, social climbing, 'popularity' and the literary market-place; always the 'true' poet – 'his bias towards poetry ... instinctive and disinterested' (305) – and not, by nature, the hack novelist toiling away in the sweat-shops of the publishing trade (what George Gissing in 1891 had pilloried as 'New Grub Street'[30]). When Hardy could afford to stop novel-writing, he did so – tainted as it was by representing his escape-route from his class origins. What *The Life* proffers, in other words, is a piece of petit-bourgeois wish-fulfilment (a publisher's reader for *The Poor Man and the Lady* had described the novel, back in 1868, as 'some clever lad's dream' [59]): an image of the 'pure' literary man Hardy desired to be.[31]

However, the explanation of why Hardy gave up fiction is rather more complex than the simple economic reason given above (although that must remain a credible factor). A further clue may lie in his comment, after the furore over *Jude*, that 'his experiences of the few preceding years [had] killed all his interest in this form of imaginative work' (286). Always preternaturally sensitive to criticism (as he was later over his volumes of poetry), he had been badly affected by the scandalized response to *Tess* and *Jude* from the late-Victorian Grundyite lobby: in no way could Tess be 'a Pure Woman' (as Hardy's provocative sub-title claimed), nor should the kinds of experience she undergoes be the stuff of fiction; and the 'immorality', 'atheism' and 'gloom' of *Jude* were the last straw.[32] Again, there is every reason to believe that he was, indeed, fed up with it all; and financial circumstances now allowing (in part, ironically, because of the very success of *Tess*), he took the opportunity to stop and do something more congenial.

But there is a further, more tangled and contentious, dimension to Hardy's decision. His fiction had, from the start, been subject to criticism of its 'improbability' (especially of plot) and of its 'awkward', 'mannered' style. Certainly, those novels, like *HE* and *A Laodicean*, which manifestly deviated from the 'Wessex' canon of 'Novels of Character and Environment',[33] were execrated on both counts. With *Tess*, and more overtly still with *Jude* and *W-B*, these tendencies were foregrounded. Hardy, in other words, was flouting – by ineptitude or design – the laws of a dominant realist orthodoxy which demanded a kind of transparent window on to 'real life'. Much in the various prefaces to the novels, in *The Life*, and in his three essays on fiction of 1888–91 suggests that it was, in fact, by *design* that Hardy's novels disrupted realist expectations. 'Candour in English Fiction' (1890) and 'The Science of Fiction' (1891), in particular, also indicate that, in his own way, Hardy was involved in the late-19th-century literary debate on Naturalism and Realism. He himself, as with Maupassant in France, opposed an 'inventory'-like transcription of facts 'from nature'; rejected a 'photographic' recording of detail; and wished to represent 'abstract imaginings'[34] by way of a 'disproportioning' (i.e. defamiliarizing) fictional writing, which would reveal the *'vérité vraie'* rather than the superficies of life. Hence, he decided, '"realism" is not Art'.[35]

The point here, surely, is – and it places Hardy foursquare in the 'transitional' category – that he was pushing up against, indeed sub-verting, the limits of realism as a fictional mode, and finding it was no longer, if ever, adequate to his purposes. But rather than pursu-ing that logic in fiction, he gives it up and returns to poetry, in which his 'moments of vision' may now find a more appropriately non-realist form. That Hardy's own word 'disproportioning', above, translates so readily into Modernist critical terminology points clearly to his later fiction, at least, as having close affinities with the work of a younger generation of novelists who *were* to follow the logic of anti-realist discourses in making Modernist fiction: D. H. Lawrence, for example, who found so much to admire (and, in part, emulate) in *Jude*.[36]

It is not insignificant, either, that the large single work Hardy un-dertook shortly after ceasing to write novels was his non-realist 'epic-drama', *The Dynasts*. Planned over a long period (*The Life* characteristically implies, throughout his years as a novelist, that it would be Hardy's truly major achievement), this enormous poetic drama involves many modes, some of which, in their affinity with cinematic techniques, again appear proto-Modernist in tendency. The first significant mention of the envisaged 'epic' in *The Life* (May 1875; 106) coincides with Hardy's writing of his uncompro-misingly anti-realist novel, *HE*, and in March 1886, a memoran-dum reflecting on the future of prose fiction proposes that

> novel-writing cannot go backward. Having reached the analytic stage it must transcend it by going still further in the same direction. Why not by rendering as visible essences, spectres, etc.... Abstract re-alisms.... The Realities to be the true realities of life, hitherto called abstractions. The old material realities to be placed behind the former as shadowy accessories.

Hardy's own response to these proposals is: 'this notion was ap-proximately carried out, not in a novel, but through the much more appropriate medium of poetry, in the supernatural framework of *The Dynasts* as also in smaller poems' (177).

Hardy's return to 'smaller poems', however, started before novel-writing had ceased. He woke before dawn on Christmas Day 1890, 'thinking of resuming "the viewless wings of poesy"' (230); and several new poems were written in the earlier 1890s. But by 1897–98, *The Life* tells us, 'he had already for some time been getting together the poems [for *WP*]. In date they ranged from 1865 intermittently onwards, the middle period of his novel-writing producing very few or none, but of late years they had been added to with great rapidity' (291–2). This first volume, then, appeared in 1898, with Hardy, typically, commenting sardonically on its reception 'by some critics [as] not without umbrage at [his] having taken the liberty to adopt another vehicle of expression than prose fiction without consulting them' (299). In addition to the monumental *Ds*, a further seven substantial volumes were to follow – some 950-plus poems in all. It is little wonder, and with some justification, that Hardy aligned himself with other 'ancients' (Homer, Aeschylus, Sophocles, Euripides) who produced major work late in life (384; see also 'An Ancient to Ancients', *LLE*); and it seems fitting to conclude here with his own epigraph in 1918 for this second career: 'A sense of the truth of poetry, of its supreme place in literature, had awakened itself in me. At the risk of ruining all my wordly prospects I dabbled in it ... was forced out of it.... It came back upon me...' (385; Hardy's ellipses).[*]

* * * * * * * *

---

[*] The reason for the essay's somewhat abrupt ending is because it then went on to explain the nature of the volume to which it serves as an introduction. More on Hardy's poetry, and its critical history, will be found in Chapter 6, below.

2

Hardy in History: A Case-Study in the Sociology of Literature

Most forms of 'historical criticism' – whether bourgeois or Marxist – have two related features in common: they are concerned with the *original* production of the text; and they tend to take for granted the *primacy* of the 'primary material', literature, as though this exists objectively and independently of the attention criticism pays to it. (We all construct our bibliographies with the texts sectionally privileged as 'primary sources'.) In comparison to history, literary studies has been naive, or disingenuous, to a degree. It lacks what I want to call, on the analogy of historiography, a *Critiography*. Now, it may be argued that the history and theory of literary criticism is literary studies' equivalent, but I do not mean merely the academic process of historicizing, demarcating and challenging different schools of criticism over time – necessary and hygenic as this is. I mean, first, the extrinsic study of the subject itself – its history, its institutions, its practices, its theoretical premises and its social relations (what is the place and function of the criticism and teaching of literature in the 1980s; what is its *'politics'*?). And second, I mean a consciousness of the constitution of the material which criticism takes as

This essay was first published in the journal *Literature and History*, 9:1 (Spring 1983). Because it is now so old and so marked by its moment of production, revising it in order to bring it up-to-date seemed a pointless task. With a very few stylistic emendations, therefore, it stands as it then stood – the synoptic initial blueprint for my later book with a similar title, and for all my work on Hardy thereafter.

'primary': literary texts – the 'facts', if I may for a moment appropriate the word, of literary studies. It is here that criticism – however
'historical' it may be – can and should learn a salutary lesson from
historiography, which recognizes that *its* 'facts' – the documents, the
primary sources, 'the Past' – are not permanent and palpable, but
are constituted in the process of *writing* history; that they are discovered, selected, suppressed, interpreted, produced and reproduced by
historians who are themselves historical and political subjects inter-
pellated into certain subject positions in a particular historical conjuncture – 'the Present'. E. H. Carr's still sharply corrective book
What is History? is helpful here. He reminds us:

> (i) that 'the facts speak only when the historian calls on them: it is
>   he who decides which facts to give the floor, and in what order
>   or context';[1]
> (ii) to 'study the historian before you begin to study the facts' (23),
>   [because the historian] 'is also a social phenomenon, both the
>   product and the conscious or unconscious spokesman of the
>   society to which he belongs; it is in this capacity that he ap-
>   proaches the facts of the historical past' (35).

This results, of course, in 'some measure of interpretation' and in
the making of 'value judgments' (79): 'the abstract standard or
value, divorced from society and divorced from history, is as much
an illusion as the abstract individual. The serious historian is the
one who recognises the historically-conditioned character of all
values, not the one who claims for his own values an objectivity
beyond history' (84). (Such a perception of the historically determined nature of 'value' would be an encouraging sign in many a
'serious' literary critic!) What Carr thus recognizes is that, as 'the
historian has no excuse to think of himself as a detached individual
standing outside society and outside history ... [he] *can and should
know what he is doing*' (139, my emphasis); and that, for Carr, is
'to master and understand [the Past] as the key to the understanding of the present' (26). Historians, in other words, quite literally
write history, constituting it in those discourses which are available
to them, and in which they can 'realize' the past in order to understand, and hence shape, the present and the future. This, let us be
clear, is a *political* activity; and history, because of its apparent
closeness to the domain of the politically 'real', has more fully
recognized its political function than criticism, which has tended to

claim for itself the ideologically innocent activity of reading its 'natural' primary material, the 'literary texts themselves', for their intrinsic, 'abstract' value, 'divorced from history'.

But what is, I hope, already clear is the consonance between history and criticism as regards a problematical 'primary material' – the difference being the absence of a critiography which confronts the partiality of critical practice. Extrapolating from Carr's historiography, however, we can readily see that literature is constituted by criticism (and other related social processes), as much as 'the Past' is by history. Literary-critical notions of canons and traditions of great literature; of inherent meanings and intrinsic value; of hierarchies of major and minor, classic and popular, texts and writers; of evaluations and discriminations of acceptable and unacceptable works within or between writers' *oeuvres*; of objective readings and definitive interpretations and editions; are historically determined and historically variable. The critic, too, is a 'social phenomenon' who selects and organizes the facts/texts according to his/her positioning in history: who (pre-eminently) makes 'value-judgements'; who, in effect, 'writes' literature from the perspective of a historical and ideological present. As with a 'historical fact', the 'primary' text is continually reconstituted by the historically changing critical attention paid to it. Neither the moment of production nor the text itself is ontologically stable, ultimately explanative, or definitive. Their 'meanings' lie not within the text, nor within past history, but in the determinate and changing sets of discursive and social relations in which they are continually reproduced in present history.

In his 1982 essay, 'Text and History', Tony Bennett clarified the positions he outlined in *Formalism and Marxism* (1979), and it is interesting to notice how similar are Bennett's remarks on the literary text to Carr's on the historical fact. He points out how both bourgeois interpretative, and structuralist, criticism have succumbed to 'the seductive facticity of the text', and how Marxist criticism has done the same by its concern with the 'conditions of production'. All, however, have 'fetishise[d] [the text] in abstracting it from the concrete and historically varying relationships in which it is inscribed during the successive moments of its history as a culturally active, received text'. He adds:

A condition of any text's continuing to exert long-term cultural effects within any society must be that it is constantly brought into connection or articulated with new texts, socially and politically mobilized in different ways within different class practices or educational, cultural and linguistic institutions and so on. ... It is only in the light of such historically concrete, variable and incessantly changing determinations – determinations which so press in upon the text as fundamentally to modify its very mode of being – that it is possible to assess, at any given moment, the effects that might be attributed to any given text or set of texts.[2]

Drawing on Derrida, Bennett suggests that a text's 'iterability' (its capacity to be constantly 're-read' and 're-written' with 'diverse meanings' and 'plural effects', beyond 'any particular set of author–reader relations' (226–7)) proscribes any notion of intrinsic meaning; that a text and its meanings are produced in the process of its consumption by variable historical readers in variable historical conjunctures and, in particular, within the discourses of criticism and education which 'especially since the 19th century ... have constituted a privileged site for the circulation of those texts which have been regarded as of special value; that is as "literary" in a specialized and restricted sense' (230). This *consciousness* of literature as historically determined and variable, Bennett argues, enables us to 'redetermine its connections with history' (235), to free it from existing discourses and to mobilize it on behalf of the present and the future. In recognizing the essentially political nature of the critic's practice, this is not at all unlike Carr's perception of the role of the historian, who 'can and should know what he is doing', and what he is doing it for. Whether this *does* describe the average critic in the 1980s is debatable – although the gender pronoun there is significant. If instead of 'he', I had said 'she', then an explicit, strategic function for criticism might not now be in question: feminist critics (as well as feminist historians) have, far beyond their male colleagues, deconstructed the myths of abstract 'value' and apolitical 'objectivity' in their respective subject-areas.

I would propose, therefore, that if there is to be a 'historical criticism' which is genuinely historical and empirical, and which 'knows what it is doing and why', then it must necessarily involve a conception of critiography. This means a study of texts *in history*; not merely as productions of their 'period', nor as receptacles of historical messages from that period which criticism decants, but as cultural productions of the 1980s. This implies, of course, an initial displacement of the apparently neutral 'primary material' from the central focus in favour of the constitutive social discourses which make it available in a determinate form as a present cultural fact. It is for this reason that I have referred in my title to a 'sociology of literature', since it may, in fact, represent a more accurate description of the practice than the ambiguous 'historical criticism'. Hardy's fiction (and I must limit myself here to this genre only) is very much present in the 1980s – and it is present as the concept 'Hardy':[3] as a cultural phenomenon defined by its place, function and parameters of intelligibility within the contemporary social formation. What I am immediately forced to ask, therefore, is how 'Hardy' got here; which texts constitute 'Hardy'; what their place in the social process may be; how those texts have been, and are, read; how they might be read and why.

I want, then, to offer a brief critiography of two of the main constitutive discourses of 'Hardy the Novelist': criticism and education, although in passing I will mention other social determinants, such as publication and reproduction in the press, on radio, television and film, which materially affect a text's availability and, through intertextuality, the ways in which it is read. Criticism itself, of course, both as 'reviewing' and as academic study, affects the availability of texts by deciding what is important or insignificant, and, by way of its usually tacit ideological presuppositions, establishes the parameters within which texts may be read; education – where criticism reproduces itself and the texts it favours as the 'syllabus' – naturalizes both the literature selected for study and the associated pedagogic and critical practices. 'Hardy' in the 1980s, I will suggest, exists as 'meaning' only in the weave of this complex set of interrelated determinations. As a focus, I shall consider the relegation of nearly half of Hardy's fiction to the status of 'minor novels', and in particular the fate of *The Hand of Ethelberta* (see also Chapter 3).

* * * * *

That 'Hardy' is a major cultural fact – for some at least – in the late 20th century, is confirmed by an article in the *Times Educational Supplement* (2.1.81), by Antonia Byatt, entitled 'Hardy Rules O.K.' Of all the novelists mentioned by prospective candidates to University College London in 1980 as amongst their favourite, Hardy was 'overwhelmingly' the first. He received 194 'mentions' out of the 520 or so applications she read (around half the year's total), with Jane Austen next at 165 and D. H. Lawrence third with 158. Fortuitously, this impression of Hardy's present importance within education is reinforced by an article in the first issue of the *LTP* journal,[4] which tabulates the number of 'mentions' authors receive in O- and A-level examination papers from the 11 examining boards over the period 1974–84. Hardy is third with 54 'mentions', only following Shakespeare with 190 and Chaucer with 56 (Dickens with 48, and Jane Austen with 46, come next). My own research on examination papers shows that this has not always been the case, but in the last ten years certainly, Hardy has been a constant presence in school education. The immediate questions are: what makes 'Hardy' so popular amongst school students at the present time; and – in so far as they do not 'set' their own set authors (indeed, the texts which are 'worthy of study' simply appear, without justification or explanation, on the syllabus) – what 'Hardy' is being read, taught and examined, and in what ways? The Hardy who rules OK is already 'made' before the student responds so positively to him. But to answer these questions first requires a brief sketch of the critical production of 'Hardy', since it is criticism (through the examination boards) which places a 'great writer' on the syllabus.

To read straight through the *Critical Heritage* volume on Hardy is to be struck by the patterns, stereotypes and commonplaces of criticism which accrete around his work in the course of his novel-writing career, and the strong sense that these remain, even now, as much a part of the construct 'Hardy' as the works themselves. A hint of this fusing of discourses is suggested unwittingly by R. G. Cox, in his Introduction to that volume, when he writes of the critical reception of Hardy's first published novel, *Desperate Remedies*: 'All the reviews agree in selecting for praise those parts of the novel which point forward to Hardy's most characteristic later work; their censure is directed against sensationalism and on over-complicated plot.'[5] Self-fulfilling prophecies! Cox is only able to perceive this 'agreement' because he too 'agrees' as to the 'most characteristic' features of Hardy's work. This shaping of the 'characteristic Hardy' as an acceptable 'great writer' takes two major forms: one, the discrimination of 'the excellent' (and therefore 'the characteristic') in his work (and the rejection consequently of that which is not as 'faults' and 'flaws'); and two, the ranking of the works into categories of 'major' and 'minor' importance, which means the excision of the latter from the canon and the syllabus. These processes, though naturalized, are by no means natural; so we must ask: what features are conceived to be good or bad, and why?

The rapidly established positive commonplaces about Hardy's work were: his description and deployment of Nature; his 'Greek' conception of tragedy, tragic characters and Fate; his 'Shakespearian' rustics; his depiction of 'Wessex'; his nostalgia for a passing rural world; his poetic style; and the 'elemental' and 'universal' significance of his characters and settings. This is, of course, the Hardy of the 'Novels of Character and Environment', and it is worth noticing that in the General Preface to the 'Wessex Edition' of 1912, Hardy himself encourages the categorization of his work and the establishment of a 'canon' by designating certain works as 'Novels of Character and Environment', whilst defining others as 'romances', 'fantasies', 'novels of ingenuity' and 'experiments' (like *HE*).[6] Hardy's emphasis only confirms the reviewers' discriminations and hierarchies hitherto, but it also reinforces them. Harold Williams, for example, by 1914 had already appropriated Hardy's terms as his own. Having identified the 'two faculties', which define the true fictional genius, as 'the gift of visualising characters who belong to the real world ... and the power of placing them in an environment', he continues, as though the General Preface had never been written, 'if we begin to measure Mr. Hardy's novels by this standard, the necessity of uncompromising differentiation becomes apparent', and he distinguishes 'five novels, in which the author keeps himself to life on the soil of Wessex, [which] stand in a distinctive place above Mr. Hardy's other books; they are *Far from the Madding Crowd, The Return of the Native, The Mayor of Casterbridge, The Woodlanders* and *Tess of the d'Urbervilles*'.[7] Reinstate *Jude the Obscure* and we have the novels dealt with by Ian Gregor in *The Great Web* in 1974 as 'Hardy's Major Fiction', and the core works in any assessment of his achievement.

The 'characteristic' faults in Hardy's work were: sensationalism; artificiality of plot; melodrama; chance and coincidence; 'flat' characterization; awkwardness and pedantry of style; pessimism or 'gloom'; didacticism (or 'ideas'); and his attempts to write about any society other than 'Wessex'. Fundamentally, these are all reflexes of a dominant – but unspoken – predilection for a realism defined by notions of 'plausibility', 'probability', 'conviction', 'credibility' and 'naturalness'. Indeed, the frequency with which the words 'probable/improbable' occur in Hardy criticism has encouraged me to coin the term 'probabilism' for the orthodox critical discourse against which Hardy is measured. What is interesting is how the critics deal with these 'faults' so that the disturbance they cause can be 'written out' of the construct 'Hardy', just as, as I shall indicate in a moment, the 'minor novels' are excised from the canon because they challenge its organic coherence. *Tess* is a good example, in so far as, for many late-19th-century critics, it is the last of the great 'tragic' novels, while already evincing the tendentiousness which was to make *Jude* a disastrous failure ('the worst novel he has ever written', L. W. Phelps wrote in 1910[8]). Edward Wright in 1904 makes a significant comparison with George Eliot (a matter I shall return to). He finds *Tess* more tragic than *Adam Bede*, but

> George Eliot's story is more simple, more natural and far more probable. If her fault is want of Art, Mr. Hardy's is artificiality. Too much machinery is employed in *Tess* to bring about the catastrophe; and in the latter part of the tale especially, disaster follows disaster in so close and yet disconnected a manner that all sense of verisimilitude is destroyed.

Equally, Hardy 'was unable, in creating his characters, to preserve the balance and the general truth to nature which is found in *Adam Bede*', these being of such 'nefarious or brutal, vicious, weak, or scornful natures' that the credulity of the most sympathetic reader is 'dispelled'.[9] And Harold Williams, in 1914, justifies the inclusion of *Tess* in *his* 'Hardy' by acknowledging that it is flawed – 'its worst faults lie in the author's obvious didacticism'; but since questions of a writer's 'philosophy' have 'nothing to do with our judgment of imaginative writing', it can still be claimed as a great 'work of art'.[10] He excises the whole intransigent dimension of Hardy's 'pessimism' because it does not fit his conception of a romantic-humanist Hardy opposing the 'old wisdom' of the rural world to the 'desolating influences' of 'modern civilization'. Indeed, a quotation from Williams's essay may serve as a fair synthesis of the critical consensus which constitutes 'Hardy' by 1914:

> The scene is laid in a secluded agricultural country where the noise of the great industrial centres hardly comes as a distant murmur, the

characters belong to the simplicity of an older and less sophisticated world than most of us are condemned to live in; but in these novels life is greater, nobler, more tragic, more fraught with tremendous issues. ... Whatever may be the limitations of Mr. Hardy's insight ... or the improbability of plot in his minor books, he can claim to have invested the tragedy of the individual with a note of universal significance as only the great masters have done. ... That the individual existence is 'rounded with a sleep' is less to Mr. Hardy than the knowledge that the essential elements of human life and character are not mortal; they endure unchangeably through the centuries.[11]

By World War I, then, 'Hardy' is a great modern tragic humanist and rural annalist, flawed by perverse tendencies, but whose five or six 'Novels of Character and Environment' represent his true achievement. It is a 'Hardy', I suggest, who is reproduced time and again, with subtle variations, in teaching and criticism right up to the present. In this context, and with the passage from Williams in mind, let me quote from an advertisement for a course on Hardy's novels in the Adult Education Department of a modern university:

Today our lives are so rushed and hectic and noisy. It is refreshing to escape into the old, traditional, rural world with the peace and calm that Hardy depicts so beautifully in his novels. His love of nature and folk-lore recreate an almost timeless world which unfortunately, even as he wrote, he saw fast disappearing. ... Although these novels are a form of escape for us from modern, urban living they still remain distinctly modern in their outlook.[12]

I cannot here chart the map of Hardy criticism since World War I, but I will make one or two observations which may help to substantiate the point. Lord David Cecil's *Hardy the Novelist* (1943) reproduces more or less exactly the late-19th-century version of Hardy, admiring all the same qualities (he is 'built on the grand Shakespearian scale'[13]), and recognizing that though a 'great writer' he is also a 'faulty writer' (111). The 'faults' are precisely those I have noted above – pessimism, preaching, clumsy style, melodrama, coincidence, etc. – and the 'minor novels' are indisputably failures. 'Improbabilism' is a major flaw: *Tess*, despite its greatness, is 'disastrously' marred by it – 'these crude pieces of machinery, tearing the delicate fabric of imaginative illusion in tatters' (116); and in *Jude*, Hardy 'breaks with probability altogether' (118). These 'faults', however, are insignificant in the light of Hardy's 'real' achievement, which is, of course, Cecil's own constitutive 'reading' or 'production' of Hardy: 'it is a tragic theme' (19); 'A struggle between man on the one hand and, on the other, an omnipotent and indifferent Fate – that is Hardy's interpretation of the human situation ... Man in Hardy's books is ranged against impersonal forces' (26); 'man's struggles as a political and social character seem too insignificant to fire his creative spark' (35);

> We are shown life in its fundamental elements, as exemplified by simple, elemental characters actuated by simple, elemental passions. ... And the fact that they are seen in relation to ultimate Destiny gives them a gigantic and universal character. Nor is the universality of this picture weakened by the fact that Hardy writes only of country people in nineteenth-century Wessex. On the contrary ... concentrated in this narrow, sequestered form of life, basic facts of the human drama showed up at their strongest. (32)

Now most people reading this will no doubt smile superciliously, (a) because they do not believe anyone any longer takes any notice of Cecil, and (b) because I am loading the odds in favour of my argument by elevating this *passé* belletrism as representative. I do not claim it is representative, but I do claim it is important in continuing to construct 'Hardy'. For example, it is the only substantial critical monograph recommended in the 'Suggested Reading' section of Methuen's 'Study Aids', first published in 1971 and available now in bookshops up and down the country. It also appears (along with three or four others) in the Pan 'Revision Aids', 'Brodie's Notes' – *first published in 1977*.

My second observation is that Leavis almost totally ignored Hardy as novelist. He is dismissed in *The Great Tradition* in a disparaging passing comment ('a provincial manufacturer of gauche and heavy fictions[14]). Given the continual comparisons with George Eliot in Hardy's lifetime, Henry James's dismissive review of *FMC*, and D. H. Lawrence's fascination with Hardy, it is surprising that Leavis did not even bother to attack him substantively. How far Leavis's influence affected the presence of, and approach to, Hardy in education from the 1940s through to the early 1970s would be an interesting question; but even more so is: why that silence on Leavis's part? I will make some suggestions towards an answer in my concluding remarks. My third observation is how little criticism there has been which has regarded Hardy seriously and historically as a social novelist concerned with the composition of the rural economy, with class, property and gender relations, etc. Merryn Williams's *Thomas Hardy and Rural England* (1972) is an over-simplified, but significantly lonely, example; and even that was criticized in a recent bibliographical essay for its 'emphatic left-wing subjectivity [which] clouds interpretation of some of the evidence'.[15] Raymond Williams and Terry Eagleton have written about Hardy,[16] and Eagleton's introduction to the 'New Wessex' edition of *Jude* is one publicly accessible countering of the conventional re-production of 'Hardy' (although the same bibliographical essay, in favourably reviewing these Introductions, omits to mention the *Jude* one at all!). But even in these cases, something of the 'Hardy' of bourgeois criticism remains in their sole address to the 'major novels'. And this leads me to my fourth observation.

Six of Hardy's 14 novels are generally regarded as 'minor': *Desperate Remedies*, *A Pair of Blue Eyes*, *The Hand of Ethelberta*, *A Laodicean*, *Two on a Tower* and *The Well-Beloved*. These are spread evenly throughout his career – *HE*, for example, appearing, to everyone's distress (then and now), immediately after his first major public success in the 'Wessex' mode, *FMC*. As I have said, none of them appears in the 'Character and Environment' category of Hardy's 1912 General Preface, but they had been marked down before that for their artificially, 'improbabilism' or deviation from the rural homelands of Hardy's Wessex. Certainly by the Edwardian period his 'society novels' are 'rather successful essays in the art of sinking', and *HE* is the least regarded of them: 'The characters are unconvincing and the plot improbable.'[17] This consensus has continued unchanged in the 20th century. Albert C. Baugh's standard *A Literary History of England* (1967) dismisses *HE* as 'only a negligible piece of frivolity';[18] for Cecil, its 'lifeless artificiality' makes it 'mainly worthless';[19] Albert Guerard, who finds the 'major/minor' classification 'unsatisfactory', nevertheless agrees that it is a 'failure';[20] in the *Critical Heritage* it is the only novel not to have even a small section devoted to it; Ian Gregor deals exclusively with the 'major fiction'; so too does Merryn Williams, never mentioning *HE* – nor does she, surprisingly, in a recent essay with Raymond Williams on 'Hardy and Social Class';[21] in three recent collections of essays[22] none of the 'minor novels' – apart from *W-B* – receives any substantive treatment at all; and even Robert Gittings's introduction to the 'New Wessex' edition

(1975) presents *HE* as 'the joker in the pack' of Hardy's novels, a 'comparative failure' and riddled with 'improbabilities'.[23] The point is, simply, that 'Hardy' as constituted by criticism is minus six out of fourteen novels – novels which do not 'fit' a conception of the humanist–realist of 'Character and Environment'. These contradictory fictions are thus excised for their 'artificiality' and 'improbability' (or, to put it another way, by their power to challenge and disturb), just as similar discourses within the 'great' novels are suppressed as 'faults' rather than treated as contradictory, but substantive, elements of the texts. I see the 'minor novels' as, in this respect, analogous to the many other forms of fiction (usually 'popular', or otherwise subversive) which are 'written out' of the literary canon.

At this point I can return to Hardy in school education, and those questions about what 'Hardy' is read, why and how. Two material determinations for his popularity in the last eight years or so may be adduced first. Although Macmillan had had a number of Hardy's novels in print in paperback for many years, in 1974/75 they published the 'New Wessex' edition including all 14 novels with new introductions, notes and prefaces, and with pictorial covers – pictures, by the by, which posed mock-Victorian 'characters' in an emphatically rural 'environment'. (Despite my remarks above about the 'minor novels', then, it is now possible to teach, say, *HE*. The simple accessibility, in other words, of these texts changes the constitution of 'Hardy', and this makes a determinate difference to teaching him.[24]) In 1975 Macmillan also published a 'Student's Edition' – aimed primarily at schools and differently packaged. This edition contained none of the 'minor novels'. Nevertheless, there were now in the mid-1970s two cheap and attractive paperback editions of Hardy available, with modern introductions and full explanatory notes. Does Hardy Rule OK, then, because in 1978, 50 years after his death, Macmillan's control of the copyright would fall in, and they had to saturate the market before others could join them? The second factor is that, at the point when Antonia Byatt does her survey, and Hardy is most intensively present on the GCE syllabus, three of the four novels set by the JMB, Cambridge, AEB and London in 1981 existed in television or film versions: Schlesinger's film of *FMC* (made in 1967 and released on EMI video in 1980), Polanski's film of *Tess* (made in 1979) and Giles's and Potter's television serial of *MC* (first shown in 1978 and repeated in 1979). Not, of course, that the GCE papers ever acknowledge that the 'text' most likely to be encountered in the student's own experience is not in the book form, 'as written by Hardy', at all.

What, then, is the 'Hardy' encountered by the A-level student; which texts and what kinds of questions reproduce the artificial construct which students come to recognize as the 'great writer' Hardy? In my sample, which includes almost complete runs of examination papers from the JMB and Cambridge since World War I, and from the AEB, London and Oxford and Cambridge selectively, and then intensively from the mid-1970s, 'Hardy' is centrally constructed around *FMC, MC* and *RN* – although until the end of the 1950s, *Under the Greenwood Tree, The Trumpet-Major* and *The Woodlanders* also appeared fairly regularly. *Tess* is not set before 1961,[25] and then only intermittently until the end of the 1970s when it becomes extremely popular; and *Jude*, significantly, only appears to have been set twice to date at A-level (AEB 1977/8). Needless to say, the 'minor novels' have never been set at all. In other words, the key texts at A-level are those at the centre of the 'Character and Environment' conception of 'Hardy', and which late-19th-century criticism had established as the apex of his achievement. The examination questions reinforce this conception – a self-fulfilling process in which critical (and ideological) assumptions select the works most appropriate to the realization of those assumptions in critical discourse (i.e. examination questions and answers). Not surprisingly, the questions are very similar across boards and over time, and they operate within a very constricted range: Nature, Fate, Tragedy, Character, and – when 'critical' – with the 'flaws' in his work:

> '"The true subject of the novel is Egdon Heath; the principal characters are much too vaguely drawn." Discuss.' (Lond. '77)/ '"Hardy is driven by some sense that human beings are the sport of forces outside themselves." Discuss and illustrate, and add a note to show how this attitude affects his greatness as a novelist.' (Camb. '39)/'To what extent do the seeds of Michael Henchard's downfall lie within his own character?' (AEB '56)/'The self-destructiveness of Hardy's characters has often been commented upon. To what extent is Michael Henchard cast in this mould?' (Lond. '79)/'How far is Michael Henchard a truly tragic figure?' (Lond. '80)/'"Hardy's characters may seem simple and rustic, but they embody universal human emotions." Discuss ... 2 or 3 characters in *The Mayor of*

Casterbridge' (Lond. '81)/'"In *The Mayor of Casterbridge* Hardy has sacrificed his characters to the mechanism of the plot." What justice is there in this charge?' (Camb. '43)/'"Although the setting of *The Mayor of Casterbridge* is realistic, the plot lacks conviction." Do you agree?' (Lond. '80)/'"Hardy's excessive use of coincidence has been criticised as a grave defect in his novels." What part does coincidence play in *Far from the Madding Crowd*, and with what effect?' (Camb. '41)/'"One of the criticisms of Hardy's craftsmanship is that too much appears to depend on coincidence and odd chances." To what extent could you apply this criticism to *The Mayor of Casterbridge*?' (AEB. '55)/'"Hardy's pessimism is so unmitigated as to be ludicrous." Consider this statement.' (Camb. '45)/'"In *The Mayor of Casterbridge*, Hardy's vision is overwhelmingly pessimistic." Do you agree?' (Lond. '81)

Although the 'Discuss' convention 'allows' the student to contradict the quotation, the 'critical' questions are invariably negatively framed so that the student is persuaded in the first instance to think in those terms. The underlying burden of all such questions, of course, is 'literary value' and an assumed agreement, between critic–examiner and critic–student, about a hypothetical model of the ultimately 'probable' novel, which in effect closes out any possible *positive* reading of those features that deviate from it. The case of *Tess* is particularly striking. I have mentioned that the early critical response was ambivalent; it is symptomatic of the way the examination system mediates literature that *Tess* has been continually represented in the same ambivalent terms. Most of the 'character questions' focus on the moral ambiguity (primarily sexual) of Tess – an issue which had exercised Mrs Oliphant in the 1890s: '"A Pure Woman". How far do you think Hardy was justified in describing Tess in this way?' (JMB '61); 'Critics disagree as to whether Tess is completely blameless or at least partially responsible for her own ultimate disaster. Make clear your own view of this matter' (JMB '81). But almost without exception, on the relatively few occasions when it has been set, there are questions on the limits of the novel's artistic achievement. In 1962, *both* the alternatives on the JMB paper were of this kind: 'Either: "Tess is the only character who is allowed to develop. The rest are static and unchanging." Discuss, etc. Or: "Melodramatic rather than tragic." How apt, etc?' In the same year, Oxford and Cambridge set: 'Consider the judgement of *Tess* as "full of faults, but a very great novel."' When it was set

again in 1980 by the same board, the question was: 'Do you consider the element of melodrama in *Tess* spoils the novel?' And in
1980, when Oxford Local set 'Despite the element of sheer bad
luck, *Tess* has a tragic inevitability', the JMB set the classic formu-
lation: '"*Tess* is a triumph despite its faults." Show to what extent,
etc.' Whether or not this startling conformity of perspective is the
reflex of a subconscious anxiety about examining a novel which is
so conscious of the sexual and social exploitation of women, or
whether it is an unthinking acceptance of long-standing critical orthodoxy, any modern student who does not find 'melodrama' amiss
(who defines it in any case, and is it necessarily bad?), or does not
recognize the 'faults' as faults (one is expected to know what they
are), or who thinks more in terms of social repression than of classical tragedy, will nevertheless be constrained to 'read' *Tess* in these
vague and alien terms. Equally as striking, perhaps, as the general
consonance of questions about Hardy, is the dearth of questions on
social issues. Only very occasionally are such questions asked, and
then usually in generalized terms ('conventions of society',
'influence of social pressures', etc.) and often as part of a 'catch-all'.
What we can deduce from all this is how restricted and determined
'Hardy' is as an educational discourse; how little of his work is on
the syllabus (that which is excised would, as with criticism, challenge and confuse it), and how this 'primary material' is reproduced
within very limited parameters of intelligibility: 'Hardy' as the
tragic novelist of character struggling heroically with Nature, Fate
or other, pre-eminently non-social, forces. Quite clearly the Hardy
who rules OK in school education at least, is 'primary material' in
only a very dubious sense.

* * * * *

But why, in conclusion, should 'Hardy' have been constituted in
this way; why made to fit uneasily into the critical discourse of
liberal–humanist realism, his 'improbabilism' criticized away, his
'minor' 'novels of ingenuity' excised, his fiction on the one hand
'rewritten' by Cecil and the examination boards, and on the other
totally ignored by Leavis even though his novels are compared to
George Eliot's – the avatar of liberal realism and the ideological
centre of Leavis's socio-critical project? My guess is that, at whatever level of consciousness, there is a recognition of just how

radically Hardy's fiction (whether intentionally or not) challenges Eliot's humanism and realism – not only in the 'minor novels', although more explicitly there, but in *all* the novels.[26] *HE*, the most 'improbable' and 'artificial' of Hardy's fiction and the one most emphatically dismissed as a negligible failure, is merely the one most uncompromisingly to demystify that social and literary ideology. Written to distance himself from Eliot after the success of *FMC* had been partly attributed to her influence, it is also the most ironically autobiographical of Hardy's fictions (including, here, Florence Emily Hardy's *The Life of Thomas Hardy*, which was written by himself), the one most obsessively and bitterly concerned with social class and alienation – to the point, indeed, where bourgeois notions of 'character' and the individual subject are deconstructed (there is no 'real' Ethelberta, she is in every sense a 'fiction'), and the one which most self-consciously displays its own artifice and fictionality. One might say that it represents the alienating fiction of class in the alienating fictiveness of the fiction.

I am, of course, now myself 'producing' *HE* – as an instance of the politics of the critiographical project – as a text which fractures the illusions of realism and of its informing ideology, and which bourgeois criticism must reject if it is not to jeopardize its own enterprise. Hardy's 'improbabilism', his flouting of realist 'conviction', challenges the whole edifice. For realism is not just a matter of literary form; it is the common-sense expression in aesthetic terms of an ideology in which the unified individual human subject 'makes sense' of his/her world by negotiation with external forces – Nature, Society, etc., which presupposes a universe that *can* be made sense of and an always potentially self-determining human subject. One form of 'making sense' of the world is through the 'probabilist' discourses of realism, in which 'plausible' characters are 'convincingly' deployed in relation to the 'credible' processes of the 'real' natural and social world. Realism, in effect, is the writing of the unified human subject on to the immensities of time, process and history, and as such is a crucial instrument in this ideology's naturalizing function. When the essential fiction of bourgeois realism – the illusion of truth – comes to be believed as the literal truth, then fiction and ideology are working very closely together, and the deception of their 'truthfulness' must be sustained at all costs. It is for this reason that non-realist modes ('gothic', 'melodrama', etc.) have been perceived as seditious by the dominant literary culture, and marginalized by the construction of 'canons' and 'great traditions' which exclude them; and that, for the same reason, potentially disruptive discourses like those of Hardy's fiction are made to fit. His 'improbabilism' draws attention to, precisely, the *illusion* of truth in humanist realism. Where George Eliot spent immense pains producing 'conviction' and 'truthfulness', and disguising the fictive contrivance involved in 'realizing' her individualist social philosophy, Hardy's fiction can be seen to parade the opposite: the fictiveness of fiction (coincidence, melodrama, etc.); a contingent, 'senseless' universe in which individuals are out of control of the social forces which exploit and victimize them; characters who are not unified human subjects, but alienated, inconsistent clusters of 'images' of the social and psychological 'circumstances' which construct them. Much of this, of course, is what is written out of the 'Hardy' constituted by criticism and education: 'improbabilism', 'pessimism'; 'minor novels'. One is reminded of how Leavis, even with George Eliot, had to excise half of *Daniel Deronda* because it flawed the novel 'Gwendolen Harleth'.[27]

The importance of a critiography within historical criticism, then, is that by studying the production and reproduction of literature in history, it denaturalizes the ostensibly unproblematical 'primary material' of the texts, showing how they are historically produced for the present, how they are constructed and appropriated by the dominant ideological institutions, and how they are naturalized in hierarchies of 'value'. In this, it also serves to free writings from that incorporation, enabling other suppressed discourses (*Tess*'s 'faults', the 'minor novels') to emerge and take their place as constituent discourses of a different 'Hardy'. The effect, for example, of reassembling the 'minor novels' with the others – free of the evaluative categories – is to release all the texts into more open and various reading, bringing into play latent potentialities for the 'major' novels which have been repressed. For the closures of the major/minor opposition do not simply exclude certain texts, they also limit the ways in which the others may be read. This is where a critiography, as with historiography, consciously asserts its political function. If 'Hardy' is recognized as *only constructed* in critical discourse, then Hardy can be *reconstructed* just as properly on behalf of an alternative interest. As with the variable facticity of the fact in history, the newly visible discourses alter the perception, the 'meaning', of the whole set of discourses. Analogously, but on a

3

Hardy and Social Class: *The Hand of Ethelberta*

Towards the end of The *Hand of Ethelberta*, there is a scene in which the heroine narrates one of her 'fictions' to the guests at Lord Mountclere's house. It is, in fact, the strangest of her fictions – the true story of her life and origins up to the point at which she enters society as fashionable widow and writer of poems:

> The narrative began by introducing to their notice a girl of the poorest and meanest parentage, the daughter of a serving-man, and the fifth of ten children. She graphically recounted, as if they were her own, the strange dreams and ambitious longings of this child when young, her attempts to acquire education, partial failures, partial successes, and constant struggles; instancing how, on one of these occasions, the girl concealed herself under a bookcase of the library belonging to the mansion in which her father served as footman, and having taken with her there, like a young Fawkes, matches and a halfpenny candle, was going to sit up all night reading when the family had retired, until her father discovered and prevented her scheme. Then followed her experiences as nursery-governess, her evening lessons under self-selected masters, and her ultimate rise to a higher grade among the teaching sisterhood. Next came another epoch. To the mansion in which she was engaged returned a truant son, between whom and the heroine an attachment sprang up. The master of the house was an ambitious gentleman just

---

This essay was Chapter 5 of *Hardy in History: A Study in Literary Sociology* (London: Routledge, 1989). It is reprinted more or less as it stood, except for the insertion of a few pages from my *Thomas Hardy* volume in the 'Writers and their Work' series (Plymouth: Northcote House, 1996).

knighted, who, perceiving the state of their hearts, harshly dismissed the homeless governess, and rated the son, the consequence being that the youthful pair resolved to marry secretly, and carried their resolution into effect. The runaway journey came next, and then a moving description of the death of the young husband, and the terror of the bride.

The guests began to look perplexed, and one or two exchanged whispers. This was not at all the kind of story that they had expected; it was quite different from her usual utterances, the nature of which they knew by report. Ethelberta kept her eyes upon Lord Mountclere. Soon, to her amazement, there was that in his face which told her that he knew the story and its heroine quite well. When she delivered the sentence ending with the professedly fictitious words: 'I thus was reduced to great distress, and vainly cast about me for directions what to do,' Lord Mountclere's manner became so excited and anxious that it acted reciprocally upon Ethelberta; her voice trembled, she moved her lips but uttered nothing. To bring the story up to the date of that very evening had been her intent, but it was beyond her power. The spell was broken, she blushed with distress and turned away, for the folly of a disclosure here was but too apparent.

Though every one saw that she had broken down, none of them appeared to know the reason why, or to have the clue to her performance. Fortunately Lord Mountclere came to her aid.

'Let the first part end here,' he said, rising and approaching her, 'We have been well entertained so far. I could scarcely believe that the story I was listening to was utterly an invention, so vividly does Mrs Petherwin bring the scenes before our eyes. She must now be exhausted; we will have the remainder to-morrow.'

They all agreed that this was well, and soon after fell into groups, and dispersed about the rooms. When everybody's attention was thus occupied Lord Mountclere whispered to Ethelberta tremulously, 'Don't tell more: you think too much of them: they are no better than you!'[1]

There are a number of points to be made about this passage. First, it recounts Ethelberta's life up to the point of the ridiculously abbreviated account, delivered in a single sentence, on the first page of the novel. Second, it stops at exactly the point where the novel itself had begun, in taking up the story of her deception of society as a young widow of good family and of her career as poet and fictionist. The reader, therefore, now has both the novelist's and Ethelberta's accounts of the 'truth' (albeit in both cases presented as fictions). Third, it 'was not at all the kind of story that [her listeners] had expected; it was quite different from her usual utterances' – one, indeed, which tells the truth about her 'real' class background, although presented as a fiction and accepted as such by her audience (her earlier stories [see *HE*, pp. 131–3] had been 'romances', although purporting to be the exact truth). We may recall here that Hardy shocked and disappointed his editor, Leslie Stephen, and the reviewers by producing *HE* after *Far from the Madding Crowd*, and that *The Life of Thomas Hardy* refers to his 'plunge in a new and untried direction' – much to 'the consternation of his editor and publishers' – which 'had nothing whatsoever in common with anything he had written before'.[2] Fourth, Lord Mountclere, the elderly aristocratic roué Ethelberta finally marries and dominates, who is himself no mean intriguer and illusionist – his house has a sham façade of stone over brick, of which the novel remarks 'as long as nobody knew the truth, pretence looked just as well' (305), and a staircase where 'the art which produced this illusion was questionable, but its success was undoubted' (304) – stops the story at the point at which the novel has begun its own narrative and advises Ethelberta about her audience: "'Don't tell more: you think too much of them: they are no better than you.'" Mountclere thus implies at once the pervasive lie of a class society, Ethelberta's merit in rising in it, and the necessity of sustaining the deception. In this respect, what we have here is not dissimilar to what *The Life* was later to do for Hardy himself (see Introduction, p. 3, and Chapter 1, *passim*, above). Fifth, the passage draws our attention to an obsession, anything but unique in the novel, with social class, with the nature of fictions and story-telling, with deception and illusion, and with the connections between all of these issues. And sixth, it underwrites (although it does not say it) the correlation between the story the novel narrates and the ironic slant of the novel itself: the fiction of a young person who achieves social success by way of making fictions – class fictions and written fictions – but in which the truth is told only as a fiction – both within the novel and *as* the novel. *HE* is, in other words, a self-reflexive novel of a highly complex order.

What I shall do here is bring into view some elements of this complexity which have been obscured by a critical orthodoxy that marginalizes *HE* in Hardy's *oeuvre*; at the same time suggesting why this orthodoxy has had to reject the novel if its conception of 'Hardy', and indeed of the 'great tradition' in fiction, are to be sustained. I shall consider the novel as a set of discourses freed of the conventional criteria of 'value' in fiction ('flat' characters, artificial plot, obtrusive style, and so on), and so hope to release potencies which those criteria make inaccessible. I shall show (while avoiding intentionalism) how *HE* self-consciously foregrounds issues of social class, gender relations, and the artifice of realist fiction writing. And I shall suggest that the exposure of the alienating lies produced by these systems is more readily perceptible in Hardy's other fiction once it has been identified in such uncompromising form in *HE*. Just as *HE* may seem to be 'the joker in the pack'[3] of Hardy's novels, but can be recuperated by conceiving it positively as a complex set of anti-realist discourses and not as a failure of literary decorum, so Hardy's work as a whole (itself uneasily placed in the canon of English literature) can only be comprehended if the interrelations between class, gender and fictionality are regarded positively as constituting the fabric of his work. Indeed, any 'reading' which does not consider these factors positively can only proceed by way of omission, excision and suppression; by stripping 'Hardy', in other words, of those subversive elements which are at play in his texts and which literary criticism cannot accommodate without endangering its own unspoken ideological presuppositions.

* * * * *

Hardy wrote *HE* immediately after *FMC*, the novel which made him successful. Its very position in his career, then, especially as it is so apparently unlike the previous novel, suggests a conscious decision on Hardy's part to do something entirely different; and indeed, as we have seen, *The Life* seems to confirm this – Hardy, nearly fifty years later, writing that he took 'a plunge in a new and untried direction'. But *The Life* as usual is curiously ambiguous about the novel and its inception. It suggests, on the one hand, that Hardy took 'the unfortunate course' of rushing into another novel 'before he was aware of what there had been of value in his previous one: before learning, that is, not only what had attracted the public, but what was of true and genuine substance on which to build a career as a writer with a real literary message'; or again, that he did it for money and in response to gossip about his social origins. On the other hand, *The Life* implies a serious purpose: 'Yet he had not the slightest intention of writing forever about sheep farming, as the reading public was apparently expecting him to do, and as, in fact, they presently resented his not doing.' It further adds that he 'had at last the satisfaction of proving ... that he did not mean to imitate anybody'; and that Hardy himself took the novel seriously: commenting (on the critics' 'chief objection ... that it was "impossible"') that 'it was, in fact, thirty years too soon for a Comedy of Society of that kind – just as *The Poor Man and the Lady* had been too soon for a socialist story, and as other of his writings – in prose and verse – were too soon for their date'.[4] (We should register here Hardy's sympathetic correlation of *HE* and that earlier, 'lost', 'socialist story' – see also Chapter 1 p. 16, above, and Chapter 7, pp. 168–73, below.) But however ambiguous *The Life* may be, we can be certain that it was a strange and self-conscious novel to write at this stage of his career, if for no other reason than because of the amount of disguised autobiography it contains.

There is little question now about the similarities between the character of Ethelberta and Hardy himself. Robert Gittings has given a useful synopsis of them in *The Young Thomas Hardy* and in the Introduction to the 'New Wessex' edition of the novel, but it is worth noting the main ones again here. There is the central structural irony of their both being lower-class people making their way in society by the profession of writing and disguising their class background; both are poets by inclination who have to turn to fiction to make a living – Hardy calling Ethelberta's poems, in the serial version of the novel, 'Metres by Me'[5] and which echo his own early 'She to Him' sonnets; Hardy's class background and his relatives' occupations and social status are reproduced for Ethelberta – servants, carpenters, schoolmistresses, and so on; there is the reference in the title to Hardy's mother's family name of 'Hand'; and in addition, there is the important point, not noted by Gittings, that at the very end of the novel Ethelberta, in her security and success, is 'writing an epic poem, and employs Emmeline as her reader' (409). Leaving aside the possibly fortuitous similarity of name with Hardy's first wife Emma, it cannot be fortuitous that Hardy was planning to write his own 'epic poem' *The Dynasts* when he could afford to stop writing fiction, and that the first reference to his earliest thoughts on this project occurs in *The Life* in the middle of the pages on *HE* and whilst he was writing that novel: 'In this same month [May] of 1875, it may be interesting to note, occurs the first mention in Hardy's memoranda of the idea of an epic on the war with Napoleon – carried out so many years later in *The Dynasts*.'[6] It seems likely, then, that Hardy was self-consciously re-presenting himself as Ethelberta, and producing an immense irony which only he could savour: his most open and accurate account of himself and his real social relations presented as a fiction in which his heroine does the same, only for both 'true stories' to be received as fictions and, in the case of the novel itself, to be criticized for being 'impossible'.

What is equally clear is the similarity between Ethelberta and Hardy in terms of their fictional theory and practice – which again suggests a high degree of self-reflexivity. *HE* is, indeed, the only novel of Hardy's in which there is substantial and explicit address to questions of fiction writing, since even *The Life* contains only passing 'notes' on Hardy's views about fiction and deals only cursorily with the novels, the reader being left to make what s/he can of the 'memoranda' about them. Nevertheless, certain notions and terms are reiterated throughout *The Life*, the 'literary notebooks', the few essays on fiction,[7] and the (often opaque) 'Prefaces' which Hardy at various times attaches to the front of his novels (including the ones for *HE*, which I shall consider below). It is not, I think, too self-fulfilling an argument to state that these circle around a problematical relation to realism and a sharp consciousness of the artifice of art, which leads Hardy at times to an embryonic conception of such modern critical notions as 'making strange' ('defamiliarization') and 'alienation' (*verfremdungseffekt*). My point simply is that, in the part of *The Life* which deals with the period from the late 1870s to the mid-1890s, when Hardy was at the height of his novel-writing career, there is continual evidence of a consciousness at work in which these issues were actively present. Whatever our attitude to 'intention', then, we cannot properly ignore the mindset of the novelist, nor can we disregard, excise or explain away fictional features in his novels which may themselves appear problematical but which are also the articulation of that mindset.

Early in *The Life*, in a letter to Hardy's sister Mary shortly after he had arrived in London, there is an equivocal comment about Thackeray (the equivocation being compounded by finding a moral tone proper for writing to a younger sister) which nevertheless initiates an iterative theme of Hardy's: 'He is considered to be the greatest novelist of the day – looking at novel writing of the highest kind as a perfect and truthful representation of actual life – which is no doubt the proper view to take.'[8] 'No doubt': but is that Hardy's 'view'? Certainly many of his later comments would seem to reject such a classic formal realism (whether it is true of Thackeray or not). The earliest of these is a memorandum (3 June 1877) in which he says:

> 'So, then, if Nature's defects must be looked in the face and transcribed, whence arises the *art* in poetry and novel-writing? which must certainly show art, or it becomes merely mechanical reporting. I think the art lies in making these defects the basis of a hitherto unperceived beauty, by irradiating them with "the light that never was" on their surface, but is seen to be latent in them by the spiritual eye.' (114)

Art is not 'mechanical reporting', but an 'irradiation' of 'a hitherto unperceived beauty'. A similar view is repeated in January 1881 when Hardy notes: 'This [perfect] reproduction is achieved by seeing into the *heart of a thing* ... and is realism, in fact, though through being pursued by means of the imagination it is confounded with invention' (147). Now it might properly be claimed here that there is nothing original or unique in Hardy's thinking, that it is in line with mainstream 19th-century romanticism. But my point is to indicate the cast of Hardy's consciousness, and to notice how increasingly sharply such commonplaces are inflected. Later the same year (July 1881), *The Life* 'reproduces' some 'notes on fiction, possibly for an article that was never written':

> 'The real, if unavowed, purpose of fiction is to give pleasure by gratifying the love of the uncommon in human experience, mental or corporeal.
> 'This is done all the more perfectly in proportion as the reader is illuded to believe the personages true and real like himself.
> 'Solely to this latter end a work of fiction should be a precise transcript of ordinary life: but,
> 'The uncommon would be absent and the interest lost. Hence,
> 'The writer's problem is, how to strike the balance between the uncommon and the ordinary so as on the one hand to give interest, on the other to give reality.
> 'In working out this problem, human nature must never be made abnormal, which is introducing incredibility. The uncommonness must be in the events, not in the characters; and the writer's art lies in shaping that uncommonness while disguising its unlikelihood, if it be unlikely.' (150)

This passage is regularly quoted in Hardy criticism, most usually to reinforce notions of Hardy's fundamental realism and to 'explain' (away) the use of contingency and coincidence in his plots; but placed together with his other comments which tend towards 'defamiliarization' as a fictional principle, his sense here of 'shaping that uncommonness' takes on a potentially non-realist resonance. A further, and related, strand in Hardy's thinking is picked out in the following note (June 1882), when he reflects: 'so in life the seer should watch that pattern among general things which his idiosyncrasy moves him to observe, and describe that alone. This is, quite accurately, a going to Nature; yet the result is no mere photograph, but purely the product of the writer's own mind' (153). What we have here in embryo is Hardy's constant presentation of his fictions as 'impressions' or 'seemings', an idea more fully enunciated in a series of highly significant jottings from the spring of 1886: 'My art is to intensify the expression of things ... so that the heart and inner meaning is made vividly visible' (3 Jan. 1886; 177). This, of course, could equally be the claim of a realist, but the phrasing ('intensify the expression', 'vividly visible') suggests an aesthetic moving beyond any notion of effecting 'a precise transcript of ordinary life'. However, the note has also to be taken in conjunction with a statement (4 Mar. 1886) which in my context here, and in any debate about why Hardy gave up writing novels after *Jude the Obscure* ten years later, must have a crucial place:

> 'Novel-writing as an art cannot go backward. Having reached the analytic stage it must transcend it by going still further in the same direction. Why not by rendering as visible essences, spectres, etc, the abstract thoughts of the analytic school?'

This notion was approximately carried out, not in a novel, but through the much more appropriate medium of poetry, in the supernatural framework of *The Dynasts* as also in smaller poems. And a further note of the same date enlarges the same idea:

> 'The human race to be shown as one great network or tissue which quivers in every part when one point is shaken, like a spider's web if touched. Abstract realisms to be in the form of Spirits, Spectral figures, etc.
> 'The Realities to be the true realities of life, hitherto called abstractions. The old material realities to be placed behind the former, as shadowy accessories.' (177)

Effectively, what Hardy is recognizing is that realism – at least for him as a novelist – is pressing against its limits, that 'abstract realisms' demand a different form to be realized as 'visible essences', and that he must move to the 'more appropriate medium' of epic poetry. He is disingenuous in suggesting that this was not 'carried out … in a novel', for the crucial problematic of Hardy's fiction (in *HE*, but also in most of the later novels) would seem to lie precisely in his attempts to find a form to 'render visible' abstract and analytic 'essences' of contemporary social relations: in particular, the 'fictions' of class and gender hierarchies. A further gloss on the inadequacy of a naturalistic realism is offered in some telling remarks about late Turner paintings in January of the following year (1887):

> 'I don't want to see landscapes, *i.e.*, scenic paintings of them, because I don't want to see the original realities – as optical effects, that is. I want to see the deeper reality underlying the scenic, the expression of what are sometimes called abstract imaginings.
>
> 'The "simply natural" is interesting no longer. The much decried, mad, late-Turner rendering is now necessary to create my interest. The exact truth as to material fact ceases to be of importance in art – it is a student's style – the style of a period when the mind is serene and unawakened to the tragical mysteries of life.' (185)

And in January 1889, again in relation to Turner, he makes the observation: 'Hence, one may say, Art is the secret of how to produce by a false thing the effect of a true' (216).

The concept of 'abstract imaginings' and the problem of their expression in art lie behind the string of related comments in the prefaces to his novels of this period (although some derive from the retrospective 1912 ones when he was editing the 'Wessex Edition'). In the 1891 Preface to *Tess of the d'Urbervilles*, he writes that it is 'an attempt to give artistic form to a true sequence of things', and in 1892 that he is concerned with 'impressions' not 'convictions', that 'a novel is an impression, not an argument'. In the 1895 Preface to *Jude*, he makes the most famous of his gnomic prefatory utterances:

> Like former productions of this pen, *Jude the Obscure* is simply an endeavour to give shape and coherence to a series of seemings, or personal impressions, the question of their consistency or their discordance, of their permanence or their transitoriness, being regarded as not of the first moment:

And in the 1912 Preface to *The Well-Beloved*, he writes:

> As for the story itself, it may be worth while to remark that, differing from all or most others of the series in that the interest aimed at is of an ideal or subjective nature, and frankly imaginative, verisimilitude in the sequence of events has been subordinated to the said aim.

Given Hardy's remarks in the *Jude* Preface above and, as we shall see, in the 1895 Preface to *HE*, the notion here that he usually pursued verisimilitude is highly dubious. Notoriously ironic and defensive as the prefaces are, there is enough continuity in their trajectory at this period (and in their relation to contemporary memoranda in *The Life*) for us to have some confidence that, at the very least, Hardy is not trying and failing to write realist fiction, and rather more that he is strategically experimenting with forms and practices which themselves crack open the discourses of realism. As he says of *Jude*, in the assumed voice of a hostile critic: 'it is not the view of life that we who thrive on conventions can permit to be painted' (Preface).

But it is in a couple of memoranda from 1890 (the year before he produced his essay 'The Science of Fiction', in which he defines realism as 'an artificiality distilled from the fruits of closest observation'), that Hardy gives most explicit articulation to a curiously prophetic statement of the aesthetics of 20th-century Formalism. Early in the year (March–April), he repeats now familiar notions: 'Art consists in so depicting the common events of life as to bring out the features which illustrate the author's idiosyncratic mode of regard; making old incidents and things seem as new' (225). By August, however, the sense of 'making strange' – of 'defamiliarizing' – and of a concomitant rejection of realism is very much more systematically stated:

> 'Reflections on Art. Art is a changing of the actual proportions and order of things, so as to bring out more forcibly than might otherwise be done that feature in them which appeals most strongly to the idiosyncrasy of the artist.'

> 'Art is a disproportioning – (*i.e.* distorting, throwing out of proportion) – of realities, to show more clearly the features that matter in those realities, which, if merely copied or reported inventorially, might possibly be observed, but would more probably be overlooked. Hence "realism" is not Art.' (228–9)

It is here, I think, that the core of Hardy's fictional aesthetic is to be found. And it is one which makes it perversely inappropriate to critically recast his fiction in the formal-realist mode – or, indeed, to perceive a 'minor novel' like *HE* as a failure of decorum in its 'uncharacteristic' content and manner, rather than to recognize it as a subversively artificial 'disproportioning' of the fictions of humanism – in the guise, here, of class relations and a 'probabilist' realism (see Chapter 2, pp. 33–4, 42–3, above).

In *HE* itself questions about realism, artifice and the illusions of verisimilitude are brought into sharp and explicit focus (I will return to the novel's enactment of them later). The main instances of this – apart from the passage with which I began – occur in Chapters 13 and 16 and concern Ethelberta's career as a fictionist. In the former, her first lover, Christopher Julian, happens on her as she is telling one of her tales (rehearsing it, in fact) to her brothers and sisters. She is presented to us – and Christopher believes it too – in these terms: 'Ethelberta's appearance answered as fully as ever to that of an English lady skilfully perfected in manner, carriage, look, and accent' (113). The implication of the artifice ('skilfully perfected') involved in manufacturing this 'appearance' (she is, in the Jamesian sense, 'the real thing') is inescapable. The tale she is telling – and Christopher arrives and eavesdrops *in medias res* – is a highly sensational, not to say gothic, romance; but, with herself as heroine, it purports to be true. Indeed Christopher believes that it is the truth, breaking into the recital with: 'For Heaven's sake, Ethelberta ... where did you meet with such a terrible experience as that?' She responds 'in a serene voice' – 'but', the novel adds, 'the calmness was artificially done' – thus pointing up Ethelberta's constant and deeply self-divisive acting of 'herself', of her artificial self-representation. Then follows this passage:

> 'But my concern at such a history of yourself since I last saw you is even more natural than your surprise at my manner of breaking in.'
> 'That history would justify any conduct in one who hears it –'
> 'Yes, indeed.'
> 'If it were true,' added Ethelberta, smiling. 'But it is as false as –'
> She could name nothing notoriously false without raising an image of what was disagreeable, and she continued in a better manner. 'The story I was telling is entirely a fiction, which I am getting up for a particular purpose – very different from what appears at present.' (114)

What the novel sets up here, then, is a complex play on questions of reality/truth/illusion/deceit, in which these moral absolutes become questionably relativized: which is the 'real' Ethelberta; is her fiction fact or not? The chapter proceeds to explain how she has been cheated out of an inheritance on the death of old Mrs Petherwin and now has to find some way of supporting her family. She cannot write poems any more, because she is 'surrounded by gaunt realities' (116): those of sustaining both the lie that is her life and the reality of her unacknowledged (because lower-class) family:

> 'I felt that to write prose would be an uncongenial occupation, and altogether a poor prospect for a woman like me. Finally I have decided to appear in public.'
> 'Not on the stage?'
> 'Certainly not on the stage. There is no novelty in a poor lady turning actress, and novelty is what I want. Ordinary powers exhibited in a new way effect as much as extraordinary powers exhibited in an old way.'...

> 'I had written a prose story by request, when it was found that I had grown utterly inane over verse. It was written in the first person, and the style was modelled after De Foe's. The night before sending it off, when I had already packed it up, I was reading about the professional story-tellers of Eastern countries, who devoted their lives to the telling of tales. I unfastened the manuscript and retained it, convinced that I should do better by *telling* the story.'...

> 'It occurred to me,' she continued, blushing slightly, 'that tales of the weird kind were made to be told, not written. The action of a teller is wanted to give due effect to all stories of incident; and I hope that a time will come when, as of old, instead of an unsocial reading of fiction at home alone, people will meet together cordially, and sit at the feet of a professed romancer. I am going to tell my tales before a London public. As a child, I had a considerable power in arresting the attention of other children by recounting adventures which had never happened; and men and women are but children enlarged a little.' (117)

There is, in fact, little difference between being the public story-teller of fictions (the novelist Hardy) and the public performance of the 'professed romancer' Ethelberta – except that the latter underscores the degree of artifice and acting involved in any fiction-making. With sharp irony, Ethelberta continues that she is going to appear in public as 'Mrs Petherwin, Professed Story-teller', although the one story she is not telling is the fiction of her life as an upperclass lady: 'As a reserved one [notice the pun 'reserved' here: more usually the word would be 'reserve'] I have the tale of my own life – to be played as a last card' (118). As we have seen, she does play it (her last *hand*?), and it is perceived simultaneously as both the truth and a fiction. Hardy too, of course, presents his true 'life' as one of his fictions (*HE*), and plays 'the tale of my own life' as his 'last card' in producing *The Life* as his true biography (a work which, I have suggested earlier (Chapter 1, p. 11), should instead be regarded as his last fiction).

What is particularly interesting in the passage above is the reference to Defoe, progenitor of the realist novel, whom Ethelberta returns to again:

> 'Now did you ever consider what a power De Foe's manner would have if practised by word of mouth? Indeed, it is a style which suits itself infinitely better to telling than to writing, abounding as it does in colloquialisms that are somewhat out of place on paper in these days, but have a wonderful power in making a narrative seem real. And so, in short, I am going to talk De Foe on a subject of my own.' (118)

We may note here the emphasis on Defoe's 'wonderful power in making a narrative seem real', reminiscent as it is of that early critic of Defoe who had remarked 'the little art he is master of, of forging a story, and imposing it on the world for truth'. But also, in this context, we should remember the two references to Defoe in *The Life* (see also Chapter 7, pp. 172–3, below): one in the section dealing with Hardy's first, unpublished, 'socialistic' novel, *The Poor Man and the Lady*, which notes that its style had the 'affected simplicity of Defoe's (which had long attracted Hardy ... to imitation of it)'; and the other in Hardy's old age (he was 79):

> A curious question arose in Hardy's mind at this date on whether a romancer was morally justified in going to extreme lengths of assurance – after the manner of Defoe – in respect of a tale he knew to be absolutely false. ... Had he not long discontinued the writing of romances he would, he said, have put at the beginning of each new one: 'Understand that however true this book may be in essence, in fact it is utterly untrue.'[9]

The irony here, in relation to *The Life* itself, is acute; but it is worth noting, too, both Hardy's use of the word 'romancer' (in the

context of the passage from *HE* above) and his obvious affinity
with the 'faking' art of the great illusionist, Defoe. *The Life* and
prefaces of course, as we have seen, are full of Hardy's own 'memoranda' on the art of making the 'uncommon' seem 'real', on the illusion of truth in fiction, and on the 'impressions' and 'seemings'
which constitute a novel's 'reality'.

The relationship between Hardy, Ethelberta, Defoe, and the
'wonderful power in making a narrative seem real', is reinforced in
Chapter 16. This is the occasion of Ethelberta's first public reading,
and the narrative stance of the novel with regard to it is to tell it in
a dispassionate reportage-like prose which emphasizes at once the
artifice and performance of Ethelberta's reading and the authority
and veracity of the novel's own account. 'What was her story to
be?' – many of the audience assume it will be 'some pungent and
gratifying revelation of the innermost events of her own life' (131);
we, as readers, know that that is her 'reserved story', and is indeed
the story the novel itself is telling. In fact, what she relates is a
fiction which purports to be authentically real:

> Ethelberta's plan was to tell her pretended history and adventures
> while sitting in a chair – as if she were at her own fireside, sur-
> rounded by a circle of friends. By this touch of domesticity a great
> appearance of truth and naturalness was given, though really the atti-
> tude was at first more difficult to maintain satisfactorily than any one
> wherein stricter formality should be observed. She gently began her
> subject, as if scarcely knowing whether a throng were near her or
> not, and, in her fear of seeming artificial, spoke too low. This defect,
> however, she soon corrected, and ultimately went on in a charmingly
> colloquial manner. What Ethelberta relied upon soon became
> evident. It was not upon the intrinsic merits of her story as a piece of
> construction, but upon her method of telling it. Whatever defects the
> tale possessed – and they were not a few – it had, as delivered by her,
> the one pre-eminent merit of seeming like truth. A modern critic has
> well observed of De Foe that he had the most amazing talent on
> record for telling lies; and Ethelberta, in wishing her fiction to appear
> like a real narrative of personal adventure, did wisely to make De
> Foe her model. His is a style even better adapted for speaking than
> for writing, and the peculiarities of diction which he adopts to give
> verisimilitude to his narratives acquired enormous additional force
> when exhibited as *viva-voce* mannerisms. And although these
> artifices were not, perhaps, slavishly copied from that master of
> feigning, they would undoubtedly have reminded her hearers of him,
> had they not mostly been drawn from an easeful section in society

which is especially characterized by the mental condition of knowing nothing about any author a week after they have read him. ... When she reached the most telling passages, instead of adding exaggerated action and sound, Ethelberta would lapse to a whisper and a sustained stillness, which were more striking than gesticulation. All that could be done by art was there, and if inspiration was wanting nobody missed it.

It was in performing this feat that Ethelberta seemed first to discover in herself the full power of that self-command which further onward in her career more and more impressed her as a singular possession, until at last she was tempted to make of it many fantastic uses, leading to results that affected more households than her own. A talent for demureness under difficulties without the cold-bloodedness which renders such a bearing natural and easy, a face and hand reigning unmoved outside a heart by nature turbulent as a wave, is a constitutional arrangement much to be desired by people in general; yet, had Ethelberta been framed with less of that gift in her, her life might have been more comfortable as an experience, and brighter as an example, though perhaps duller as a story. (131–3)

There are three points to note here. First, there is the emphasis again on Defoe, 'that master of feigning' whose 'method of telling' Ethelberta copies to achieve 'the one pre-eminent merit of seeming like truth'. What is striking is that only 15 pages previously the novel tells us more or less exactly the same about Defoe, including that his style was 'infinitely better [suited] to telling than to writing' (see above, p. 57). There is one important difference, however: before it was Ethelberta speaking to Christopher Julian, now it is Hardy informing the reader. What this betrays, in the painstaking account of her 'method of telling' and the emphasis on the deceptions of realism, is both Hardy's own interest in Defoe's 'amazing talent ... for telling lies' and the consanguinity of author and heroine: they are both 'professed story-tellers' and 'romancers', in fact and in fiction. Ethelberta's life as illusionist, in terms both of her class origins and of her profession, is no more than a displaced version of Hardy's, and the novel then becomes the fictive account of a real life: the author's own. Second, we may register the comment, in the final paragraph, on the effect of this 'romancing' on Ethelberta's character: in 'performing this feat' (of creating a 'true' fiction by art) she discovered 'the full power of that self-command' which was to help her play and win in society's stakes: so too, of course, had the Hardy of *FMC* who was now about to enter the social and intellectual life of London on his own terms. The lie of fiction and the lie of 'the life' are intimately connected: Ethelberta 'makes it' by way of fictions – both written and personal – to a cynical marriage with Lord Mountclere which underwrites her social position and gives her the 'freedom' to write an epic poem; Hardy also makes it – by way of similar fictions – to a cynically ambiguous relationship with society and the freedom to write an epic poem. Third, we may savour the strange final sentence of the passage in which, we learn, Ethelberta's ability to dissemble her real self makes the 'story' of her life less dull, but her life itself less 'comfortable'. The alienated image of the fragmented and disconnected elements of her personality in 'a face and hand reigning unmoved outside a heart by nature turbulent as a wave' has a note of personal bitterness which we may judge to be Hardy's. Fiction-making of this order costs a great deal; and that, in effect, is what *HE* is all about. As D. H. Lawrence wrote of the novel in his cryptic and penetrating comments on Hardy, it is

> the hard, resistant, ironical announcement of personal failure, resistant and half-grinning. It gives way to violent, angry passions and real tragedy, real killing of beloved people, self-killing; [it is] the one almost cynical comedy [marking] the zenith of a certain feeling in the Wessex novels ... the end of the happy endings.[10]

In this, and especially in the notion of 'self-killing', Lawrence identifies both the fiercely self-ironic thrust of the novel and its pivotal place in the development of Hardy's fiction.

There is an equally ironic coda to Chapter 16 in which Hardy literally 'reproduces' the critics' reviews of Ethelberta's performance. One of these is made to notice (aptly) that the event owes 'its chief interest to the method whereby the teller identifies herself with the leading character in the story'; another – once released from 'the magic influence' of the narration – 'perceive[s] how *improbable, even impossible,* is the tissue of events to which we have been listening with so great a sense of reality, and we feel almost angry with ourselves at having been the victims of such utter illusion' (my italics). And a third, like Christopher Julian earlier, believes Ethelberta's story to be true:

> The combinations of incident which Mrs Petherwin persuades her hearers that she has passed through are not a little marvellous; and if

what is rumoured to be true, that the tales are to a great extent based upon her own experiences, she has proved herself to be no less daring in adventure than facile in her power of describing it. (135–6)

The fact that it is Hardy himself writing these 'reviews'; that the stylistic parody is very exact; that he uses the conventional words 'improbable' and 'impossible' (which, as we know, his own novel was to be continually labelled); that he parades the terms 'reality' and 'illusion'; and that he once again foregrounds the central paradox about truth and deception in fiction and in life – suggests just how self-reflexively obsessed with artifice this novel is.

Everything I have indicated so far, indeed, suggests a strategic and self-conscious intervention on Hardy's part concerning class mobility and the making and writing of fictions. What Hardy's intentions were, we cannot of course know (although we can guess); but even if we did, we would still face the problem that we face with that ultimate proof of the intentionalist fallacy, *The Life*: would we believe what he says? What we can identify, however, is the degree of self-consciousness in the written discourse of the novel, and infer, therefore, that its mode and style are not accidental, but are themselves central to the strategy of the book, whatever that may be. Hardy himself, as always, is both suggestive and opaque, although his self-consciousness is everywhere apparent. The title itself, with its multi-layered play on the word 'hand', should alert us: 'hand' as in marriage; 'hand' as in cards; 'hand' as in writing; 'hand' as in paid worker; 'hand' as in Hardy's mother's maiden name. And the sub-title also – 'A Comedy in Chapters' (which had to be dropped from the serial version because it might suggest that Hardy was a 'professional joker'(!)[11] but which, significantly, was restored for book publication) – draws attention to the staged artificiality of the novel.[12] The Preface, written much later (1895), together with the 1912 'PS', is conscious of its central problematics – while being, in Robert Gittings's ingenuous phrase, 'curiously defensive'.[13] Hardy admits the 'somewhat frivolous' nature of the narrative, but himself questions whether 'comedy' is quite the right word to describe it, and in 1912 he suggests that it is 'more accurately, satire', thus pointing to a purposive animus which the word 'comedy' does not carry (see also Chapter 7, pp. 173–4, below). He further claims that 'a high degree of probability was not attempted in the arrangement of the incidents'; and in the 'PS' makes the baldly 'neutral' remark: 'The artificial treatment perceptible in many of the pages was adopted for reasons that seemed good at the date of writing for a story of that class, and has not been changed.' Is 'artificial' used positively or negatively here? 'Adopted for reasons that seemed good at the date of writing' suggests an intended 'artifice/-iality', but what were the 'reasons', and do they or do they not still 'seem good'? What constitutes the 'artificial treatment' anyway, and why was it suitable for 'a story of that class'? Does that last phrase mean 'of that type' or 'about that social class'? All we can know for certain is that Hardy was conscious of 'improbabilist' criticism and of the 'artifice/-iality' of the novel. But what the Preface and 'PS' also draw attention to was the critics' irritation at *HE*'s 'unexpectedness' after *FMC*, and Hardy's belief that in its 'reversal of the social foreground', it 'appeared thirty-five years too soon'. Taken together with his remarks on

> its choice of medium, and line of perspective ... to excite interest in a drama – if such a dignified word may be used in the connection – wherein servants were as important as, or more important than, their masters; wherein the drawing-room was sketched in many cases from the point of view of the servants' hall,

this would seem to suggest that, many years later, Hardy was still acutely aware of both the class-consciousness and the aesthetic self-consciousness of the novel.

However by 1912, as I have shown in Chapter 2, the contemporary critical consensus had already sifted Hardy's work to produce a canon of major works which fitted orthodox conceptions of the novel, in the process excising *HE*, amongst others, as irretrievably 'minor'. Hardy's own General Preface of 1912 had, of course, helped to reinforce this categorization by seeming to elevate the 'Novels of Character and Environment' over the 'Romances and Fantasies' and the 'Novels of Ingenuity' (otherwise 'Experiments') like *HE*. It is noteworthy, too, that Hardy there again mentions their 'not infrequent disregard of the *probable* in the chain of events' and 'the *artificiality* of their fable' (my emphases). Whether he intended to disparage them and confirm the critics' predilections, once more we cannot know; but what is clear, is Hardy's consciousness of their modal experimentality and his unease with the constraints of 'probabilism'. These two tendencies, of course, have become the permanent grounds on which criticism deals with *HE*:

improbable plotting, artificiality of treatment, thin characterization, scant knowledge of upper-class London society, strained satire, awkward and mannered style. Most criticism, in other words, either ignores the novel totally or rejects those features which most insistently and pervasively comprise the fabric of its discourse. In accepting 'artificiality' and 'improbability' as unproblematically pejorative terms with which to dismiss the novel, criticism operates myopically within parameters which are themselves drawn up on partial premises.

* * * * *

Before turning more extensively to those insistent discourses of class and artifice in the novel itself, I want briefly to consider Robert Gittings's and Richard Taylor's treatment of *HE*.[14] Gittings has a chapter entitled 'Ethelberta' in *Young Thomas Hardy*, has edited and introduced the 'New Wessex' edition, and writes sympathetically and perceptively – although finally obtusely – about the novel. He well exemplifies how even perceptions which follow the logic of the novel's discourses can be blocked and obscured by the predetermining critical criteria of fictional 'propriety' and literary 'excellence'. In the biography, Gittings deals with Hardy's growing dissociation from his relatives and the necessary concealment of his origins as he married the middle-class Emma Gifford and became successful with *FMC*, and he suggests that Hardy made a 'surprising' and 'very personal' decision that his next novel would deal with 'the situation in which he found his own life, as a writer of humble origins acclaimed by a society which might, if knowing, have found them contemptible'. So, Gittings deduces: 'perhaps from an inborn necessity to write the teasing problem somehow out of his system, was evolved the most uneven and contradictory of all Hardy's novels.'[15] Two assumptions inform this: one, that Hardy had to 'write the problem out of his system' – not that it might remain the ground bass for all his subsequent fiction; and two, that the novel is aesthetically damaged. Much of Gittings's chapter, however, is a detailed and convincing account of how much autobiographical material the novel contains; of how Hardy edited the serial version (and indeed extensively revised the first book edition of 1876 for the 1892 republication) to conceal the extent of his own background in it; and of how his marriage to Emma Gifford in

1874 both affected the novel and exacerbated the tensions of his class deception. But Gittings is unable to move beyond these factual *aperçus* to a positive analysis of the novel: the chapter is shot through with the word 'improbable', and where he (rightly) points to 'the theme of class concealment' as 'an obsession', he can only add that 'it throws the novel out of balance in a way which puzzled all reviewers' (292). Where he speaks perceptively of Ethelberta as 'this synthetic character and her dilemmas [which] were meant to express, in secret guise, Hardy's own', he can still only see the novel as 'this manufactured and cryptic book' (293): 'synthetic' characters, 'manufactured' and 'cryptic' writing – which might be symptomatic of Hardy's own tensions – are all implicitly condemned on aesthetic grounds. Again, Gittings rightly notes the similarity between Hardy and Ethelberta as thwarted poets, commenting on Hardy's failure to get into print at this stage – 'so yet another prime passion of his life was driven underground' (297). But personal traumas, for Gittings (as for so many other psycho-biographers), produce a writer-hero who 'from this time ... shows evidence of the violence that this uprooting from the past had done to his essential being. ... It was this strain and fixed gloom that pursued him, like a haunted person, all the rest of his long life' (298). Gittings could well be right, but the idealist notion of Hardy's 'essential being', together with the absence of any conception of 'ideology' and of a critical apparatus which can deal with the 'improbable', means that he can only see the novel as Hardy's 'last gesture from the class to which he really belonged. He wrote out of his system the Hardy who was one of the people who toiled and suffered. From now onward, he surveyed such people as one who had escaped from their world' (295–6). Gittings is right to say that Hardy's class position changes, but wrong to imply the shift was so simple: Hardy never 'really belonged' to one class, but was precisely one of the 'metamorphic classes' he mentions in *HE* (320); it is that which underlies the 'strain' of his work thereafter. The novel is less a farewell to his 'real' class than a recognition of the contradictory position in which he was now situated.

Gittings's later introduction to the 'New Wessex' edition brings these issues into sharper focus. Much of the biographical material is the same, but the check-rein of critical orthodoxy now holds back the earlier perceptions about class and writing; the framing essay to the only accessible modern edition of the novel [in 1989], therefore, is one which perpetuates all the old-established commonplaces. Its final sentence synopsizes the critical perspective within which the novel is viewed: having discovered that at certain moments the character of Ethelberta comes alive (Gittings has earlier noted that what Hardy 'drew best' in his fiction was 'the full-scale portrait of a real woman'),[16] he concludes: 'It is in moments such as this that the "Comedy in Chapters" transcends its artificial and private framework to touch the universality of the greater novels' (28). It is within this almost self-parodying literary-critical frame, then, that Gittings sees *HE* as 'the joker in the pack' of Hardy's novels which 'fascinates by its very strangeness' (15). Puzzling though its provenance immediately after *FMC* may be, he can only state: 'It is as if written by a different hand and, it must be added, by a far less competent one' – explanations as to why this 'joker' should come next being reduced to a suggestion that Hardy may have been imaginatively exhausted (16–17). (Gittings does, however, suggest that Hardy's 'negative' reason for writing the novel, which largely accounts for its 'comparative failure', was his reaction to comparisons with George Eliot (21–2).) The main aspects of this 'failure' are, not surprisingly, the familiar truisms of Hardy criticism: Ethelberta's situation is not 'even remotely plausible'; 'a large part of *Ethelberta* is badly written'; 'even more disconcerting, Hardy returns to *what we know to be the faults* of his very first novels' (my italics); Hardy had 'reverted' to the 'class bias' criticized by Alexander Macmillan in *The Poor Man and the Lady*; Hardy was 'trying a realistic portrayal of the society into which he himself in real life had just made a move'; there are 'the most delightful and realistic' moments when Hardy is 'completely ... at home' writing about the lower orders; 'the total improbability of many incidents in the novel'; and the 'incredible plot and obsessive criticism of society and conventional manners'.[17] It is notable how the novel's attitudes to social class and the aesthetics of 'improbabilism' are hunted down together by conventional criticism. There is one point finally, however, which indicates the almost perverse misrecognition fostered by realist-humanist criticism, and this is Gittings's interesting suggestion that *HE* is really in the tradition of the 'old-fashioned novelette': rather than being in advance of its time – as Hardy claimed in both *The Life* and the 1895 Preface – the novel 'could have been written for a romantic-magazine audience at any time in the last hundred years'. Historically dubious though this

Furthermore, Taylor realizes that the novel 'originates in that most consistent of Hardy's preoccupations: class division' (68); that it 'is a study of the physical and personal deracination which later leads to the personal and social tragedies in *Tess* and *Jude*' (71); and 'what a seminal novel [it] may be in the Hardy canon; his deepest concerns are packed in, and nowhere else are his social beliefs set out with such clarity' (71).

Why, then, is the essay ultimately so blandly conventional and disappointing? The answer may lie in the fact that Taylor cannot put his perceptions together in a radical reading which follows their logic, precisely because he is controlled by the critical parameters of 'Thomas Hardy' and the ranking of his work. For example, he continually privileges the 'great novels' – in comparison with which (Taylor has intimate knowledge) 'Hardy did not intend [*HE*] to be taken as seriously' (57). Nor should we 'expect characters on the scale of those in the Novels of Character and Environment': *HE* is 'more modest and its tone is different' and 'if it is not as good as *The Return of the Native* ... that is partly to say that Hardy is better at writing a different kind of novel' (74). Within such a critical discourse, therefore, *HE* is locked unquestionably into position – 'we can', says Taylor, 'glimpse *a more characteristic* Hardy novel running like a stream below the surface' (64, my emphasis) – and in this context, the novel's perceived radical characteristics will clearly be turned and blunted. So that despite the force of Ethelberta's character, she 'just misses the stature of some of the better-known heroines, since she is trimmed to fit the mode of the novel' – 'the heroine of a comedy, mocked and undermined' whom Hardy does not finally endorse: her 'suppression of emotion by reason and will-power is no solution ... and he turned away from it' (64–6). Equally, the 'radicalism' of the novel (which had 'over-reached itself' in *The Poor Man and the Lady*, but was 'reasserted more powerfully' in *HE*) is nevertheless 'tempered with humour', so that it becomes 'not a socialist manifesto, but ... a humanitarian and compassionate work ... making a plea for personal dignity while regretting the ironies of prevailing conditions' (68). In this reading (which, as we shall see, the novel nowhere makes as self-evident as Taylor assumes), Ethelberta only 'gets on' by 'dissociating herself from the honest endeavour represented by her family'; and the novel, in its 'outcry against unfair privilege and social advantage, urban pretensions and hypocrisy', becomes 'a celebration of the spiritual and moral superiority of country life' (71). Not only is this an astonishing and unrecognizable claim as regards the 'determinate text' of the novel we have before us, it is also a classic instance of the late-20th-century reaffirmation of Hardy as rural humanist. However, the incorporation of even such 'social messages' within the mannered and artificial modality of the novel is 'one of the reason for [its] comparative failure' (71); Ethelberta is too large for it and 'we may prefer to wish her in a more serious work'; the mode of the novel is 'basically inimical to Hardy's tragic imagination'; and this clash produces tensions which 'at least partly dissipate the dramatic stature of the work' (74). The novelist of *HE*, therefore, is turned back once again to face his real self: not just rural humanist, but also tragic realist. For all his rehabilitation of Hardy's 'lesser fiction', then, Taylor can only do it by showing how, below a novel like *HE*, 'runs like a stream' the 'more characteristic' (real) Hardy of character and environment, and not by allowing its socially and formally radical artifice to be both surface and depth.

* * * * *

But whatever the recuperative processes of criticism, and whatever Hardy's intentions may have been, the text of the novel, from the outset, unmistakably draws attention to its own artificiality and to its playfulness about literary forms and expectations. A fiction which so self-consciously includes disquisitions on fictions should have its own narrative discourses regarded with great care. And indeed the novel plays on, exploits, parodies and exposes the conventions of both romantic and realist fiction throughout: from the extraordinary first page on which Ethelberta's prehistory is baldly summarized and her 'romantic' marriage and widowhood dealt with in a single reductive sentence ('He, a minor like herself, died from a chill caught during the wedding tour, and a few weeks later was followed into the grave by Sir Ralph Petherwin, his unforgiving father, who had bequeathed his wealth to his wife absolutely' (33), to the equally contrary ending in which Ethelberta does not marry her young lover Christopher Julian (he receives a windfall inheritance which is, ironically, not enough – 'a tantalizing sum' [404] – and marries Ethelberta's sister Picotee, whose face 'had grown to resemble her sister's' [408]. Instead, she becomes the wife of the wicked old aristocrat, Mountclere (whom she reforms), takes over the running of his estate, provides for her family, and now 'lives mostly in the library' pursuing her career as an epic poet (409). The novel constructs its ironic and parodic animus in a number of ways: by direct mockery of the conventions; by its mannered and self-conscious style; and by its own wilfully self-destructive fictional strategies and contrivance – chance, coincidence, sensationalism, caricature, authorial intrusion, and so on. Hints of the first of these – of overt exposure of romantic conventions – are apparent early on when Ethelberta, after her renewed acquaintance with Christopher Julian, is described as going 'where all ladies are supposed to go when they want to torment their minds in comfort – to her own room' (44), and again in the following passage:

> The hour grew later, and that dreamy period came round when ladies' fancies, that have lain shut up close as their fans during the day, begin to assert themselves anew. At this time a good guess at Ethelberta's thoughts might have been made from her manner of passing the minutes away. Instead of reading, entering notes in her diary, or doing any ordinary thing, she walked to and fro, curled her pretty nether lip within her pretty upper one a great many times, made a cradle of her locked fingers, and paused with fixed eyes where the walls of the room set limits upon her walk to look at nothing but a picture within her mind. (45)

The curiously external stance of the writing suggests a mockery of the genre of female romance, whilst also producing a sharply alien-ated sense of Ethelberta's character: there is something mechanical about her here, which, as we shall see, can be perceived throughout the novel. Again, her effect on Christopher is rendered thus: '[she] might soon become ... an indestructible fascination – to drag him about, turn his soul inside out, harrow him, twist him, and other-wise torment him, according to *the stereotyped form of such processes*' (67, my emphasis). Much later, during Ethelberta's trip to Rouen (where most of her suitors ridiculously follow her), she muses about Mountclere: 'Thus backed up by Sol and Dan, her aunt, and Cornelia, Ethelberta felt quite the reverse of a lonely female persecuted by a wicked lord in a foreign country' (269–70) – although, in a way, this is an accurate description of her situation at this point. What the novel is doing, of course, is drawing ironic at-tention to the very fictional convention it is at the same time ex-ploiting, just as it does in the case of Mountclere's marriage to

Ethelberta (which both families are trying to stop) by way of the words of a society lady:

> 'What a funny thing!' said the lady, with a *wretchedly factitious smile*. 'The times have taken a strange turn when the angry parent of the comedy, who goes post-haste to prevent the undutiful daughter's rash marriage, is a gentleman from below stairs, and the unworthy lover a peer of the realm!' (345, my emphasis)

I shall return later to the relation between fictional and class reversals, a confluence which may be said to represent the principal discourse of the novel.

Hardy's style, when it is 'pedantic', 'awkward', and self-conscious, is commonly regarded as one of his major 'flaws'; and Gittings, in the essay considered above, includes it amongst 'what are known to be' Hardy's faults in *HE*, identifying it as the result of his early penchant for Harrison Ainsworth.[19] Certainly the novel's style is pervasively self-conscious, but its very consistency makes it more a strategic mannerism – one which intensifies the defamiliarizing ('disproportioning') effect of the whole work (note the italicized phrase in the quotation above) – than a failure of control. For example, a 'town young man' is described (in terms which call to mind Dickens's reifications of character) as having 'a Tussaud complexion and well-pencilled brows half way up his forehead, so that his upper eyelids appeared to possess the uncommon quality of tallness' (56–7); a letter in which Ethelberta begins to tell Christopher the truth about her class background but then burns, is emblematized as being 'poked and stirred ... till a red inflammation crept over the sheet' (97); and London under moonlight is rendered in extravagantly over-wrought prose: 'ordinary houses were sublimated to the rank of public buildings, public buildings to palaces, and the faces of women walking the streets to those of calendared saints and guardian-angles, by the pure bleaching light from the sky' (156). Again, Alfred Neigh, the cosmopolitan man of letters, finding himself in love with Ethelberta, paces his room in distress and is undercut by the narrative voice: '"O, the deuce, the deuce!" he continued, walking about the room as if passionately stamping but not quite doing it because another man had rooms below' (164); and his name, which the novel constantly uses for jokes, gives rise to extreme self-conscious facetiousness when Ladywell expostulates: '"No, Neigh – never!"' (163). Equally, Ethelberta's attitude to Neigh is presented in the following chapter-opening as: 'The question of Neigh or no Neigh had reached a pitch of insistence which no longer permitted of dallying, even by a popular beauty' (219); and her quandary over whether to marry him and be honest with him or not is presented – partly as her own musings, partly as the narrative's – in elaborately mannered terms:

> One palliative feature must be remembered when we survey the matrimonial ponderings of the poetess and romancer. What she contemplated was not meanly to ensnare a husband just to provide incomes for her and her family, but to find some man she might respect, who would maintain her in such a stage of comfort as should, by setting her mind free from temporal anxiety, enable her to further organize her talent, and provide incomes for them herself. Plenty of saleable originality was left in her as yet, but it was getting crushed under the rubbish of her necessities.
>
> She was not sure that Neigh would stand the test of her revelations. It would be possible to lead him to marry her without revealing anything ... yet Ethelberta's honesty shrank from the safe course of holding her tongue. It might be pleasant to many a modern gentleman to find himself allied with a lady, none of whose ancestors had ever pandered to a court, lost an army, taken a bribe, oppressed a community, or broken a bank; but the added disclosure that, in avoiding these stains, her kindred had worked and continued to work with their hands for bread, might lead such an one to consider that the novelty was dearly purchased. (220)

What is noteworthy here, aside from the abrasive analysis of marriage and class, is the detachment of tone and the ornate language of the passage which severe to emphasize the deeply alienated position of 'the poetess and romancer' who has 'plenty of saleable originality ... left' and who is presented as though she were no more than a series of 'considerations' which can be adduced in coldly calculating prose. I will return to the novel's mechanistic presentation of Ethelberta's 'character' in a moment.

But by far the most obtrusive manifestations of the novel's artificiality are the various narrative strategies employed to get the story told at all. What criticism would call 'improbabilism' is rife here; but because *HE* is primarily concerned with class deception and the relativity of fiction and truth, the overtly fictive mode of articulation is central to the whole statement the novel makes: fiction here represents fictions. The modes of narration are diverse, but they invariably 'alienate' the reader by placing her or him where they can actually see the perspective the novel is offering them and by the uncompromising artificiality of the device. One such recurrent perspective is that of characters' views of other characters within the book, often from unseen points of vantage which effectively transmute those observed into actors in a performance or show. An early example of this is in Chapter 3 where Ladywell and another 'gentlemanly person' observe Picotee from 'a small square hole' in The Weir House, waiting in the rain for Christopher Julian to pass her in his characteristically unperceiving way (55–6). There is no reason why they should see her thus, nor does the episode have any direct bearing on the plot; but the effect, in keeping with so much of the rest of the novel, is to intensify the staged and artificial social relations of people in this society. Similarly, Christopher and his sister Faith, supplying the music for a dance at which Ethelberta is a principal guest (and who has been instrumental in getting them the job), observe the dancers from behind a 'screen of ivy and holly': 'the whole spectacle deriving an unexpected novelty from the accident of reaching their eyes through interstices in the tracery of green leaves' (62). Here, the (perceived) perspective serves both to emphasize 'Ethelberta Petherwin's performance' (64) and to further distance the upper-class Christopher, who has come down in the world, from the lower-class Ethelberta who is deceptively a lady: in other words, to reinforce the sense that the alienating fiction of class actually proscribes a relationship between the only two people in the novel who might have loved each other with spontaneity and passion.

But by far the most extended and structurally ironic of such scenes is the one in Chapter 29 which depicts a dinner-party at the London home of Mr and Mrs Doncastle, where Ethelberta's father is the butler, and where Ethelberta – as the well-connected widow, Mrs Petherwin – is to dine. It will repay some detailed attention. None of Ethelberta's Society acquaintances, of course, know of her 'real' background, nor that she is the butler's daughter. Her sister, Picotee, who is herself passed off as Ethelberta's maid, has wanted to see her '"sitting at a grand dinner-table, among lordly dishes and shining people, and father about the room unnoticed!"' (223; we may notice in passing Hardy's slyly ironic inversion of adjectives here: for it is the dishes which are 'lordly' and the people 'shining' –

with their new and meretricious 'polish' – rather than the other way round). It is arranged, with the help of a servant of the house, that Picotee will secretly observe the scene:

> Through the partly-opened door there became visible a sideboard which first attracted her attention by its richness. It was, indeed, a noticeable example of modern art-workmanship, in being exceptionally large, with curious ebony mouldings at different stages; and, while the heavy cupboard doors at the bottom were enriched with inlays of paler wood, other panels were decorated with tiles, as if the massive composition had been erected on the spot as part of the solid building. However, it was on a space higher up that Picotee's eyes and thoughts were fixed. In the great mirror above the middle ledge she could see reflected the upper part of the dining-room, and this suggested to her that she might see Ethelberta and the other guests reflected in the same way by standing on a chair, which, quick as thought, she did.
>
> To Picotee's dazed young vision her beautiful sister appeared as the chief figure of a glorious pleasure parliament of both sexes, surrounded by whole regiments of candles grouped here and there about the room. She and her companions were seated before a large flower-bed, or small hanging garden, fixed at about the level of the elbow, the attention of all being concentrated rather upon the uninteresting margin of the bed, and upon each other, than on the beautiful natural objects growing in the middle, as it seemed to Picotee. In the ripple of conversation Ethelberta's clear voice could occasionally be heard, and her young sister could see that her eyes were bright, and her face beaming, as if divers social wants and looming penuriousness had never been within her experience. Mr Doncastle was quite absorbed in what she was saying. So was the queer old man whom Menlove had called Lord Mountclere.
>
> 'The dashing widow looks very well, does she not?' said a person at Picotee's elbow. (233)

A little later, Picotee has related to her Alfred Neigh's after-dinner account of how Ethelberta had checked out his (non-)estate (in Chapter 25), and hears the '"Ha-ha-ha-ha-ha-ha"' of the 'boozy men' laughing at it. We immediately register, in the above scene, the opulence of the furniture, especially that 'noticeable example of modern art-workmanship', the sideboard: its 'exceptional' size; its 'curious ebony mouldings' (where 'curious' can mean 'finely-worked' or 'intricate', but also 'odd', 'extraordinary'); its various other eclectic decorative features; and its massive solidity – all of which encodes its showy *nouveau-riche* bad taste. What is less obvious is that Hardy surely has in mind the Veneerings in Chapter 2 of Dickens's *Our Mutual Friend*, those wonderfully 'bran-new people in a bran-new house in a bran-new quarter of London', who also own a sideboard: 'The great looking-glass above the sideboard, reflects the table and the company. Reflects the new Veneering crest, in gold and eke in silver.' By this artful intertextual reference, Hardy reinforces the specious artificiality of the new middle and upper classes. This is compounded by the description of the dinner-party proper. The grandiosely overstated image of 'a glorious pleasure-parliament ... surrounded by whole regiments of candles' parallels, in its bombastic grandiloquence, the excessive extravagance of the hosts and their guests – a trope repeated in the hyperbolic absurdity of the table decoration: 'a large flower-bed, or small hanging-garden'. Notice, too, that the company are more interested in 'each other' than in 'the beautiful *natural* objects' (my emphasis) of the display. In the midst of all this, sits Ethelberta, 'the chief figure' in the scene, her 'clear voice', 'bright' eyes, and 'beaming' face, in fact, of course, part of her *performance* as a well-to-do, well-bred 'lady' – a performance disguising, as the text, in a sudden serious modulation, is quick to remind us, 'divers social wants and looming penuriousness'. Indeed, as we shall see below, the presentation of Ethelberta's face as mask-like is reiterated throughout the novel – as though she lives her real life behind it, while it becomes a sign of her falsity and alienation. This is brought out in the present passage by the final comment of Picotee's 'conductor': '"The dashing widow looks very well."' 'Dashing widow' itself combines two contradictory terms – with the flashy brilliance of 'dashing' reminding us of the 'shining people' earlier – but 'looks very well' is more subtle. The phrase can mean 'in good health' and also that she 'looks good' (i.e. beautiful or well-turned-out); but in this context, it also focuses attention at once on her *appearance* (of being a 'lady') and on the sense in which 'looks' implies 'seems' – i.e. 'looks' something she is not. In this respect, the wonderfully ironic sentence I have earlier drawn attention to – '[her] appearance answer[ing] as fully as ever to that of an English Lady skilfully perfected in manner, carriage, *look* and accent' (113, my emphasis, and see below, p. 84) – may act as a gloss on the present one, in so far as it is difficult to know whether that phrase denoting premeditated and rehearsed artifice – 'skilfully perfected' – refers to

Ethelberta's 'appearance' (her 'look') or to the generic 'English Lady's'. Such sentences are, indeed, characteristic of Hardy's layered prose – if we read it with care.

'Looks very well', however, also reminds us that the most contrived and self-conscious feature of the passage is the way *it* and *we* are 'looking', too. The dinner-party, and Ethelberta centrally, are 'seen' by way of a complex set of voyeuristic displacements: the 'partly-opened door' allows Picotee to peep into the dining-room and see the sideboard on which the 'great mirror' reflects the guests, but it is only by climbing on a chair that she can see them, with Ethelberta as 'chief figure'. We too, as readers, let us be clear, also only 'see' Ethelberta – reflected in a mirror – by being balanced on that chair and through the gap in the doorway. But in *our own seeing* of this manner of 'seeing' we may come to realize how the scene formally enacts, in its own presentational strategies, the deception and alienation of a class-system, which the whole novel – and I would argue, most of Hardy's others – exposes. Not only are Picotee and the father/butler dissociated from their own relative by the 'fiction' of class-position, but Ethelberta herself has become no more than an image displaced in a mirror, seen obliquely through a half-open door, and the subject of an after-dinner *story*. This, however, is very much her 'reality'; she is indeed (false) 'appearance', 'performance', 'look', contrived and exposed in the self-displaying fictiveness of the discourses which, at the same time, constitute and claim her as 'real' – those of the novel itself. Our theatre-like positioning as observers of the performance here, should, in the other (Brechtian) sense of 'alienation', make us at once 'see' both the performance and that it *is* performance. And if we take the hint, much of Hardy's other fiction will release markedly similar strategies of looking and seeing.

Equally self-conscious is the novel's use of letters. The presence of further 'writings' within a novel so concerned with the writing of fictions is immediately conspicuous and compounds its self-reflexiveness. For the most part, the letters are used to convey the 'truth' about Ethelberta's real position: Mr Chickerill's letter to her in Chapter 7, for example, finally reveals her background to the reader, while simultaneously raising questions about the veracity of literature and about the problems of upward class mobility (83–4); and Mrs Chickerill's letter in Chapter 34 explains how Menlove the servant has penetrated Ethelberta's secret and is likely to reveal the deception, at the same time reinforcing the cynically opportunistic approach to marriage of which Ethelberta herself is inescapably the creature: "'O, this false position! – it is ruining your nature, my too thoughtful mother!'" (273–4). Most significant in my context here, however, are Ethelberta's two letters to Christopher in Chapter 9, one of which tells the truth about her background, which she destroys; the other simply compounding the 'fiction'. It is a striking instance of the novel's self-consciousness that it can proffer both versions of the 'truth' about Ethelberta (and about Hardy), 'destroy' one and retain the other – while in fact preserving both for the reader: it is, in effect, the apotheosis of Hardy's own legerdemain in writing this 'fiction' about his own ('real') class position. Finally, as an example of the extraordinary flouting of the 'probable' in this novel, we may notice the exchange of letters (and the authorial intrusions) between Ethelberta and Lord Mountclere in two more or less adjacent inns in Melchester, negotiations about their possible marriage being conducted, at this point, entirely by letter. After the receipt of one such the following passage occurs:

> 'Ho-ho-ho – Miss Hoity-toity!' said Lord Mountclere, trotting up and down. But, remembering it was her June against his November, this did not last long, and he frantically replied: – MY DARLING, – I cannot release you – I must do anything to keep my treasure. Will you not see me for a few minutes, and let bygones go to the winds? Was ever a thrush so safe in a cherry net before! (317)

The novel moves, here – as it does elsewhere – into a kind of absurd farce, making no pretence of realism. But as an exposure of the shams, deceptions, subterfuges, stratagems and exploitations involved in the social (class and gender) relations of marriage, it is no more 'unreal' than the conventional fictional representation of courtship and marriage in novels contemporary with it. Its fictions simply do not purport to be 'real'; and, in the process, it calls in question the 'reality' of those other social and fictional representations which *do*.

HE is, indeed, largely constituted by such uncompromisingly fictive contrivance (Ethelberta, with nice irony, herself claims: 'I am a rare hand at contrivances' (226), and she is elsewhere described as knowing 'the ins and outs of contriving' (407)). Coincidence, chance, contingency, improbability and absurdity smack the reader in the face – to the point, in fact, where it becomes perverse to apply realist criteria at all. There is the ironic coincidence of the guests at Mr Doncastle's commenting on the butler's face after they have unknowingly discussed his daughter's poems in front of him (80-1). There is the implausible scene when Ethelberta, disguised and in the company of her two workman brothers, visits the Royal Academy exhibition to see Ladywell's picture of her and overhears two men discussing how she is to be Neigh's wife – before he has even begun to court her (194). There is the grossly improbable moment when Ethelberta observes the trees which hinder her view of the sea being felled on Mountclere's orders to satisfy her whim: 'One of the trees forming the curtain across it began to wave strangely: it went further to one side, and fell' (255-7). There is the absurd contingency of Mountclere's yacht meeting Ethelberta's boat on the way to France (an event too far-fetched to be an 'error' of fictional decorum); and the ridiculous farce in the hotel in Rouen when three of Ethelberta's suitors are all attending on her in different rooms, and two of them, leaning out of their windows, recognize each other while overhearing the third's conversation with her:

> Upon a balcony beneath [Neigh] were the speakers, as he had suspected – Ethelberta and the viscount. Looking right and left, he saw projecting from the next window the head of his friend Ladywell, gazing right and left likewise, apparently just drawn out by the same voice which had attracted himself.
> 'What – you, Neigh! – how strange', came from Ladywell's lips. (284-5)

'Strange' indeed. But no more so than the inexplicable chapter in which Ethelberta, thinking throughout the night about whether she should marry Mountclere or not, looks up 'a well-known treatise on Utilitarianism', and later a chapter – significantly on '"the *disciplina arcani*, or, the doctrine of reserve"' – in 'an old treatise on Casuistry', from which the arguments are rehearsed with literal quotations (295-7). There is, too, the wildly contingent plotting of the journey that Lord Mountclere's brother and Sol Chickerill undertake together to try and prevent the marriage, which includes a sea trip to Knollsea (and the coincidence of a storm sending them back the way they had come (348-54), at the end of which Mr Chickerill and Christopher Julian, who have been travelling together without knowing it, meet up with Sol and Mr Mountclere – all of them arriving too late (365-9). Finally, there is the crazy gothic 'business' of Ethelberta's note, passed through a window into the wrong hands, and the foiling therefore of her attempt to escape from Mountclere:

> The voice was so different from her brother's that she was terrified; her limbs quivered. In another instant the speaker had struck a wax vesta, and holding it erect in his fingers he looked her in the face.
> 'Hee-hee-hee!' The laughter was her husband the viscount. (394–9 *passim*)

Mountclere then tells her 'a story' – '"I have learnt the art from you"' – after which they agree to negotiate, with Ethelberta congratulating Mountclere on his plot: '"It was stratagem against stratagem. Mine was ingenious; yours was masterly! Accept my acknowledgment. We will enter upon an armed neutrality"' (400–2). By these later scenes, the novel is not bothering with the illusion of realism at all: the contrivance is naked, the fiction manifestly fictive. But just as the callous deceptions and illusions of class and gender hierarchies are exposed, as we shall see, by this caricatured melodramatic fiction, so too are the mystifications of a 'probabilist' realism which are no less contrived – and often more so – in their pursuit of verisimilitude. 'Improbable' *HE* may be, but that does not mean it is less 'truthful'.

* * * * *

I want now, therefore, to show how the fictional contrivance of the novel exposes the alienating fictions of class and gender relations. Unlike most of Hardy's fiction, so criticism would seem to imply – although my focus here is to question that assumption – *HE* is obsessively and exclusively concerned with social class and, within that, the gender relations involved in courtship and marriage. The *donnée* of the plot – a young woman who deceives society about her class origins and operates successfully within its codes – establishes this from the outset. But the texture of the whole novel is composed, almost line by line, of an extreme sensitiveness to the nuances of class position – a sensitiveness that derives from a perspective which looks both up and down with equal familiarity and with equal unease. At one point the novel registers, parenthetically, a passing reflex of Ethelberta's: 'a word of Christopher's about somebody else's mean parentage, which was spoken in utter forgetfulness of her own position, ... had wounded her to the quick nevertheless' (174). This, in a sense, identifies the ruling consciousness of the novel as a whole. Characters are invariably placed, for example, in exact class stations. Picotee appropriately (and we should remember Hardy's sister and cousin) is a pupil-teacher, and Ethelberta – intended by her parents for a governess (124) – thinks, in a moment of despair, of teaching as a career (292), which would indeed be, but for her writing, her 'correct' class occupation. Christopher, who has come down in the world, earns a meagre living by his music, but his sensibilities, attitudes and actions are always those of a leisured gentleman: when he first meets Picotee he immediately perceives her status and 'lowered his method of address to her level at once' (52); and his attitude to Ethelberta, despite her superiority to him in many ways, is often patronizing: for instance, he is enamoured by 'the romantic ubiquity of station that attached to her' – a response accounted for by the novel because 'his faith in society had departed with his own social ruin' (122). Ethelberta's young husband's father, who dismisses the 'homeless governess' when he sees the way the wind is blowing, is 'an ambitious gentleman *just* knighted' (307, my italics – Hardy's irony is very precise). Ethelberta's own consciousness, in particular, continually registers relationships in class terms. She perceives that Neigh and Ladywell 'were both too near her level to be trusted to bear the shock of receiving her from her father's hands'; but goes on to recognize that 'though her genesis might tinge with vulgarity a commoner's household, susceptible of such depreciation', a peer's family might be able to stand it (295) – although earlier she has worried that Mountclere's 'interest in her was not likely, under the ordinary influences of caste feeling, to continue longer than while he was kept in ignorance of her consanguinity with a stock proscribed' (268–9). What is notable in the novel, then, is the iterative and minutely sensitive registering of the characters' class differences. But equally, scenes, places and gatherings of people are always presented with their class co-ordinates in the foreground. Knollsea, at the beginning of Chapter 31, is immediately identified in these terms: 'Everybody in the parish who was not a boatman was a quarrier, unless he were the gentleman who owned half the property and had been a quarryman, or the other gentleman who owned the other half, and had been to sea' (243). A dinner-party at the Doncasters' – 'who lived in a moderately fashionable square' – is framed by a satirical analysis of smiles and laughter as notations of social class:

And again, later, Sol says:

> 'Upon my life I should be inclined to laugh, if I were not so much
> inclined to do the other thing, at Berta's trick of trying to make
> close family allies of such a cantankerous pair as you and I! So much
> of one mind as we be, so alike in our ways of living, so close
> connected in our callings and principles, so matched in manners and
> customs!'...

> Mountclere faintly laughed with the same hideous merriment at the
> same idea, and then both remained in a withering silence, meant to
> express the utter contempt of each for the other, both in family and
> in person. (368)

What we see here, I think, is how the novel's farcical discourse itself
articulates the absurdly irrational nature of a class society.

In general, however, the novel's satirical animus – which so upset
Hardy's contemporaries and plenty of later critics – is directed
against the upper classes. It may well be because of this that he is
criticized for his 'ignorance' and 'improbable' rendering of society,
and is patronized for being 'at home' only with lower-class rural
characters. But Hardy, of course, is no more of one class than the
other, and no more 'naturally' realistic about one than the other;
indeed, the defamiliarization of class relations perceptible in HE
(and, in fact, most of his fiction) is determined by his peculiarly
contradictory class insertion as *arriviste* professional writer in metropolitan society. What the novel emphasizes in particular about
the upper classes is that their superiority is as much a fiction as
Ethelberta's own. Christopher Julian, for example, is always shown
to be weaker than Ethelberta and without the energy to succeed as
an artist, although he is constantly aware of his superior social
class; Ladywell, the painter, is condemned in similar terms; guests
at various parties are frequently revealed to have been elevated by
way of trade or fortuitous circumstance; and their literary and artistic education, significantly, is invariably inferior to Ethelberta's:
when she visits Milton's grave in Cripplegate Church, for instance,
with the Belmaines and Neigh, it is she who knew it was not in
Westminster Abbey and she who reads from his poetry – being 'the
only one present who could properly manage blank verse' (212).
Alfred Neigh in particular, the society *beau* and man of letters, is
revealed, in Ethelberta's 'disillusive discovery', to rest his social

standing on the horse-knackering business (see *HE*, 200); this is the reality behind his façade of breeding, superiority and misogyny, and it leads to Ethelberta's perception that they are 'too nearly cattle of one colour' for him to be able to forgive her her class background (*ibid.*).[20] Finally Lord Mountclere, although of genuinely noble descent, is presented melodramatically as the decadence of a noble line, who is said to have an unspeakable past and has let his estate go to ruin. He inhabits a house for which 'art' has been purchased to produce 'illusion' and which is mainly a modern sham – 'a stone mask worn by a brick face' (304)[21] – and keeps a mistress (calling herself 'Lady Mountclere') in a cottage in his grounds. Ironically, however, it is him Ethelberta marries, because he has the cynical realism and the status not to mind her origins or her class deception. As my opening quotation shows, having listened to Ethelberta's 'fictional' account of her real life-story, Mountclere tells her not to expose herself to the other guests who 'are no better than you', and pronounces with cynical honesty:

> 'But my father and friends?' said she.
> 'Are nothing to be concerned about. Modern developments have shaken up the classes like peas in a hopper. An annuity, and a comfortable cottage –'
> 'My brothers are workmen.'
> 'Manufacture is the single vocation in which a man's prospects may be said to be illimitable. Hee-hee! – they may buy me up before they die! And now what stands in the way? It would take fifty alliances with fifty families so little disreputable as yours, darling, to drag mine down.' (308–9)

In a sense, Mountclere appears as the grotesque exposé of the basic premise of a class system: that it must disguise its artificiality and perpetuate the illusion of being natural.

It is in Ethelberta herself, however, that we feel the full force of the novel's obsessive consciousness of class, and it is in her 'character' that the mannered artifice of the fiction and the contradictions of class position most strongly intersect. To discuss Ethelberta as 'a character' at all is difficult, and this problem itself is an important aspect of her significance: because she is so divided – as Ethelberta Chickerill, as Mrs Petherwin, as Professed Story-Teller, as the 'beloved' of four different men – and because the reader experiences her in all these roles, no one of which can be identified definitively as the 'real' Ethelberta, 'her character', if the term still means anything, must comprise all of these roles. She is fashioned by circumstance, and is constituted by the social roles consequent on it: that is her reality. But it is a reality, equally, which is overtly fashioned by the text: at a number of levels, 'Ethelberta' exists only as a fiction (as a 'lady', as a 'romancer', as a character in the novel), and as such she resists and challenges the character analysis – based on the notion of an individual 'real' personality or unitary subject – of humanist realism and its affiliated critical praxis. If 'Ethelberta' is seen to be composed solely by fictional discourse – as 'representation' – then she draws attention to the fact that so too are all other heroines, however much their 'round', 'knowable', extra-textual 'reality' is admired by literary criticism. Shortly after Ethelberta has become a success by way of her poems, she is the subject of a conversation at the Belmaines' between two society ladies:

> 'She is one of those people who are known, as one may say, by subscription: everybody knows a little, till she is astonishingly well known altogether; but nobody knows her entirely.'...
>
> 'She has apparently a very good prospect.'
> 'Yes; and it is through her being of that curious undefined character which interprets itself to each admirer as whatever he would like to have it. Old men like her because she is so girlish; youths because she is womanly; wicked men because she is good in their eyes; good men because she is wicked in theirs.'
> 'She must be a very anomalous sort of woman, at that rate.'
> 'Yes. Like the British Constitution, she owes her success in practice to her inconsistencies in principle.'
> 'These poems must have set her up. She appears to be quite the correct spectacle. Happy Mrs Petherwin!' (94)

What is emphasized here is Ethelberta's unknowability, the 'inconsistencies' of her character(ization), her being whatever men choose to make her, and her status as 'spectacle'. These are, indeed, all the terms in which she is represented by the novel: as a series of perceived images, of 'seemings', of 'impressions', her reality being that of a social and literary fiction (significantly, a few lines later, during an ironic conversation with Mrs Belmaine about the upward social mobility of servants, Ethelberta refers to original pedigree as 'the first edition' [95]). Her deception as to her class background is constantly presented as playing a part: Christopher, playing music at the dance, watches 'Ethelberta Petherwin's performance' (64), although it is no more than her ordinary social behaviour; and when he next comes across her, rehearsing her fiction to the children in the country (see above, p. 55), she is described as at the centre of a 'natural theatre', her 'appearance answer[ing]', as we have heard, 'as fully as ever to that of an English Lady skilfully perfected in manner, carriage, look, and accent' (112–13). The sense of strategic artifice in the phrase 'skilfully perfected' is compounded by its syntactical ambiguity in the sentence: is the phrase in apposition to 'her appearance' or to 'an English lady'? The implications are quite different. The ambiguity of 'being a lady' also crops up with Neigh, who says: '"directly I saw you I felt that nobody ever came so near my idea of what is desirable in a lady"' (203). The irony is complex here, for Neigh – later described by Ethelberta as 'one of those horrid men who love with their eyes' (241), that is, who turn women into visual objects – is himself a sham who misrecognizes Ethelberta as 'the real thing'. But what is significant again is the syntax of the sentence, in which Ethelberta comes as near as anybody ever did to his 'idea of what is desirable in a lady' – nearer, indeed, than the real thing ever could. Ethelberta's 'act' is indeed fetishized by Neigh's perception of her; but effectively, also, her reality is what she seems – the alienating effects of which the novel's prose draws attention to in the description of her face when Neigh tells her he knows she has visited his estate:

> Her face did not change, since a face must be said not to change while it preserves the same pleasant lines in the mobile parts as before; but anybody who has preserved his pleasant lines under the half-minute's peer of the invidious camera, and found what a wizened, starched kind of thing they stiffen to towards the end of the time, will understand the tendency of Ethelberta's lovely features now. (204)

The detached language and ironic stance – combined with the reference to the new 'mechanical' visual art of photography – turn 'Ethelberta's lovely features' into an object dissociated from her being; just as, in the scene at the Belmaines' above when the topic of servants arises, the novel says: 'The face of Ethelberta showed caution at once'; and then: 'The face of Ethelberta showed venturesomeness' (94), where the full genitive, in place of 'Ethelberta's face', implies the mask-like reification of her features. Earlier, during a conversation with Christopher in which he is deceived about her class, there is a moment when 'Ethelberta smiled a smile of many meanings' (41) as though smiling strategically and instrumentally; and much later, negotiating with Mountclere, she is presented in the following terms: 'But none of this reached her face'; 'Ethelberta flung at Lord Mountclere a look which clipped him like pincers'; 'Ethelberta's show of passion went as quickly as it had come' (314–15). The point is that, because of the deception she practises, Ethelberta can never be an integrated being; she is always an alienated 'performance'.

This alienation is given most emphatic focus in Ethelberta's relations with her family. The unnaturalness of the deceit required by the codes of class society is evidenced by the 'improbability' of her living two discrete lives – one as a member of her family and the other as a total stranger to it: lives which are not allowed to meet except as they traverse the 'Ethelberta' the novel itself realizes. Picotee strikes the note when she says to Ethelberta: '"I have told nobody that we are sisters, or that you are known in any way to me or to mother or to any of us"' (71); and her little sister tells Christopher: '"She lives there along wi' mother and we. But she don't want anybody to know it, sir, cause she's celebrate, and 'twouldn't do at all"' (110–11). This destructive split is re-emphasized by her carpenter brothers who draw attention at once to the dehumanizing deception of Ethelberta's own life, to their (and indeed the whole family's) complicity in it and to Ethelberta's contradictory liking for it:

> '"Twould demean her to claim kin wi' her in London – two journeymen like us, that know nothing besides our trades.'
> 'Not at all,' said Christopher. 'She would be pleased to see any straightforward honest man and brother, I should think, notwithstanding that she has moved in other society for a time.'
> 'Ah, you don't know Berta!' said Dan, looking as if he did.
> 'How – in what way do you mean?' said Christopher uneasily.
> 'So lofty – so very lofty! Isn't she, Sol? Why she'll never stir out from mother's till after dark, and then her day begins; and she'll traipse about under the trees, and never go into the high-road, so that nobody in the way of gentle-people shall run up against her and know her living in such a little small hut after biding in a big mansion-place. There, we don't find fault wi' her about it; we like her just the same, though she don't speak to us in the street; for a feller must be a fool to make a piece of work about a woman's pride,

when 'tis for her good that he should not. Yes, her life has been
quare enough. I hope she enjoys it, but for my part I like plain
sailing. None of your ups and downs for me.' (124)

Later, Sol brings into high relief the 'absurdity' of this family relationship – and the reiteration of the word 'absurd' reverberates well
beyond the limited sense it has within the conversation in the text:

> 'So Berta and Mr Julian, if you'll go on and take no more notice o'
> us, in case of visitors, it would be wiser – else, perhaps, if we should
> be found out intimate with ye, and bring down your gentility, you'll
> blame us for it. I get as nervous as a cat when I think I may be the
> cause of any disgrace to ye.'
> 'Don't be so silly, Sol,' said Ethelberta, laughing.
> 'Ah, that's all very well,' said Sol, with an unbelieving smile; 'but if
> we bain't company for you out of doors, you bain't company for us
> within – not that I find fault with ye or mind it, and shan't take any-
> thing for painting your house, nor will Dan neither, any more for
> that – no, not a penny; in fact, we are glad to do it for 'ee. At the
> same time, you keep to your class, and we'll keep to ours.'...

> The two brothers then turned their backs upon their visitors, and
> went on working, and Ethelberta and her lover left the room. 'My
> brothers, you perceive,' said she, 'represent the respectable British
> workman in his entirety, and a touchy individual he is, I assure you,
> on points of dignity, after imbibing a few town ideas from his
> leaders. They are painfully off-hand with me, absolutely refusing to
> be intimate, from a mistaken notion that I am ashamed of their dress
> and manners; which, of course, is absurd.'
> 'Which, of course, is absurd,' said Christopher.
> 'Of course it is absurd!' she repeated with warmth, and looking keenly
> at him. But, finding no harm in his face, she continued as before: 'Yet,
> all the time, they will do anything under the sun that they think will
> advance my interests. In our hearts we are one. All they ask me to do
> is to leave them to themselves, and therefore I do so.
> 'Two more sisters of mine, whom you have never seen at all, are also
> here. They are older than any of the rest of us, and had, broadly
> speaking, no education at all, poor girls. The eldest, Gwendoline, is
> my cook, and Cornelia is my housemaid. I suffer much sadness, and
> almost misery sometimes, in reflecting that here are we, ten brothers
> and sisters, born of one father and mother, who might have mixed
> together and shared all in the same scenes, and been properly happy,
> if it were not for the strange accidents that have split us up into sec-
> tions as you see, cutting me off from them without the compensation
> of joining me to any others. They are all true as steel in keeping the

secret of our kin, certainly; but that brings little joy, though some satisfaction perhaps.' (139–41)

The passage reveals the consonance between 'the absurd' and 'alienation' in a class system which dissociates like from like by the fictions of differential status. The novel keeps returning us to the question: which is the real Ethelberta? The answer this passage gives is 'both'. Her reality is the split personality apparent here in Ethelberta's emphasis on the family's common humanity ('in our hearts') and her ability simultaneously to use obviously acquired and condescending class language about her brothers (who 'represent the respectable British workman in his entirety') and her sisters ('poor girls').

It is this deeply divided consciousness of Ethelberta's which dominates the novel. As an earlier quotation suggests, she is made up of 'inconsistencies'; she herself says: '"Experimentally, I care to succeed in society; but at the bottom of my heart, I don't care"' (141). The novel enacts the polarity of 'society' and 'heart' – just as the passage above with her brothers shows that, although she may hang on to both terms, they are in fact irreconcilable. On a number of occasions, Ethelberta wishes she could die:

> Often at such conjunctures as these, when the futility of her great undertaking was more than usually manifest, did Ethelberta long like a tired child for the conclusion of the whole matter; when her work should be over, and the evening come; when she might draw her boat upon the shore, and in some thymy nook await eternal night with a placid mind. (218)

This, however, is a 'Comedy in Chapters' in which physical death is not an option. But the desire to pull out of her deception and return to simplicity is insistent:

> 'I wish I could get a living by some simple humble occupation, and drop the name of Petherwin, and be Berta Chickerill again, and live in a green cottage as we used to do when I was small. I am miserable to a pitiable degree sometimes, and sink into regrets that I ever fell into such a groove as this. I don't like covert deeds, such as coming here to-night.' (225)

And again:

> 'I have decided to give up romancing because I cannot think of any more that pleases me. ... I will never be a governess again: I would

rather be a servant. If I am a school-mistress I shall be entirely free from all contact with the great, which is what I desire, for I hate them, and am getting almost as revolutionary as Sol. Father, I cannot endure this kind of existence any longer. I sleep at night as if I had committed a murder: I start up and see processions of people, audiences, battalions of lovers obtained under false pretences – all denouncing me with the finger of ridicule. Mother's suggestion about my marrying I followed out as far as dogged resolution would carry me, but during my journey here I have broken down; for I don't want to marry a second time among people who would regard me as an upstart or intruder. I am sick of ambition. My only longing now is to fly from society altogether, and go to any hovel on earth where I could be at peace.' (293)

What these passages reveal is Ethelberta's destructive consciousness of the falsity of her life (her 'self-killing', in D. H. Lawrence's phrase, see above, p. 60) and her longing to return to an earlier self, another 'reality', which pre-exists the one that now constitutes her life – one which is theoretically her 'true' self. But what the trajectory of the novel confirms is the delusion of these dreams: she cannot escape the logic of her life. Indeed she marries Lord Mountclere – the ultimate symbol of her incorporation by the fiction of class, and the agency which, while enabling her to fulfil her 'duty' to her family, alienates her most completely from them; so that, by the end, she controls the estate, runs all her family's lives, but has herself disappeared from the novel – except as a distant figure who passes in a coach and is talked about with awe by her sister and erstwhile lover. Ethelberta is what the fiction has made her: a woman with a 'will of iron', severe on the servants, respected by everyone, and writing that 'epic poem' (409). In the course of this process, she is presented as the creature of circumstance: at once the victor and the victim of social class. Her 'character' is susceptible to 'those devious impulses and tangential flights which spoil the work of every would-be schemer who instead of being wholly machine is half heart' (306); and she registers 'that old sense of disloyalty to her class and kin by feeling as she felt now which caused the pain, and there was no escaping it' (179). At the same time, she knows she must cynically continue to construct the fiction of herself, a class image which makes her acceptable to that other class of which she is also a part (185). She is honest with herself about her plight – 'melancholy and mistaken thoughts of herself as a counterfeit had brought her to this' (205); but she is also the dehumanized victim of her own deception: 'She had at this juncture entered upon that Sphinx-like stage of existence in which, contrary to her earlier manner, she signified to no one of her ways, plans, or sensations, and spoke little on any subject at all. There were occasional smiles now which came only from the face, and speeches from the lips merely' (217; note here both the reified 'smiles' once more, and the suggestion of an automaton in the use of 'the' instead of 'her'). When she does tell the 'truth' about herself, as we have seen, it is taken as a fiction and is curtailed by the cynical realist she marries for convenience, before all has been revealed. Increasingly she sees herself as 'a thing' (251), as 'public property' (280), as 'ready for my role' (297), as so totally alienated from 'herself' that, in one highly significant passage, she thinks of herself as a different woman to the one she thought she was:

> In looking back upon her past as she retired to rest, Ethelberta could almost doubt herself to be the identical woman with her who had entered on a romantic career a few short years ago. For that doubt she had good reason. She had begun as a poet of the Satanic school in a sweetened form; she was ending as a *pseudo*-utilitarian. Was there ever such a transmutation effected before the action of a hard environment? It was not without a qualm of regret that she discerned how the last infirmity of a noble mind had at length nearly departed from her. She wondered if her early notes had had the genuine ring in them, or whether a poet who could be thrust by realities to a distance beyond recognition as such was a true poet at all. Yet Ethelberta's gradient had been regular: emotional poetry, light verse, romance as an object, romance as a means, thoughts of marriage as an aid to her pursuits, a vow to marry for the good of her family; in other words, from soft and playful Romanticism to distorted Benthamism. Was the moral incline upward or down? (297)

We may notice in passing the effects of a 'hard environment' and 'realities' on the career of a 'true poet', and remember Hardy as a similar protagonist in *The Life*. But more to the point here, the passage fractures any conception of 'character' as unitary subject: 'Ethelberta' – within her story and within the novel – is no more than what class and the novel make her: a set of contradictory discourses artificially held together by the 'illusionism' of both these fictions. And is there any more definitive answer to the passage's concluding question, which raises again the relativity of absolutes, than there is to the one the novel continuously poses: which *is* the 'real' Ethelberta?

* * * * *

At this point, and in conclusion, I return to Robert Gittings and Hardy's 'negative' reason for writing *HE* (see above, p. 65): that his irritation at the comparisons with George Eliot after *FMC* led him to write a novel totally dissimilar to hers. Gittings comments characteristically:

> The novel's part-failure comes from this negative pattern. In it, Hardy cut himself off very largely from the deep, ancestral, archetypal Dorset family past, on which he always drew so successfully. *Far from the Madding Crowd* had been entirely written in the low, large cottage, his birthplace, only a few miles from all the scenes of the novel. It is full of the fireside influence and folk-memory of Hardy's mother, the most powerful inspiration of his life. To allot such a small space in *Ethelberta* to these essential influences was to maim the story at the outset. Again, to produce a brittle, semi-theatrical novel of ingenuity, in an attempt to be unlike the deep and philosophic texture of George Eliot's novels, once more weakened Hardy by substituting negative reasons for positive.[22]

We see here, at their most explicit, a number of the tendencies I have earlier identified in the production of 'Hardy' as 'great writer': *HE* is 'maim[ed] ... at the outset' by not dealing with the 'essential influences' of the rural life Hardy knew best; Hardy's own phrase from the 1912 General Preface – 'novel of ingenuity' – is used without attribution, thus granting it unproblematical and definitive status; the novel is characterized as 'brittle' and 'semi-theatrical', and is then compared to the 'deep and philosophic texture' of George Eliot's fiction – Hardy's reaction being seen as 'negative'. In effect, George Eliot's humanist realism is being used as a measure of Hardy's work when it is not about Wessex; *HE*, therefore, is found wanting and can be deemed a 'minor' deviation from the main thrust of the 'great' works – a necessary tactic for a humanist-realist criticism based on liberal-bourgeois conceptions of 'character' and common-sense 'probabilism' if its own 'fictions' are not to be exposed and demystified.

On the other hand, I do not wish to suggest that Hardy intentionally wrote a novel which challenged George Eliot's fiction at every

point; I have merely tried to look 'positively' at *HE*, to read its discourses beyond the limiting perspectives of humanist-realist criticism, and to note how radically, in the event, it challenges the work
of, say, George Eliot. Eliot's fiction affirms, even in the late works,
the possibility of moral maturation in individual human subjects
which contains the seeds of the reform of the social organism as a
whole – a world-view conveyed by way of 'rounded' and 'consistent' characters who 'live' in the discourses of a 'convincing' and
'truthful' realism. The account given of their lives and of their
moral triumphs in the complex web of a class society purports to be
authoritative and authentic, and therefore underwrites the belief
that human individuals (of 'character') are effective in resisting and
reforming the structurally exploitative and unjust mechanisms of a
capitalist class society. By parading the fiction of class, and by
articulating this in a fiction which foregrounds its own artifice, *HE*
exposes both how destructive of the individual the class system is
(alienation equals impotence), and how illusory is the conception of
'character', of the unitary, efficacious human subject, in humanist-
realist fiction. At a stroke, as it were, the novel threatens the coter-
minous notions of 'the individual' and of 'character' which lie at the
heart of bourgeois liberal-humanist ideology and its dominant literary form. 'Artificiality' parallels 'alienation', 'fiction' parallels
'class'; and the character 'Ethelberta' is no more than the amalgam
of discourses which structure her in the novel. To ask who is the
'real' Ethelberta, or which is the 'true' story of her life (indeed,
what is the real 'Hardy'), is to receive the answer: the fictional discourses which determine and represent them – contradictory, dis-
continuous, fractured, 'unreal'. And if the 'character/individual' is
perceived to be no more than this – either in fictional or social
terms – then the whole organicist world-view of humanist realism is
called to account. But to bring to bear on the novel a critical paradigm derived from such a world-view will indeed be to render it a
'failure', a 'joker', an 'improbable' fiction; will be to exorcize its
subversive force as a text bitterly inscribed by hostility to the destructive illusions of a class society and the literary ideology which
sustains them. Throughout this chapter I have, instead, deployed a
different paradigm to show how, in its aggressive fictionality, *HE*
can be made to yield its force, while at the same time demonstrat-
ing, by extensive quotation, that the determinate discourses of the
text permit this strategy. I have not, however, suggested that Hardy

4

Hardy's 'Quite Worthless' Novel: *A Laodicean*

In Albert C. Baugh's *A Literary History of England* (1967), the following comment appears: 'criticism of *A Laodicean* ... is disarmed by the fact that, having been contracted for, it was composed during convalescence from a severe illness. It is quite worthless.'[1] What does it mean to make such an absolute negative judgement? At bottom, that the novel simply does not fit the critical stereotype of Hardy as the great tragic novelist of 'Character and Environment' and of 'Wessex'. Indeed, together with *The Hand of Ethelberta*, *A Laodicean* is probably the most execrated and disregarded of all Hardy's novels. Even more recent sympathetic editors and critics have presented it as 'certainly not one of Hardy's great novels'; 'an experiment that failed'; as providing 'little evidence of the imaginative fire which characterizes Hardy at his best'; grudgingly, 'not the complete failure it is usually taken to be'.[2] What these commentators commonly propose is that the novel is, nevertheless, part of the great man's work; and so its 'very crudities have an interest, and invite comparison with the finer workmanship in other novels'; 'it possesses an intrinsic interest to any student of his mind and methods of writing ... but ... more important ... a number of the technical problems which he set himself, but failed to

A version of this piece will act as the Introduction to the new 'Everyman's Library' edition of *Laod.* – forthcoming. The present essay has been revised and extended, including the incorporation of several pages from my *Thomas Hardy* volume in the 'Writers and their Work' series (Plymouth: Northcote House, 1996).

solve here, found more complete and satisfactory expression in *The Mayor of Casterbridge* and *Jude the Obscure*.[3] Please note – for I will return to the point – that the 'crudities' and 'failed technical problems' are not regarded as fundamental components of Hardy's fictional discourse, but simply as showing up the 'finer', 'complete and satisfying expression' of later and/or greater works.

Nevertheless, *Laod. is* an odd novel; and it is perfectly easy to see how the critical orthodoxy has been arrived at – although my aim in this essay will be to try and prise it free of just that. It *was* written during a severe illness (between October 1880 and May 1881): having a contract for its serialization in the first European edition of the American *Harper's New Monthly Magazine*, and having composed the first 13 chapters by the time he was ill, Hardy was too far on to be able to back out (the serial, in 13 parts, began to appear in December 1880), and most of the rest of it was dictated to his wife, Emma, whilst he was lying on his back with his feet higher than his head. It was finished on 1 May 1881, and continued to appear in *Harper's* until December of that year. Book publication was in November and December 1881, in New York and London respectively, but the London edition was remaindered within two months. Hardy later destroyed the manuscript, largely because so much of it was in Emma's hand and because she was to claim, in years to come, that she had had much input to several of his novels. The serial version was heavily revised for the book edition of 1881; several hundred further changes were made for the Osgood, McIlvaine first Collected Edition of Hardy's works in 1896; and many more again for the 1912 Macmillan 'Wessex Edition'.[4] *Which* text, therefore, represents the 'essential' *Laod.* is impossible to say, and effectively knocks on the head the notion of the determinate and inviolate 'text in itself' so beloved of formalist critics. In fact, the two most readily available contemporary paperback editions of the novel to date underline this problem, in so far as the 'World's Classics' edition uses the 1881 version as source-text, while the 'New Wessex' reproduces the 1912 edition.[5]

It is also true that many of the criticisms of the novel's 'crudities' do appear to have a certain substance. There *is* a disconcerting shift of focus from Book I to Books II and III; there is general agreement that the 'travelogue' round Europe in Books IV and V (drawing heavily on the Hardys' own tour of Normandy the previous summer) is long-winded and slackly composed – even the doughtiest apologistic heart fails when yet another chapter opens: 'They next deviated to Amiens ...', and Captain de Stancy yet again resumes his unrequited wooing of Paula: '"Do be a little *more* of my way of thinking!" rejoined de Stancy passionately.'[6] Much of the writing is also either obtrusively overdone – 'the length of time that he sat there was so remarkable as to raise that interval of inanition to the rank of a feat' (381) – or as flat as a pancake: 'After the Baden slopes the flat thoroughfares of "Charles's Rest" seemed somewhat uninteresting, though a busy fair which was proceeding in the streets created a quaint and unexpected liveliness' (322). The character of both the weak men who are in love with Paula is curiously unrealized: George Somerset, the diffident Hardy-like architect, shows not one tiny characteristic to explain why Paula does, indeed, fall in love with him – unless it be the 'moustache all-sufficient to hide the subtleties of his mouth, which could thus be tremulous at tender moments without provoking inconvenient criticism' (38); and Captain de Stancy, a world-weary cavalry officer, after a period of self-imposed abstinence from wine and women, undergoes what we would now recognize as symptoms of the male menopause: he pours his bottles of mineral water out of the window (their contents 'dribble in a small stream on to the gravel below'), murmurs: '"To Paula!"' – as he drinks 'a glass of the ruby liquor', and ejaculates: '"A man again after eighteen years" ... shutting the sash and returning to his bedroom' (202). The novel is, indeed, as several critics note,[7] written in 'a mixture of modes', including 'melodramatic intrigue' and 'improbable' sensationalism. Hardy himself, in his 1896 Preface, implies that, unlike some of the 'Wessex' novels, this one's readership will be youthful and romantic or 'comfortably' elderly, and that its 'predetermined cheerful ending' was 'strenuously' pursued. It is, of course, one of the three novels in his own third (and lowest?) category in the 'General Preface' to the 1912 'Wessex Edition': 'Novels of Ingenuity' or '"Experiments" ... written for the nonce simply.'[8]

Further oddities about the book, which critics often represent negatively but which I merely wish to point to neutrally for the moment, may be identified as follows. There is the strange presence of William Dare, the boy/man of indeterminate age and nationality, who speaks snippets of several European languages – '"as they say at Madrid"/"as the Italians have it"' (130, 137); has 'DE STANCY' tattooed on his breast because he is Captain de Stancy's illegitimate son; and who is, as far as I am aware, the first – possibly the only – photographer in 19th-century British fiction. I will return to the importance of photography in the novel later. Dare also carries a pistol and grows a moustache as a disguise (in the serial version, he has a false one in his pocket which he dons at one point; Hardy changed that in the book editions). Equally odd is the arrival in the novel of Paula's long-lost uncle, Abner Power – 'a stranger, with the manner of a Dutchman, the face of a smelter, and the clothes of an inhabitant of Guiana' (265) – who 'has been quite a lost man to all of us for nearly ten years – ever since the last time we last heard from him' (267–8), and who is later referred to – by the narrative voice – as 'that breathing refrigerator, her uncle' (274). It transpires that he has been a mercenary bomb-maker for anarchists in Geneva, has had a bomb blow up in his face, and has been on the run ever since from both them and 'all the heads of police in Europe' (379). He too carries a pistol, and has a bizarre stand-off with Dare in a church vestry before disappearing back to Peru. Despite all this, and apart from accompanying the ladies around Europe while (inexplicably) seeming to encourage de Stancy's bid for Paula's hand, Uncle Abner has absolutely no function in the plot – *nothing* happens or is changed by his presence: he is simply introduced and despatched as a grotesque figure in the later parts of the novel. Whether Hardy was, in some sense, parodying the conventions of the genre of sensational fiction by thwarting expectations here may well seem more credible in the light of what I have to say later. A further 'sensational' aspect of the book is its unexpected, melodramatic, but striking, ending in which Dare piles the de Stancy portraits into a bonfire and burns the castle down. It is also worth noting that where the novel finally puts Charlotte de Stancy in an Anglican convent and the Captain leaves the area with his artillery battery, it discloses *absolutely nothing* about Dare: does that 'citizen of the world' (166), that 'cosmopolite' (101, 169), who seems to be the evil genius of this modern world, perish in the fire; remain in Markton to hamper George's and Paula's happiness; or join Uncle Abner in Peru? As one instance among many of its oddity, the novel does not say.

* * * * *

Before I ask – and attempt to answer – my central questions: what kind of a novel is *Laod.*? and what does it in fact offer us as fiction?

– a brief account of its theme may be in order. The multiple titles point us to it: '*A Laodicean*[9] or, The Castle of the De Stancys. A Story of To-Day'. Part of our problem as modern readers is that 'To-Day' is now very much 'Yesterday', and the 'modern' appurtenances – the telegraph, railways, photography, religious debate, architectural restoration, etc. – which the novel emphatically foregrounds are by no means so topically striking as they would have been in 1880. Nevertheless, its project, very clearly and explicitly, is to examine the *mentalité* of a contemporary society in transition between 'the ancient and the modern' – a phrase it uses more than once. This theme is inflected in a number of more or less obvious ways. The Baptist Chapel, for example (43–4), built by the railway magnate Mr Power's new money, is contrasted (not entirely unfavourably) with the ancient English village church George is sketching as the novel opens. Old Sir William de Stancy now lives in a modern villa (an example of 'mushroom modernism'), is himself uncompromisingly 'modern', and loathes the 'lumber' of the past (72, 75). It is 'the modern Paula' (248) who installs the telegraph – a central motif in the novel – in the ancient de Stancy castle: George discovers that its humming wire 'vanished through an arrow-slit into the interior. This fossil of feudalism, then, was [its] journey's end' (22); and she has also put a 'new and shining' clock in the castle tower, because 'the old one ... only told the hours. Paula says that time, being so much more valuable now, must of course be cut up into smaller pieces' (54, 64). Railways, of course, are central to the novel: Paula's father has made his fortune building 'half the railways in Europe' (118) and bought with it the de Stancy castle, its portraits and furniture – 'a clash', says George, for our explicit edification, 'between ancient and modern' (62). But the curves of the tunnel Mr Power has built locally 'are said to be a triumph of science' (119) and, as a significant affirmation of Hardy's positive attitude to modernity – confounding the conventional representation of him as only championing traditional ways of life – the narrative voice comments: 'the popular commonplace that science, steam and travel must always be unromantic and hideous, was not proven at this spot' (120).

Indeed, the novel's own ambivalence about the relative values of 'ancient' and 'modern' is an exemplification of its theme. Despite being 'emphatically a modern type of maidenhood' (46), Paula is susceptible to the 'weird romanticism' of the de Stancy 'spell' – 'as if the historic past had touched her with a yet living hand' (227): she wishes she *was* a de Stancy; wants to restore the castle she has 'inherited' as authentically as possible; and only encourages the Captain's suit because the match would, in a sense, put everything right. The text constantly draws attention to her hybridity: the description of her boudoir (65–7) emphasizes its 'thoroughly modern Milly'-ness, but also notes that it 'were as if a stray hour from the nineteenth century had wandered like a butterfly into the thirteenth, and lost itself there' (66); and George reflects on her as a 'modern flower in a medieval flower-pot … and upon the incongruities that were daily shaping themselves in the world under the great modern fluctuations of classes and creeds' (67) – a phrase I shall return to. A short passage which has, apparently, proved to critics Hardy's pathetic lack of grasp in this novel[10] – but whose manifestly arch tenor suggests other explanations – uses the telegraph again to make a similar point:

> The cheering message from Paula to Somerset sped through the loop-hole of Stancy Castle tower, over the trees, along the railway, under bridges, across four counties – from extreme antiquity of environment to sheer modernism – and finally landed itself on a table in Somerset's chambers in the midst of a cloud of fog. (232)

'Sheer modernism' is also a striking phrase, reminding us, perhaps, of that more famous tragic one in *Tess of the d'Urbervilles*: 'the ache of modernism'. But the uncompromisingly modern telegraph is itself subjected to ambivalence: in comparison to 'the fairer side of feudalism', the novel notes that 'the modern mental fever and fret which consumes people before they can grow old was also signified by the wire' (52). Registering the echoes here of Matthew Arnold's 'sick hurry and divided aims' in 'this strange disease of modern life',[11] we may again look forward to that more destructive condition in *Jude*: 'the modern vice of unrest'. Lastly, in the context of the novel's counterpointing of 'ancient' and 'modern', there is Paula's and George's debate on Mr Power's status as a modern railway engineer, and on the respective merits of 'art' and 'science', of designing castles or railways. Does Paula 'represent the march of mind – the steamship, and the railway, and the thoughts that shake mankind' (118), or a romantic '*prédilection d'artiste*' (136) for the de Stancys and the castle? Do George's preferences lie with early English architecture or with the dynamics of modern engineering?

exposes the modes, directions and possibilities of Hardy's fictional *corpus*, and makes his techniques visible in their overt crudity of display. And while I would not claim that the novel is, in fact, a fully controlled and coherent articulation of its themes, it is nevertheless worth considering that since we are not by now dealing with a journeyman novelist – *The Return of the Native*, for example, precedes it by three years – these effects may suggest that their overwrought and unresolved juxtapositioning represents a more conscious formal 'Experiment' to catch the problematics of an eclectic 'modernism'.

It is difficult for us, now, to 'see' Hardy in 1880, encrusted as he is by his critical and cultural mythologizing since. In order to get underneath this, and speculate about what Hardy looked like while writing *Laod.*, let us go along to some extent with his self-presentation of himself as poet first and by no means a 'born novelist'; as a writer who, at least initially, had to earn a living in the rough world of the Victorian literary market-place; who had to learn to become, above all other considerations, 'a good hand at a serial' (his own words); who, as *The Life of Thomas Hardy* (disingenuously) claims, always regarded novel-writing as a 'trade', not an art.[16] What we see, then, is a writer with many choices facing him, rather than the 'Wessex' novelist of 'Character and Environment' already formed and waiting only to emerge from the chrysalis. In fact, Hardy's first real popularity had only arrived in 1874 with *Far from the Madding Crowd* (which some critics initially thought was by George Eliot), after which he immediately wrote *HE* (1876) – 'A Comedy in Chapters' – this giving him, *The Life* informs us in a telling sentence: 'the satisfaction of proving, amid the general disappointment at the lack of sheep and shepherds, that he did not mean to imitate anybody'.[17] Indeed, 'Wessex' only becomes a more or less focused conceptual 'region' with *RN* (1878), a novel which, at the time, received a lukewarm reception, and which was followed by the much more popular historical pastoral, *The Trumpet-Major* (1880). Then comes *Laod.* and, immediately afterwards, Hardy's third novel in three years, *Two on a Tower* (1882) – a mixture of comic romance, anti-clerical satire and unexpected pathos. At this point, the young Havelock Ellis, in a perceptive survey-review of all Hardy's fiction to date, predicts that he will continue to develop along the lines set down in his ironic social comedies and write more in that mode.[18] The point I wish to make is that, in 1880, in the complex and volatile world of the fiction market, a relatively unestablished novelist, not yet inscribed with the indelible 'Wessex' signature, had many kinds of fiction open to him, and *Laod*. displays several of them in operation – modes which in other novels are *also* used, perhaps less heterogeneously, to articulate the 'ache[s] of modernism'. Here, in the agitated textual crust of *Laod*., is acutely perceptible the revealing clash of fictional plates more or less visible – as fissures and cracks open up and close – beneath the unstable 'realist' surface of Hardy's fictional terrain as a whole.

* * * * *

What the novel identifies is that, at this point, three subjects in particular are prominent in Hardy's repertoire: not 'Wessex', 'Character' and 'Environment', but 'modernity', 'class' and 'sexuality'. And it is arguable that these remain his prime concern, albeit hidden under the 'acceptable' surface of his so-called 'major' novels.[19] For example, the terrible destructiveness of the 'clash between ancient and modern' that was later to be shown in *Tess* is not brought out here, but the 'romanticism' of a finished, but still seductive, past which 'modern spirits' must negotiate is announced in both novels by way of (meretricious) present-day scions of 'old' families: both William Dare and Alec d'Urberville being presented as melodrama 'villains' – thus exemplifying the factitiousness of a 'reproduction' past. The contemporary remnants of decayed families both live in modern houses (old Sir William's 'mushroom modernist' 'Myrtle Villa' – 'almost new, of streaked brick' – anticipates Alec's 'almost new' 'rich red' house, 'The Slopes', in *Tess*); and in both novels, family portraits and tombs are used at once as cranks for the plot and symbolically: for example, Captain de Stancy, in a bizarre scene, turns himself into a family portrait (212), just as Alec, equally bizarrely, leaps up from the d'Urberville vault, having pretended to be the recumbent figure on a sarcophagus. My point simply is that, both in theme and formal enactment of it, *Laod*. is by no means the 'sport' in Hardy's *oeuvre* it has often been taken to be, but rather brings clearly into view that his fictional strategies are common to both 'major' and 'worthless' texts.

Following on from that first, 'lost' novel, *The Poor Man and the Lady*, the 'tendency' of whose writing was 'socialistic, not to say revolutionary',[20] much of Hardy's fiction is, in fact, driven by cross-class relationships and registers the transitions of a rapidly changing class society. *Laod.* is no exception. For its 'surface' theme of the destabilizing mix of 'romanticism' with 'modernism' is actually premised on new *class* positions – and we may recall George's phrase here: 'the great modern fluctuations of classes and creeds' (67). Paula is, indeed, an estate-owning 'Lady', but only by way of inherited 'new money'. The novel reiterates the insecurity of her position as a nouveau-riche arriviste amongst the rural gentry: her dinner-party guests will 'include people of old cavalier families who would have treated her grandfather, … and even her father, with scorn for their religion and connections' (125); and George is unable 'to estimate precisely the disqualifying effect, if any, of her non-conformity, her newness of blood … among the old county families established round her' (124). Her entire relationship with the de Stancys is based on an inversion of the established class hierarchies (in a sense, Paula, here, is the Alec of *Tess*), and the novel, as we have seen, calls in question the 'romantic' fantasy of a *passé* feudalism 'surviving' into a world of telegraphy and photography. Significantly, it is the preternaturally alienated, modern bastard, the 'sinister' Dare, who understands exactly his family's class position: 'a worn-out old party. … We represent conditions of life that have had their day. … Our one remaining chance was an alliance with new aristocrats; and we have failed. We are past and done for' (429). Dare survives by transmuting himself into an amoral, displaced entrepreneur who might well prosper in Peru. Conversely, it is George, from an established professional middle-class background, who makes the 'alliance' with the 'new aristocrat' at the end. But he, too, is acutely conscious of the 'modern fluctuations' in class relationships: he feels Paula's 'social position as a woman of wealth … a perceptible bar to that full and free eagerness with which he would fain have approached her' (341); and at the very moment when Paula forces a proposal of marriage out of him, Hardy gives himself away by the explanation he puts in George's mouth for his 'delicacy' about asking her: '"the woman is rich, and the man is poor"' (422). Hardy's obsession with class – first articulated in the title of *The Poor Man and the Lady* – and his minutely nuanced presentation of it, is rendered more visible throughout his fictional *oeuvre* when we are made to see it so clearly in the mannered textuality of *Laod.*

Paula's 'if you want to marry me … you must say so; for I am here to be asked' (423) also directs us to the continual interrelationship of class and sexuality in Hardy's fiction. Here, we have a fascinating heroine – the 1912 'Postscript' to the Preface calls her 'really lovable' – who has all the erotic investment of Tess. Our introduction to her establishes this early – in a passage reminiscent of the way Angel is to view Tess at Talbothays (see also the scene where de Stancy watches Paula in the gym, analysed below, pp. 107–11):

> She wore a summer hat, beneath which her fair curly hair formed a thicket round her forehead. It would be impossible to describe her as she then appeared. Not sensuous enough for an Aphrodite, and too subdued for a Hebe, she would yet, with the adjunct of doves or nectar, have stood sufficiently well for either of those personages, if presented in a pink morning light, and with mythological scarcity of attire. (87)

Where Tess has a 'mobile peony mouth', Paula has a 'mobile bosom' (88); but Tess's oral eroticism is also evident: 'Paula, moulding her cherry-red lower lip beneath her upper one in arch self-consciousness at his act, turned away' (131). She is presented as an ('eclectic') mixture of extreme modern competence, romantic dreaminess and earnest intellectual aspiration, as flirtatious coquette, shy lover and determined young woman: '"He'll never forgive you" ... "Won't he!" said Paula, with soft faith. "I'll see about that"' (404). But we should also not forget her surname – Power – and that she is 'a woman of wealth'. In many respects, she is another of Hardy's 'new women' (Ethelberta, Tess, Sue Bridehead, in their different ways), and as such is another destabilizing factor in the transition from 'ancient' to 'modern'. Typically (the phrasing is again echoed in *Tess*), her womanliness and strength are emphasized: 'Miss Power seemed not only more woman than Miss de Stancy, but more woman than Somerset was man' (96; note that 'seemed' for later comment). Certainly, the novel is at pains to present her as stronger than both her suitors. She roundly tells George that he is 'too faint-hearted' in his pursuit of her (285); and in a moment, surely, of male sexual fear at the threat of women's 'power' (so common in later 19th-century patriarchy), he admits the 'curious impression' that 'he could not see himself as the husband of Paula Power in any likely future. He could not imagine her his wife. ... [T]hough he could picture her as queening it over him, ... he could not see her in a state of domesticity with him' (288). Equally, de Stancy's feelings for Paula are thrown into 'the most foolish boyish shape' (317), and he, too, is subject to her scorn: '"Well, love is natural to men, I suppose. ... But you must love within bounds; or you will be enervated. ... Men allow themselves to be made ridiculous by their own feelings in an inconceivable way"' (315–16).

However, there is a difference between 'strength' and 'power'; and it is quite within the bounds of possibility that there is a telling pun in the name 'Miss Power' – for Paula *does* 'miss power' simply by being a woman within partiarchy. Barbara Hardy has commented perceptively that in *Laod.*: 'Hardy is showing the powerlessness of a typical woman's life, the more sharply because she is endowed with a kind of power', noting also that this 'heiress [of] fortune and romantic energy' is paralleled by Isobel Archer in Henry James's *The Portrait of a Lady*, which was being serialized simultaneously (October 1880–November 1881). Whatever notional power Paula may have, she is in fact heading inexorably towards marriage – her only real choice being that between two 'mentors' (one 'romantic', the other 'modern'). This, combined with Hardy's emphasis on her physical charms and intelligence – which turns her into 'a more appealing sexual object' for George, de Stancy and author – reveals, for Barbara Hardy, his 'failure to see what was really wrong with his heroine': that 'she inherits everything from her father except the one thing – his sex – which could endow her with some power of choice'.[21] Whether Hardy did 'fail to see' Paula's real powerlessness is a moot point; more significant is the fact that this novel, as with so many of his others, and the society they critically reflect, in effect neutralizes the 'power' of the heroine it has so dynamically engendered.

One last point about Paula will lead into my final topic here: her characterization – or rather, the lack of it. In his 1912 prefatory 'Postscript', Hardy reflects that Paula is 'individualized with some clearness ... though she is of that reserved disposition which is the most difficult of all dispositions to depict, and tantalized the writer by eluding his grasp for some time'. In fact, the text itself emphasizes her inscrutability – on one occasion referring to her explicitly as 'an enigma' (155), and on others self-consciously abjuring responsibility for the task of depicting her by such devices as 'Miss Power seemed ...' or 'It would be impossible to describe her ... '. Havelock Ellis, in his 1883 review mentioned earlier, makes the (italically pointed) quotation above, then there must be a real question as to how far the 'crudities' *are* lapses in decorum and control, and how far they are, instead, strategic – even parodic – displays of the palette's range of effects. Hardy, let us remember, had already written *FMC* and *RN* and knew what he could do in that mode. It is barely credible, therefore, ill as he may have been, that he was blind to the obtrusive artificiality of much of the novel. But the whole text is, in fact, very much more self-conscious than the 'poor-ill-Hardy' school of criticism has ever allowed, and in two significant ways: its own awareness of the fictional strategies it deploys, and its iteration of tropes of imaging and representation.

The novel abounds with self-reflexive utterances: on George witnessing the telegraphic 'conversation' about him between Charlotte and Paula before he has met the latter, the narrative comments: 'the machine went on with its story. There was something curious in watching this utterance about himself under his very nose, in language unintelligible to him'; '"Dear me"', says George in the middle of it, '"the plot thickens ... How could she know about me?"' (71); in relation to the plainly contrived 'character' of de Stancy, the novel muses: his 'peculiarly bifold nature ... was something rare in life, and perhaps happily so' (230); on the fortuitous reappearance of Uncle Abner noted earlier, Paula is made to comment: '"The return of my uncle is so extraordinary that it ought to be told in a less hurried way than this"' (267); Dare notes that it is '"by the merest chance"' that he has a pack of playing cards in his coat pocket (187); the text, having effected a coincidence of monumental shamelessness, comments: 'and this, by a coincidence common enough in fact, though scarcely credited in chronicles' (209); on the *second* occasion that George – by chance – does not receive an invitation to one of Paula's parties, he exclaims: '"Too late!" [actually it turns out not to be] ... "To think I should be served this trick a second time!"' (240); a further coincidence is referred to as giving 'an added point to the satire' (255); George is 'so struck by the circumstance' of Dare also arriving in Carlsruhe on the same train that he almost forgets to alight (324; in the 1881 version, it is 'the phenomenal circumstance'). And so on. Such 'externalized' treatment of coincidence and chance may give us some clues as to whether or not it is also one of Hardy's involuntary 'flaws' in the 'major' novels. The degree of self-consciousness announced here is further reinforced by a number of obtrusive textual 'devices' (not unfamil-

iar, again, in *Tess* and particularly *Jude*): the formulaic description
of the artillery brigade entering Markton (171; in the 1881 edition
again, more typographically emphasized); the capitalized 'DE
STANCY' tattooed on Dare's breast (186); a playbill reproduced in
the text (244–5); the two interpersonal 'conversations' mechanically
carried out – and reproduced textually as – by telegraph (262–4,
288–9).

But to give a fuller illustration of both aspects of the self-
conscious fictionality of Hardy's writing in this novel noted above,
let us look in detail at a passage which brings sharply into view
both his narrative positioning of the reader as complicit in the alienated *looking at* of a character, and his mannered ironic style – this
time with heavily charged sexual undertones. The scene, in Book
the Second, Chapter Seven, has been described by one critic of
Hardy's 'lesser novels' as the 'most widely mocked'[25] of the novel's
unintended comic absurdities. 'Mocked' it may have been by critics
concerned to read Hardy as a wayward and 'flawed' realist genius,
but whether the comic absurdity is *unintended* remains to be seen.
William Dare, William de Stancy's illegitimate son, has arranged
for his 'dad' to see the lovely heiress, Paula, so that he will be
seduced away from his self-imposed vow of fidelity to his dead
lover (Dare's mother), pay court to Paula, marry her, and thus
restore the family to its rightful inheritance (the castle, etc.). Paula
is working out in her modern gym deep in the woods, entirely un-
conscious that she is being spied upon; Dare has engineered a hole
in the gym wall through which can be seen '"quite a curiosity, and
really worth seeing"' (196); de Stancy moves forward, now slightly
the worse for drink – which, the text obligingly tells us, 'would
have been *comical to an outsider*' (196; my emphases, and mine
throughout the passage which follows):

> and *looked through the hole into the interior* of the gymnasium.
> Dare withdrew to some little distance, and *watched* Captain de
> Stancy's face, which presently began to assume an expression of
> interest.
> What was the captain *seeing*? A sort of *optical poem*.
> Paula, in a pink flannel costume, was bending, wheeling and undulat-
> ing in the air *like a gold-fish in its globe*, sometimes ascending by her
> arms nearly to the *lantern*, then lowering herself till she swung level
> with the floor. Her aunt Mrs Goodman, and Charlotte de Stancy, were
> sitting on camp-stools at one end, *watching* her gyrations, Paula

occasionally addressing them with such an expression as – 'Now, Aunt, *look at me* – and you, Charlotte – is not that shocking to your weak nerves,' when some adroit feat would be repeated, which, however, seemed to give much more pleasure to Paula herself in *performing* it than to Mrs Goodman in *looking on*, the latter sometimes saying, 'O, it is terrific – do not run such a risk again!'

It would have demanded the poetic passion of some joyous Elizabethan lyrist like Lodge, Nashe, or Greene, to fitly phrase Paula's *presentation of herself* at this moment of absolute abandonment to every muscular whim that could take possession of such a supple form. The white manilla ropes clung about *the performer* like snakes as she took her exercise, and the colour in her face deepened as she went on. Captain de Stancy felt that, much as he had *seen* in early life of beauty in woman, he had never *seen* beauty of such a real and living sort as this. A bitter recollection of his vow, together with a sense that *to gaze* on the festival of this Bona Dea was, though so innocent and *pretty a sight*, hardly fair or gentlemanly, would have compelled him to *withdraw his eyes*, had not the *sportive* fascination of *her appearance glued them there* in spite of all. And as if to complete *the picture* of Grace personified and add the one thing wanting to the charm which bound him, the clouds, till that time thick in the sky, broke away from the upper heaven, and allowed the noonday sun to pour down through *the lantern* upon her, *irradiating* her with a warm light that was incarnadined by her pink doublet and hose, and *reflected in* upon her face. She only required a cloud to rest on instead of the green silk net which actually supported her reclining figure for the moment, to be quite *Olympian*; save indeed that in place of haughty effrontery there *sat on her countenance* only the healthful sprightliness of an English girl ....

Looking in a side direction, [Dare] *saw* Havill idling slowly up to him over the silent grass. Havill's knowledge of the appointment had brought him out to *see* what would come of it. When he neared Dare ... the former simply pointed to de Stancy, upon which Havill stood and *peeped* at him. 'Is she within there?' he inquired.

Dare nodded, and whispered, 'You need not have asked, if you had *examined his face*'....

To *precisely describe* Captain de Stancy's admiration [*look* in the 1881 version] was impossible. A sun seemed to rise in his face. By *watching* him they could almost *see the aspect of her* within the wall, so accurately were her changing phases *reflected in* him. He seemed to forget that he was not alone.

'And is this,' he murmured, in the manner of one only half apprehending himself, 'and is this the end of my vow?'

Paula was saying at this moment, 'Ariel sleeps in *this posture*, does he not, Auntie?' Suiting the action to the word, she flung out her arms behind her head as she lay in the green silk hammock, idly *closed her pink eyelids*, and swung herself to and fro. (196–8)

In the Victorian context, as also in our jaded own, the scene is inescapably erotically charged: at once in its celebration of Paula's potent physical sexuality – even if innocent in itself – and, conversely, in its corrupting of that innocence by the scopophilic framing of it by what we would now call 'the male gaze' (my emphases will have drawn attention, amongst other things, to the passage's iteration of words and phrases to do with 'seeing', 'looking' and 'picturing'). That Hardy was fully conscious of the eroticism of the passage is evidenced by the revisions he made to it in the various versions of the novel. For example, Paula's costume in the serial publication uncompromisingly 'showed to perfection every curve of her figure', a clause deleted in the book edition; where the book version has, as here, '"shocking to your weak nerves"', the serial has Paula saying '"is not that pretty"'; the 1896 book edition added 'innocent and', as here, to the serial's 'though so pretty a sight'; conversely, where the serial had 'strange fascination', the book changed the adjective to 'sportive', as here – with its connotations of being 'roguish', 'wanton', 'amorous'. Furthermore, it does not take an especially prurient mind to register the overt sexuality of the whole description: Paula is 'bending ... and undulating'; is giving way to *'absolute abandonment to every muscular whim* that could *take possession* of such a *supple form'* (my emphases); the 'white manilla ropes' cling about her 'like snakes'; 'the colour in her face deepened as she went on'; 'Bona Dea' (literally 'the good goddess') is the Roman goddess of chastity – but also of fertility – who was worshipped only by women, although, by an erotic inversion, not so here; the spectacle should have compelled de Stancy to *'withdraw* his eyes', but Paula's 'sportive' appearance *'glued* them there in spite of all' (my emphases); the sun 'pouring down' through the 'lantern' (both skylight and, suggestively, an early film projector) bathes her in a kind of artificial lighting: 'irradiating her with a warm light that was incarnadined by her pink doublet and hose, and reflected in upon her face' – 'incarnadine' means having the pinkish colour *of flesh*, and pink, especially in Hardy's poetry, invariably signals the erotic.

Consider, too, the physical implications of Paula's tightly pink-clad figure, either with ropes clinging 'like snakes' round her 'supple form' or 'reclining' (i.e. lying on her back) 'supported' by a 'green silk net': our contemporary soft-porn photographers (and let us not forget that William Dare is one of the earliest photographers in English fiction) could scarcely dream up a more explicit way of exhibiting female flesh. But the following word 'Olympian', beyond its surface sense of 'goddess-like', may also invoke Edouard Manet's nearly contemporary (1865) sensual painting of a courtesan, 'Olympia', who is also reclining nude on a bed, with one hand prudishly but provocatively lying over her pudendum – a painting which had been a *succès de scandale* when first exhibited.[26] Leaving aside the 'sun ris[ing] in [de Stancy's] face', unable to 'withdraw' his eyes which are 'glued' to Paula's 'body', we may conclude this account of the passage's visual erotic fantasy by noting Paula's surely auto-orgasmic 'posture' in the final lines: 'she flung out her arms behind her head as she lay in the green silk hammock, idly closed her pink eyelids, and swung herself to and fro'. This is a late Victorian centrefold in all but name.

However, it is also noteworthy that the language of the passage, on two occasions in particular, draws attention to the theatricality of Paula's display in a scene which is itself inescapably theatrical: 'Paula's *presentation of herself* at this moment of absolute abandonment', and, just below – with the ropes clinging around her – she is called 'the performer' (she is also described as 'performing' one of her feats). This, together with de Stancy's viewing position in the first line of the passage, is surely not a fortuitous, *unintended* invocation of the 'peep-show' – of 'What the Butler Saw'? Other evidence in the passage also points to a high degree of self-consciously arch alienation in the narrative stance and style. We have noted in passing above how Dare 'frames' the scene by calling it 'quite a curiosity', and how de Stancy is burlesqued as potentially 'comical to an outsider'; but in answer to its own stylized question as to what the Captain was 'seeing', the narrative answers with the equally mannered and self-reflexive phrase: 'a sort of optical poem' – which at once offers a definition of the scene in the gym but also of the novel's own *representation* of that scene. Later, the passage grandiloquently invokes 'the poetic passion of some joyous Elizabethan lyrist' (note the oddity of the word – not 'lyr*ic*ist') in pretending to avow its own inadequacy to the task of doing justice to the scene. Similarly, it draws attention to its own descriptive incapacity when it claims that 'to precisely describe Captain de Stancy's admiration was impossible' (note my comments on Paula's 'characterization' above, p. 104; and note too the ambiguity of Hardy's revised earlier word 'look': both de Stancy's appearance *and* his 'loo*king*' – his transfixed male 'gaze'). The passage further undercuts itself by a kind of mock-heroic bathos when Paula, requiring 'only ... a cloud to rest on ... to be quite Olympian', is brought suddenly to earth instead by being described as exuding 'only the healthful sprightliness of an English girl'.

Finally, we may note that the present scene has an overt negative analogue in an earlier chapter (Book the First, Chapter Two), where George's '*gaze* into the lighted chapel' (45, my emphasis) sees the recusant Paula, this time 'clothed in an ample robe of flowing white' (46), refuse to enter the baptismal pool – and so, we must assume, *fails to see* the clinging, wet robe reveal her 'supple form'. For George, 'there was but one scene: the *imagined scene* of the girl herself as she sat alone in the vestry' (49, my emphasis). The fact that the erotically realized Paula-in-the-gym episode so closely parallels and inverts this chaste, sexually repressed and 'imagined' scene is surely further evidence, if any were needed, that we are in the presence of highly self-reflexive composition in this novel and of writing which is very conscious of the artifice of fiction. Whether we see the narrative stance in the gym passage as finally complicit in the eroticized fantasy of the male gaze, or as ironically subverting it, is a moot point – as it is with the similarly erotic presentation of Tess in the later novel. What seems to me incontrovertible here, however, is that any 'comic absurdity' is indeed 'intended', and directed towards the reader – especially (male) ones who do not get the joke.

But the most striking aspect of this narrative self-consciousness – and perhaps the *point* of it – is the text's persistent foregrounding of false (or mis-)representation. As with most of Hardy's fiction, *Laod.* is packed with instances of 'looking' and 'seeing', often from odd angles of vision (see, for example, Paula's garden-party in Book the First, Chapter Fifteen), or of spying and peeping – the most obvious being de Stancy's voyeuristic gazing on the pink-clad Paula analysed above. Invariably and significantly, it is the male characters who occupy these superior and furtive vantage-points, and in relation to Paula in particular, this reinforces the 'enigma' of her 'character', representing her only as reflected images of the male gaze. Even more to the point are the motifs of factitious representation scattered throughout the novel: it opens (line 4) with the 'eclectic' George sketching a *'transitional'* style of church doorway (my emphasis); the de Stancy portraits – an emphatic presence at many points – are first introduced by George wondering 'how many of the lofty foreheads and smiling lips of this pictorial pedigree could *be credited as true reflections of their prototypes. Some were wilfully false no doubt; many more so by unavoidable accident and want of skill*' (55; my emphasis). And this is immediately succeeded by a narrative intervention of what appears to be, in my context here, acute self-reflexivity: 'Perhaps a *true account* of the sweetest and softest among those who looked so demurely at him over their pearl necklaces was *a story* which, *related in its bareness*, would be *hardly credible* to the more self-repressing natures of the present day' (55; my emphases; note the slippage from 'account' to 'story'). An 'account of the sweetest and softest' (Paula), 'related in its bareness' (as the novel does), and 'hardly credible' to those 'more self-repressing natures of the present day' (Hardy critics), is, of course, an excellent description of *Laod.* itself. But please note: the 'bare', 'hardly credible' account, here, is the *'true'* one (as is, perhaps, this non-realist novel's own 'story').

Later, Dare is described as 'a sort of counterfeit of Miss Power' (82), and, in a sense, they *are* both false heirs to de Stancy castle – George also wondering if Paula 'might have been imitating' one of the 'bygone beauties' in the portrait gallery (97). The 'cosmopolite' photographer,[27] Dare, who has a trace of the de Stancy physiognomy (101), is characterized, in a significant pun, as 'a complete negative' (101); the 'original photograph' of him – 'the transcript of [his] features' – is burnt to protect him from the police (180); and he begins to '*wear* a moustache' as disguise (214; my emphasis) – as though it were an artificial appendage (see also p. 96, above). De Stancy imitates the figure in one of the ancestral portraits, asking '"Is the resemblance strong?"' (212); and, in an even more complex trope, as part of his campaign to win Paula, he has Dare photograph all the portraits of his ancestors – whether 'true reflections' or 'wilfully false' – the photographs presumably becoming a 'true' record of 'false' images. It is also, of course, one of Dare's doctored photographs which helps alienate Paula from George for a while, and the narrative commentary on it is again worth attention:

It was a portrait of Somerset; but by a device known in photography the operator, though contriving to produce what seemed to be a perfect likeness, had given it the distorted features and wild attitude of a man advanced in intoxication. No woman, unless specially cognisant of such possibilities, could have looked upon it and doubted that the photograph was a genuine illustration of a customary phase in the young man's private life. (332)

'Contriving ... what seemed ... a perfect likeness' is surely a contradiction in terms – but that, nevertheless, is what Realism claims for itself; and the notion of the photograph as 'genuine illustration' – the 'camera never lying' – is, of course, one of the most potent myths of modern life. Doctored photographs are later in the novel explicitly described as 'misrepresentations' and 'libellous', while being further identified as the productions of the '*ingenious*' Mr Dare (389; my emphasis): we should not forget that *Laod.* was categorized by Hardy as one of his 'Novels of Ingenuity'.

* * * * *

Laod., in my view then, becomes a parodic attack – by way of its own performative anti-realist textuality – on the (mis)representations passed off as 'telling things as they really are' by fictional Realism. The number of occasions on which my quotations throughout have contained the words 'seemed' or 'perhaps' – *Jude*, we may recall, was described by Hardy as 'a series of seemings' – bear witness to this, as do the evasions and disclaimers about being able to 'describe' the characters. By this stage in his writing career, as his journal entries throughout the 1880s make clear, Hardy had come to believe that novel-writing had to 'transcend' the merely inventory-like recording of surface realities: 'Art is a disproportioning – (*i.e.* distorting, throwing out of proportion) – of realities, to show more clearly the features that matter in those realities, which, if merely copied or reported inventorially, might possibly be observed, but would more probably be overlooked. Hence "realism" is not Art.'[28] It is also worth noticing, in conclusion, that in an essay on fiction which Hardy produced while preparing to write *Tess*, he argued fiercely – against the claims of Realism – that a fictional art which goes beyond the 'transcript ... of material fact' is 'more true than history or nature can be'.[29] In this he echoes Maupassant, who wrote in 1888: 'the realist, if he is an artist, will seek to give us not a banal *photographic* representation of life, but a vision of it that is fuller, more vivid and more compellingly truthful than even reality itself'.[30] For Hardy in *Laod.*, I would argue, Realism had become not merely 'banal', but as potentially pernicious – in its 'misrepresentations' of modernity, of 'character', of class and sexual relations – as the 'ingenious' William Dare's photographs are.

5

'Moments of Vision': Postmodernizing *Tess of the d'Urbervilles*:
or,
Tess of the d'Urbervilles Faithfully Presented by Peter Widdowson

Anyone who has read *Tess of the d'Urbervilles* (and certainly any modern criticism about it) will be in no doubt that the novel is emphatically visual in many of its effects. There are those famous set-piece 'descriptions' of rural Wessex (not quite Dorset, let us remember); the inescapably scenic moments, such as the May-dance at Marlott as the novel opens or sunrise at Stonehenge towards the end, which render talk about Hardy's proto-cinematic techniques more than merely chic; and the narrative's obsessive voyeuristic gazing at Tess herself (especially that famous 'mobile peony mouth'[1]) which has made so many readers *wonder* a little about Thomas Hardy. But there is also a great deal of visual imagery in the novel of a rather more self-reflexive sort – a kind of metadiscourse about looking, seeing, perception, representation, imaging.

This essay, almost entirely as it stands, was published in Charles P. C. Pettit (ed.), *New Perspectives on Thomas Hardy* (London: Macmillan, 1994). A slightly different earlier version was the Introduction to my edited collection, *Tess of the d'Urbervilles* (London: Macmillan, 'New Casebooks', 1993).

This is not new or unique to *Tess*, of course: it is everywhere apparent in Hardy's fiction – from the subtitling of *Under the Greenwood Tree* as 'A Rural Painting of the Dutch School' to the presence (betimes) of a photographer in *A Laodicean*; from the staged artificiality of the tableaux vivants in *The Hand of Ethelberta* to the blindness of Clym in *The Return of the Native*; from the astronomer's telescope in *Two on a Tower* to striking 'moments of vision' (a phrase I shall return to) such as that in *Desperate Remedies* (Hardy's first published novel) where Cytherea Graye, watching her father and some masons at the top of a church spire – 'it was an *illuminated miniature, framed in* by the dark *margin* of the window' (my emphases) – suddenly sees him fall to his death: 'he reeled off into the air, immediately disappearing downwards'.[2] And there are the typographical signs and devices scattered throughout the text of *Jude the Obscure* – a novel significantly characterized by its author in his Preface to the first edition (1895) as 'a series of seemings, or personal impressions'.[3]

But self-conscious techniques of visualization are particularly insistent in *Tess*, a novel also prefatorily described by Hardy as 'an impression'[4] – a significant word, perhaps, given his fascination with the late 'impressionist' paintings of J. M. W. Turner.[5] Chapter 2, for example, opens with a reference to a 'landscape-painter', and from there on – as J. B. Bullen has pointed out – the novel abounds with overt or covert references to pictures.[6] There is also the complex ambiguity of the narrator's point of view or stance – towards Tess in particular. For instance:

> As she walked along to-day, for all her *bouncing handsome womanliness, you* could sometimes *see* her twelfth year in her cheeks, or her ninth *sparkling from her eyes*; and even her fifth would flit over the *curves of her mouth* now and then.
> Yet *few* knew, and *still fewer* considered this. *A small minority*, mainly strangers, would *look long at her* in casually passing by, and grow momentarily fascinated by her freshness, and wonder if *they* would ever *see* her again: but *to almost everybody* she was a *fine and picturesque* country girl, and no more. (43)

My emphases draw attention to the voyeurism of the passage, but the uncertainty of focus ('you ... few ... still fewer ... a small minority ... almost everybody') and the peculiar logic of the syntax in the second paragraph ('Yet ... but ... and no more') make it very difficult to say who sees her like this and whether the narrative is attempting to distance itself from the erotic imaging the passage in fact delivers or is fully complicit in it. Furthermore, there is the continual presentation of Tess in terms of the way she is 'seen' by others – most especially, of course, Alec and Angel – until her 'character' seems to be composed entirely of other people's images of her (a point I will return to later). And there are the many other instances where the narrative deploys strikingly visual devices and motifs, from the filmic long-shots (the farm-girls picking swedes at Flintcomb-Ash) and close-ups (Tess's mouth), to the final scene where Angel and Liza Lu, 'their eyes rivetted' to the gaol's flag-pole, watch the 'black flag' unfurl, which denotes that Tess has been hanged (notice how, at this point, a novel which has fetishized Tess's visual presence throughout now signals its absence by her displacement into a black flag).

It is quite possible to think, therefore, that *Tess* is actually in some way *about* seeing and representation. After all, Hardy himself describes it in the Preface to the first edition – although we can never really trust that wary old ironist and least self-revealing of writers – as 'an *attempt to give artistic form* to a true sequence of things' (my emphasis). And he also claims, by way of the novel's hugely contentious subtitle ('appended', he would have us believe in a Prefatory Postcript of 1912, 'at the last moment' and with no premeditation), that his 'Pure Woman' is '*faithfully presented* by Thomas Hardy' (my emphasis). Does the phrasing here suggest just how ironically conscious he was of representation as a potent source, precisely, of *mis*representation? Had the image, as we all now know in these postmodern times, already substantively replaced 'the thing itself' for Hardy? Was he already discrediting the notion that there is an ultimate reality, or true essence, outside history and discourse – such as 'human nature', for example, or even perhaps: *pure woman*? But a discussion of this key term in Hardy's disingenuous subtitle – and a central theme of critical commentary on *Tess* – must wait for a moment, although, as we shall see, the 'pure woman' and her attendant debate in fact focus the issues of seeing and representation which I have suggested the novel so insistently raises. Certainly a good deal of recent criticism emphasizes these issues as crucial terms in discussing *Tess* – an emphasis which derives principally from two very contemporary critical sources: feminism and poststructuralism. In order to explain what I mean here, I need to reflect briefly on the general state of the last two decades of Hardy criticism, before returning to the problems of 'seeing', (mis)representation and pure women.

While selecting work from the past twenty years for the Macmillan 'New Casebook' on *Tess*, I found that with a few honourable exceptions, all the really interesting material came after 1980. It appeared that work from the 1970s, even that of high quality and sophisticated in its own terms, somehow 'belonged' to an earlier critical phase[7] – rather like those cars which are still being made new and still function adequately, but which, when you lift the bonnet, clearly betray a prior generation of technology. I do not mean to be gratuitously dismissive, nor to foster a 'Whig' view of literary-critical history as continually 'progressive', nor do I wish to be wilfully partial and partisan, but so much critical writing on *Tess* in the 1970s, with its emphases on plot, 'poetic structure', character, 'ideas' and imagery (sometimes symbolism), *does* now seem passé, beside the point, going nowhere – except over well-trodden (some might say exhausted) ground.

What gradually becomes apparent, despite an obsessive innovativeness and self-presentation of *difference*, is that by far the greatest proportion of criticism on Hardy's fiction in the 1970s was held within the (by then) traditional parameters of critical intelligibility.[8] These were fundamentally humanist-realist in origin, promoting notions of a unified human subject ('the individual', 'character') at the centre of the general scheme of things – metaphysical, natural and social ('environment') – and of the artist's prime responsibility and achievement as being to represent this relationship with veracity (or with 'realism'). This, in turn, implies, on the one hand, the existence of an external reality to be copied – a given 'real world' and 'characters' both knowable and describable – and, on the other, the possibility of deploying a language which could accurately *describe* – not mediate – that reality, one which had a precise referentiality and would 'tell things as they really are'. What lies at the heart of such an essentialist world-view is a belief that everything has an ultimate ontological reality, an irreducible essence, quite outside its material, historical or discursive circumstances (things as they *really* are). The commonest (and most ideologically potent) expression of this is the notion of 'Human Nature' – the proposition that whatever the circumstances, and with the best will in the world, human beings cannot change their basic nature, or have it changed for them: that they are, as it were, trapped by their own very human-ness. But it is, of course, this 'essential' human nature which artists are most praised for depicting, and their 'realism' is, paradoxically, at once their ability to represent the contingent reality of everyday life, *and*, by way of this, the essential unchanging reality of 'Human Nature' itself. In its attempt to render this essence visible by describing it in referential language, realism too is essentialist.

Hardy, against the grain of much of his writing, has, from the earliest reviews, been hauled into consonance with such a worldview and such an aesthetic. Borrowing his own phrase, 'Novels of Character and Environment',[9] to praise what are generally regarded as his 'major' novels, critics have characteristically seen Hardy, 'at his best', as the tragic humanist-realist of Wessex, finding essential human nature in the lives of his rural protagonists (and in his 'rustic chorus') pitted in conflict with 'Fate' or 'Nature' (much less often with 'Society'). This, together with his descriptions of nature and his evocation of a 'passing' rural community, has been regarded as his major achievement, and accounts for the elevation into canonic texts of about eight out of his fourteen novels (the six 'minor novels' fail in various ways to fit this mould[10]). Even so, Hardy presents problems, and it is noteworthy how much damage-limitation criticism has had to go in for in order to wrench this 'flawed genius' into the canon and tradition. Hardy's 'faults' are said to be: his tendency to 'melodrama'; the excessive use of chance and coincidence in his plots; his 'pessimism'; his parading of 'ill-digested' ideas; his at times pedantic, awkward, mannered style; and, over and above all these – indeed subsuming them – his tendency to 'improbability' and 'implausibility'; in other words, his failure to be 'realistic', or, to put it yet another way, to represent 'essential reality' accurately. These 'faults' and 'flaws' bedevil even his major works, where they have to be ignored or explained away, but they are the principal cause of his 'failure' in the 'minor novels'.

All too often, and however sophisticated the particular inflexions of critical inquiry in the 1970s, many of these governing co-ordinates remained unchallenged. Certainly there were innovative approaches, with a kind of high-powered humanistic formalism (emphasizing imagery, symbolism, 'poetic structure', and so forth) replacing the older 'character'/'Fate'/Tragedy/rural-elegy nexus, but fundamentally similar underlying assumptions (about Hardy's

humanism, about his 'flaws', and especially about his 'uneasy' relation to realism) continued to determine the critical positions taken
up. There was little attempt, for example, to rethink the tendency to
reject large chunks of Hardy's texts simply as bad writing; little
sense that viewing them through a realist lens might result in them
appearing 'improbable', and that perhaps the lens was wrong; little
inquiry into the nature and function of Hardy's language (except
perhaps its 'poetics'); little inquiry into his 'inadequate' characterization (because 'character' itself remained an unproblematic
concept) or his contingent plotting; little thought that perhaps
Hardy was an *anti*-realist, challenging and demystifying the limits
and conventions of realism and humanist essentialism. But the fundamental inadequacy of most of the 1970s criticism which I have
been generalizing about is not so much its residual subscription to
the conventional critical stereotypes of Hardy's fiction, but rather
its failure to admit, disguised by grandiloquent evaluations and
judgements, that it was inadequate to the task of dealing with the
entire textuality of the literary works it had in hand. All novels, but
Hardy's especially so, are riddled with contradictory discourses, are
inscribed throughout with fault-lines thrown up by the clash of
competing discursive 'plates' just below the text's surface, and it is
surely the job of criticism, not to reject them as 'failures of taste',
but to explore and explain the significance of the work *as a whole*.
It is instructive to compare criticism from the 1970s with the many
1980s essays[11] which focus on the dynamically unstable textuality
of Hardy's fictional writing: its plural discourses and competing
styles, its irony, mannerism and self-deconstructing artificiality, its
self-conscious vocabulary and modes of address, its language of
tension. But the perception of these features is the reflex, I have suggested particularly, of feminist and poststructuralist initiatives and
it is to these that we will return in a moment.

However, there is one impressive piece of scholarship from
the 1970s which should first be acknowledged as fundamentally
influential in the contemporary redirecting of attention to Hardy's
textuality in relation to *Tess*: J. T. Laird's *The Shaping of Tess of
the d'Urbervilles* (1975), a book which traces the evolution of the
novel from its earliest stages of manuscript composition, through
various editions and revisions, to the 'quasi-definitive' version of
the 'Wessex Edition' of 1912. Despite a rather unnerving self-
contradiction when Laird seems to suggest, *contra* his own exhaus-

tive proof of the instability of the text, that 'studying the author's creative processes ... eventually leads to a surer and deeper understanding of the meaning of *the definitive text*' (my emphasis),[12] his work nevertheless reveals the extent and significance of Hardy's revisions and emendations, how conscious their effects were, and how a detailed examination of the textuality of *Tess* reinforces the sense that 'representation' and notions of a 'pure woman' are bedrock issues in the novel. Much criticism since 1975 has been deeply beholden to Laird in its pursuit of textual *cruces* to explain the signifying effects of *Tess*, and his work has been taken further since – most particularly in the monumental Oxford edition of the novel edited by Juliet Grindle and Simon Gatrell[13] – and in the latter's *Hardy the Creator*, whose critical method its author calls 'textual biography' and which establishes how extensively and radically Hardy revised his texts in a subversive, experimental practice of writing, a practice which, as Terry Eagleton has put it, shows a 'novelist whose work ... is always on the point of breaking through its own containing forms'.[14]

But it is with the intervention of feminism and poststructuralism that Hardy criticism significantly begins to retool. From the start of his novel-writing career, of course, critics noticed and focused upon 'Hardy's Heroines', and there are many essays entitled thus (or alternatively 'Hardy's Women'), most of which reproduce, not surprisingly, the sexual stereotyping of dominant gender ideology.[15] *Feminist* criticism, conversely, aims to decode the sexual/textual politics of literary texts, and has therefore been especially concerned with the *representation* of women; with the whole construction of gender in discourse; and with the notion of the 'male gaze', its consumption of women and its tendency to reproduce its own images and fantasies as female sexuality. In this respect, Hardy's novels are an ideal site on which to explore such issues – and not by any means necessarily from a position of hostility to his representation of women, but rather from a recognition of the complexity and innovativeness of what he seems to be doing.

Alternatively, poststructuralist criticism, most obviously in Deconstruction, has re-emphasized textuality as the primary concern of criticism – though not as evidence of the integrated wholeness of the text as great work of art so beloved of New Criticism, but on the contrary, as a fissured, riven, deranged, unstable linguistic terrain. In this case, too, Hardy's texts – and in

particular their evident artificiality, self-reflexiveness about modes
of perception and reproduction, and their contradictory constituent
discourses – offer themselves as fertile ground for analysis.

A seminal early essay,[16] in the contexts of both textuality and
gender, is one by John Goode called 'Woman and the Literary Text'
(1976), in which he suggests that we can only see the 'political implications' of a work by attending to its 'formal identity', and that
in relation to *Tess* what we witness (and are implicated in) is 'the
objectification of Tess by the narrator', especially by way of making
her 'the object of consumption' of Alec and Angel (and then of us
as voyeuristic readers consuming with our eyes both the text and,
hence, Tess herself). The effect is to make us 'the subject of her,
and thus guilty of the object images whose contradictions she is
subject to'. In other words, Tess is composed of all the 'object
images' the novel defines her as, primarily deriving from male
lookers and including the narrator/Hardy and us as readers in our
collusion with those images: nubile country-girl, plump arms, erotic
mouth, etc. Goode comments that this is why, 'whatever Hardy's
own ideological commitment, no frame will hold his novel in place',
or, to put it another way, why the text's discourses *have to be* accepted as contradictory. These themes are extended in Goode's later
(1979) essay, 'Sue Bridehead and the New Woman', where he suggests that Sue is an 'exposing image' in the 'taking of reality apart'
which *Jude* effects – most particularly of the mystifications inherent
in conventional notions of love and marriage.[17] More recently,
Goode's pioneering and radical recognition of the textual/sexual
politics and subversive anti-realism of Hardy's fiction have received
sustained expression in his *Thomas Hardy: The Offensive Truth*, a
book described by Terry Eagleton as 'alert to Hardy's fiction ... as
transformative practice, disruption, intervention, texts which ...
often enough meditate on the act of writing as a metaphor of their
preoccupations, [and which show] astonishing ... radicalism of
gender as well as class'.[18]

What is happening to Hardy, as a reflex of his new critical reproduction in the 1980s and 1990s, is that he is in the process of being
postmodernized. The foregrounding of sexual politics in *Tess*, and
of the tensions incident on a late-19th-century male novelist writing
so ambiguously about his 'pure women' heroine, about the destructive maleness of his two heroes' relations with her (especially the –
apparent – ambiguity of seduction and rape), and about marriage,

separation, bigamy, extra-marital sex and childbirth, all imply a writer whose 'consciousness' is in some sense being recast in the mould of feminist thinking about sexuality and patriarchy.

More obviously poststructuralist in their variously stylistic, semiotic and deconstructive analyses of the complex, riven, heteroglossic textuality of *Tess*, equal amounts of contemporary criticism all point to the unstable play of the signifier as the nodal experience of the novel. In other words, we have a text which has indeed become a disruptive 'series of seemings', one which, in its destabilizing formal dynamics, 'disproportions' (Hardy's own word – see below, p. 127) reality by revealing how slippery language is, how 'meaning' (and hence ideology) is constructed within discourse, and, precisely therefore, how representation becomes *mis*representation. By disturbing and displacing 'reality' (together with its servant, Realism) in the defamiliarizing discourse of his own texts, Hardy exposes (or, more exactly, as a creature of postmodernism *is made to* expose) the mystifications, naturalizations and (mis)representations by which the dominant ideology and culture sentence us all to lives of false being.

However, before I alchemize Hardy once and for all as postmodernist (and throw away the stone), let me more properly register – so that I can bring it into sharper focus in the following section – that in his own historical period, and certainly when he was publishing his poetry, Hardy was indeed a contemporary of the Modernists. It may be that the critical industry, already in his lifetime busily at work on him as both poet and novelist (combined, let us admit, with not a little self-fashioning[19]), had so constructed him as the great proto-Georgian poet, as the humanist-realist rural-tragedian, as Grand Old Man of English Letters, that the *modernist* in Hardy could not then or later easily be perceived. Of course, it is a critical truism to say that he is a 'transitional' writer, but I wonder now just *how* transitional, or whether Hardy was not in fact already *there*, already a Modernist. D. H. Lawrence recognized it in the *Study of Thomas Hardy* (1914), written as he launched into the work which was to become *The Rainbow* and *Women in Love*, and Ezra Pound hailed him as a contemporary poet; but still, it is only with hindsight and the clearing of the critical trees that the innovative anti-realism and self-conscious modernity of much of Hardy's fictional *oeuvre* comes into view. Which is why, I suggest, it has been so simple for recent criticism to find the ingredients in him for a transmogrification into postmodernist.

Well, you might say, who would have thought it: 'good little Thomas Hardy', the poet of Wessex and the English countryside, the great humanist tragedian of the 'Novels of Character and Environment', the elegist of a passing rural tradition, etc., suddenly becoming subversively postmodern. But then, literary criticism never *could* quite handle Hardy: didn't make it to F. R. Leavis's Great Tradition; always 'flawed' by contingency, melodrama and improbability; neither securely 'Victorian' nor 'modern'; uncertain whether he is primarily novelist or poet. But in neither genre has Hardy ever really been made to *fit* (except by a lot of critical man-handling and dismissal of recalcitrant elements), which makes one think, doesn't it, that our disruptive postmodern Hardy may, after all, be nearer the mark. It is with this in mind that I now return to my two focal themes: 'seeing'/representation and the notion of Tess as '(a) pure woman'.

* * * * *

With characteristic ambiguity of utterance, Hardy entitled one of his later volumes of poetry *Moments of Vision* (1917). The ambiguity of the word 'vision' is readily apparent: at once the literal 'seeing/sight' (as in '20/20 vision'), the metaphysical notion of imaginative revelation ('she had a vision'), and the proleptic ability to see through or beyond the immediately determinate ('he has vision', 'her vision of the future'). The ambiguity of the cluster of inflections around 'moments', however, is rather less obvious. Of course, 'moments' are brief fractions of time, usually implying stopped fragments in the temporal process (as in 'wait a moment', 'magic moments' or 'moment of truth'), and this is certainly the upper meaning in Hardy's title: particular instances of 'vision'. But there are two other senses which also haunt the fringes of the word: first, that of serious consequence ('momentous', 'matters of pith and moment'); second, and for my purposes here more significant, that within physics which means the measure of a turning effect (as in 'the moment of force'). So Hardy's title may imply that the instants of 'vision' are important ('moments' of great 'moment'), but also that the vision is somehow itself in motion, turning, swinging round a point, pivoting.

If we think for a (dare I say) moment of the effect of a turning vision – in the most literal sense – then we must conceive of a 'seeing' which moves round its object (consider astronauts observing Earth from their circulating spacecraft), and which can theoretically move round it through 360 degrees in any direction, i.e. in three-dimensional mode. Move round your chair, *looking* at it, and you will, at various stages, see it from all sides and all angles (downwards, upwards, sideways, etc.). In other words you will be able to apprehend it as a totality, a three-dimensional object. But two things may strike you: one, if you 'stopped' the moment when you were theoretically looking straight up at it from below (chair suspended absolutely vertically above you), the 'image' from that 'moment of vision' would look remarkably unlike one's standard received image of a chair (think of the kind of trick-photography which takes familiar objects from unfamiliar angles: where a bucket, for example, taken from directly above, becomes no more than a set of concentric circles). Two, how on earth (and I use this phrase, here, not *merely* as a manner of speaking) would you represent, *in visual terms*, your total apprehension of the total, three-dimensional chair – the chair in all its chairness? How, indeed, would you 'see' it all, all in one moment? Two senses of 'moment' – turning and stopped instant of time – clash here in fundamental contradiction: one is, precisely, *in motion*, in time; the other, equally precisely, is still, 'stopped', out of time. Is there any way of resolving this physical impossibility? Well, yes – if we return to the other term in Hardy's title: 'vision'.

For vision, in what I have called its metaphysical senses, allows us (but especially the creative artist) to break out of the space/time trap of the third dimension, and enter that zone of relativity beyond the determinate factors of time and space. Put simply and crudely, 'vision' allows us to 'see' the future, or 'envisage' another world; it would also enable us to see, in one totalizing 'moment' (in this case, *both* stopped instant *and* full circular movement), all of our chair at the same time. It is not without point, here, when approaching so visual an artist as Hardy (and, indeed, one who draws heavily on painting for both his terms of reference and his imagery[20]), to note that this liberation from space/time, this envisioned *simultaneity* of experience, was the principle on which the modernist painters, only a dozen years after *Jude* (why don't we think of Hardy and Picasso as contemporaries? – Picasso was well into his 'Metamorphic' phase when Hardy died in 1928), based their dislocations of conventional (realist/mimetic) form. That is why one can see both profiles of a face simultaneously in Cubist portraits, or a violin dismantled with all its planes simultaneously displayed on the two-dimensional picture-surface of a modernist still life.

'Vision', then, both as momentary revelation (what James Joyce, only ten years after *Tess*, was to call an 'epiphany') and as 'turning' or destabilizing perception, is a way of breaking out of the conventional, the normative, the familiar, the naturalized fictions of 'common sense'. Indeed it ruptures a (bourgeois) world constructed very largely by the cultural ideology of a Realism which 'tells things as they really are' and has a profound antipathy to the 'improbable' or 'implausible' – qualities which are themselves frequently the result of, precisely, 'vision' and 'the visionary'. For Hardy, vision in this binary sense ('double-vision'?) is a way of 'defamiliarizing', of 'making strange' – and I strategically choose the formalists' terms to signal once again his consanguinity with modernism – the naturalized world of conventional perceptual reality, of 'seeing things as they really are'. It is subversive in many ways, and not least in its anti-realist stance – which may help to explain the troubled history of Hardy's place in the conventional canon of English fiction and the difficulty many critics have had in comprehending the apparently schizophrenic textuality of his novels. It is worth adding here that Hardy himself was not just 'doing defamiliarization' by chance – as an automatic and unwilled reflex of his (unconscious) proto-modernist mind. On the contrary, he was thinking about it throughout his writing life, but especially from the 1880s onwards; and his last, highly self-reflexive and self-conscious work of fiction, 'Florence Emily Hardy's *The Life of Thomas Hardy*' (he composed it himself, before his death, in the 1920s[21]), is full of concepts and phrases which at once define 'vision' as what we would now call 'complex seeing' and which would, had they been written by a 20th-century cultural theorist, have equal currency with terms like 'defamiliarization' and 'baring the device' or the Brechtian notion of 'alienation'.

Prior to the 1880s, Hardy's views show a more purely Romantic conception of the visionary function of art: 'irradiating ... with "the light that never was" ... a hitherto unperceived beauty ... seen to be latent ... by the spiritual eye'.[22] But by 1886 Hardy is reflecting: 'novel-writing as an art cannot go backward. Having reached the analytic stage it must transcend it by going still further in the same direction. Why not by rendering as visible essences, spectres, etc., the abstract thoughts of the analytic school?' And later in the same passage he proposes the use of 'abstract realisms', significantly stating that this project was actually carried out, not in a novel, but in 'the more appropriate medium' of his immense epic poetic-drama, *The Dynasts* (177). What is clear, if nothing else, is that Hardy was being pressed against the limits of conventional realism. The following year, in expressing his admiration for the paintings of 'the much-decried, mad, late-Turner', he rejects 'the original realities – as optical effects, that is' in favour of the 'expression of ... abstract imaginings' (185). Taken in conjunction with his remarks about 'impressions' and 'seemings' in the prefaces to the novels of the 1890s referred to earlier, it is clear that notions of 'vision', and how to realize it formally, were much on Hardy's mind. But it is in a couple of memoranda from 1890 (while he was completing *Tess*) that his most prophetically modernist utterances are made:

> Reflections on Art. Art is a changing of the actual proportions and order of things, so as to bring out more forcibly than might otherwise be done that feature in them which appeals most strongly to the idiosyncrasy of the artist.

> Art is a disproportioning – (*i.e.* distorting, throwing out of proportion) – of realities, to show more clearly the features that matter in those realities, which, if merely copied or reported inventorially, might possibly be observed, but would more probably be overlooked. Hence 'realism' is not Art. (228–9)

It is here, I think, that the core of Hardy's fictional aesthetic is to be found, and the informing frame of reference for a reading of *Tess*: art is a 'disproportioning' of reality – realism is not art. In other words, 'vision' (abstract imaginings), swinging round its 'moment', makes visible 'essences' (the notion of a 'pure woman', for example). But at the same time, vision 'distorts', 'disproportions', those representations of reality ('copied or reported inventorially') which are the naturalized (mis)representations of Realism, in order to expose essentialist misrepresentation for what it is (how can there, in fact, be 'a pure woman' or 'pure woman'?), and to illuminate another truth which those misrepresentations obscure: that 'reality' is only ever *discourse* – 'seemings', 'imaginings', 'impressions'.

'My art', Hardy wrote in 1886, 'is to intensify the expression of things ... so that the heart and inner meaning is made vividly visible' (177). *Tess*, that most 'vividly visible' of novels, may be an example of Hardy 'intensifying the expression' in order to bring into view precisely that 'expression' – the discourses of representation themselves – for scrutiny and demystification in order to exemplify the fact that 'expression' is its own very 'heart and inner meaning', that the 'reality' of an image *is* the image itself, that its only reality is what it constructs through representation. 'Expression' does not copy 'things as they really are', it forges images in its artifice. Tess may indeed be 'a pure woman', but *only as she is imaged*, only as the 'artificial' construct of representation – and who knows whether this is true or false: except, unless we miss the irony (for Hardy knows full well the claim is nonsense), when she is '*faithfully* presented by Thomas Hardy'.

Let us now turn, at last, to that subtitle itself, and consider it as the pivot of a 'moment' around which *Tess* swings in exemplification of Hardy's disproportioning art discussed above. The two main senses of the phrase 'a pure woman' are readily evident: the ethical/sexual (the use of which in relation to Tess as fornicator-murderess so incensed Hardy's Victorian critics), and the ontological/archetypal (in which she would be, were Bob Dylan her bard, 'just like a woman' in every respect). There is also the further related sense of the generic as 'ideal' – again, perhaps, in two inflexions: both prototypical and perfect. I am not primarily concerned here with the ethical sense, although for Hardy at the time it was clearly a strategic assault on the moral attitudes of his readers and *their perception* of purity. It is that other essentialist meaning that is of interest to me, and especially in relation to Hardy's concern with making 'visible essences' noted above. The novel is full of phrases which indicate that he was thoroughly conscious of this second sense and probably more interested in it than the contemporary moral issue. Let me start with the two most obvious examples: at Talbothays, in the early morning idyll with Angel, Tess is described as 'a visionary essence of woman – a whole sex condensed into one typical form' (170); and later, as she approaches Flintcomb-Ash, the narrative, in an odd shift of tense and focus, presents her in this way: 'Thus Tess walks on; a figure which is part of the landscape; a fieldwoman pure and simple, in winter guise' (326) – where the phrase 'pure and simple' *could* mean a pure, simple field woman, but clearly actually implies the essential stereotype. (Much earlier, during the harvesting at Marlott, the narrative has already given us this generalization: 'A field-man is a personality afield; a field-woman is a portion of the field; she has somehow *lost her own margin*, imbibed the *essence* of her surrounding, and assimilated herself with it' [123, my emphases] – so that Tess, too, the 'fieldwoman pure and simple', must also be subsumed within this characterization – or rather, *de*-characterization.) Further, as we have seen, when Tess is first introduced in Chapter 2 she is described as 'a fine and picturesque country girl, and no more' (43, note that word 'picturesque' and the phrase 'and no more'), and later again, just after the generalization about field-women above, she is called, in an oddly contradictive phrase, 'an almost standard woman' (126). Elsewhere, the narrative regularly generalizes about women – for example, on Tess's 'rally' after the death of her child, it muses: 'Let the truth be told – women do as a rule live through such humiliations, and regain their spirits, and again look about them with an interested eye' (141) – a sentence remarkable both for its patriarchal patronizing (do men – by implication, of finer sensibility – not 'regain their spirits', then?) and for that revealing phrase 'an interested eye'. Again, in relation to the dairymaids' passion for Angel at Talbothays, we are told they are involuntarily overwhelmed by 'an emotion thrust on them by cruel Nature's law'; and, in an even more insulting instance of chauvinistic essentialism, 'the differences which distinguished them as individuals were abstracted by this passion, and each was but portion of one organism called sex' (187) – 'pure women' indeed, and just like the field-women who have lost their 'own margin'. For Angel, of course (and for the narrator too?), Tess is archetypally this 'organism' in the famously erotic passage when she has just awoken on a summer afternoon:

> She had not heard him enter, and hardly realized his presence there. She was yawning, and *he saw the red interior of her mouth* as if it had been a snake's. She had stretched one arm so high above her coiled-up cable of hair that he could see its satin delicacy above the sunburn; her face was flushed with sleep, and her eyelids hung heavy over their pupils. The brim-fulness of her nature breathed from her. It was a moment when *a woman's soul* is more incarnate than at any other time; when the most spiritual beauty bespeaks itself flesh; and sex takes the outside place in *the presentation*. (210, my emphases)

Is this what Hardy means by 'a pure woman' in his subtitle? But notice again, as in all these quotations, how he seems to be doing the very opposite of establishing Tess's 'character'; that, conversely, in rendering her as essence – 'a woman's soul' – he is making her an enigma, unknowable, subject only to speculation (rather as Hardy's later disciple, John Fowles, was to do with Sarah Woodruff in *The French Lieutenant's Woman*), and inimical, therefore, to the *raison d'être* of a fictional realism which finds its very heart in well-rounded 'character'.

But, of course, it is the continuous textual 'presentation' (notice Hardy's use of the word at the end of the last quotation above) of Tess that makes the obsessive (and usually erotic) imaging of her as something to *look at*, as something *seen*, as a visual *object*, so inescapable. Space prevents a full account of the number of occasions her mouth (again, see the above quotation) is fetishistically focused upon – for example, 'To a young man with the least fire in him that little upward lift in the middle of her red top lip was distracting, infatuating, maddening' (190). But her smile and her eyes also receive continual attention ('her rosy lips curved towards a smile' [69], 'a roguish curl coming upon her mouth' [223], 'her eyes enlarged, and she involuntarily smiled in his face' [92]), as do her neck, her arms, her hair and general deportment ('Tess stood there in her prettily tucked-up milking gown, her hair carelessly heaped upon her head' [223]). Equally heavily emphasized is the 'bouncing handsome womanliness' of her figure (see the quotation at the beginning of this chapter); even Angel at his most idealizing – in the passage where he sees her as the 'visionary essence of woman' (see above, p. 128) – is still aware that there weren't many women 'so well endowed in person as she was' (169); and for Alec she is of course the true *femme fatale* (not, by the by, necessarily a scheming woman or 'siren', merely 'irresistibly attractive'): 'She had an attribute which amounted to a disadvantage just now; and it was this that caused Alec d'Urberville's *eyes to rivet themselves upon her*. It was a luxuriance of aspect, a fulness of growth, which made her appear *more of a woman* than she *really* was' (71, my emphases; note both the male gaze and the physical essentialism implied by the phrases 'more of a woman' and 'really'.) And later it is this voluptuousness which starts the process of de-converting Alec as preacher: 'his eyes, falling casually upon the familiar countenance and form, remained contemplating her. ... "Don't look at me like that!" he said abruptly' (356) – an inversion which must surely be the most brilliant evocation in fiction of male perfidy and the double standard, for who, after all, is doing the looking? It is further worth noticing in passing that it is not just Tess who is made into a sex-object by the text: Car Darch, just before Alec has sex with Tess, is described thus: 'she had bared her plump neck, shoulders, and arms to the moonshine, under which they looked as luminous and beautiful as some Praxitelean[23] creation, in their possession of the faultless rotundities of a lusty country girl' (100).

In late-20th-century terms, the above descriptions would surely amount to 'soft' pornography, or at least to accurate representations of the titillatory visual devices employed therein. And the text further emphasizes this voyeuristic stance in its recurrent verbal and narrative objectification ('the presentation') of women in the novel. The 'club-walking' girls in Chapter 2, for instance, are taking part in 'their first *exhibition* of themselves' (40, my emphases here and below); the Clare brothers are 'on-lookers' at 'the *spectacle* of a bevy of girls dancing' (43); Tess, after her first visit to Trantridge, 'became aware of the *spectacle* she presented to [her fellow-travellers'] surprised vision: roses at her breast; roses in her hat; roses and strawberries in her basket to the brim' (73); Mrs Durbeyfield, 'bedecking' Tess for the sacrifice to Alec, is so proud of 'the girl's *appearance*' that she is led to 'step back, *like a painter from his easel,* and survey her work as a whole'; and in order to let Tess 'zee' herself, she hangs a large 'black cloak [surely the 'black flag' of Tess's hanging] outside the casement, and so made a large reflector of the panes' (79). On other occasions the text pans back from Tess and reduces her (once again de-characterizing her in the process) to an insignificant dot on the landscape: 'Tess stood still upon the hemmed expanse of verdant flatness, like a fly on a billiard-table of indefinite length, and of no more consequence to the surroundings than that fly' (142); 'the two girls crawl[ed] over the surface of [the 'desolate drab' field] like flies' (331).

Throughout the novel, then, Tess in particular is highly visualized as an object of 'vision' in the swinging 'moment' of the text's gaze. Only on two significant occasions does she disappear from view: once, when she is hanged, with Angel and Liza-Lu's eyes 'rivetted' (like Alec's on her body) to the gaol flagpole, and she becomes merely 'a black flag' (449); the other when, in the old phrase precisely, Alec commits 'the act of darkness' with her: 'The obscurity was now so great that he could see absolutely nothing but a pale nebulousness at his feet, which represented the white muslin figure he had left upon the dead leaves. Everything else was blackness alike' (107). It is as if, paradoxically and pointedly, the novel implies that the essence, the 'pure woman', can only be 'presented' as visualizations, only as she *appears*, but that the basic 'realities' of her existence (sex, death) are unknowable, unrepresentable – like those innermost secrets of 'character' that no one quite comprehends or can describe in other people, however well they know them.

And let us be clear: we know almost nothing substantive about Tess's 'character', for the novel never attempts to penetrate her secret being. It may tell us things *about* her (she 'spoke two languages' [48]); give us her views (about the 'blighted star', for example); and show her spirited moments of mettle (to Alec's male cliché, '"that's what every woman says"', she retorts in implicit rejection of 'pure woman' essentialism: '"Did it never strike your mind that what every woman says some women may feel?"' [112], just as she tells Angel to 'call me Tess' when he insists, in the 'visionary essence' scene, on idealizing her with names like Artemis and Demeter [170]). The novel may further appear to try and characterize her state of mind – 'she looked upon herself as a figure of Guilt intruding into the haunts of Innocence ... she fancied herself such an anomaly' (121) – but only, we note, at a detached psychologistic distance; it may try and explain her love for Angel ('its single-mindedness, its meekness; what long-suffering it guaranteed, what honesty, what endurance, what good faith' [255]), but the more the text produces phrase after defining phrase, the more a palpable sense of her love recedes – just as earlier, despite all its words, the narrative signally fails to describe her eyes: 'neither black nor blue nor gray nor violet; rather all those shades together, and a hundred other ... around pupils that had no bottom' (126). For all this 'characterization', then, we really 'know' Tess very little indeed – which is presumably why so much critical argument has raged over whether she is 'passive' or not, whether she is 'pure' or not, indeed whether she is a 'fully-rounded character' at all.

Which is, I would suggest in conclusion, to beg the question. For *Tess* is precisely *not* a novel attempting to offer us a 'knowable' character, but rather one which exposes *characterization* itself as a humanist-realist mystification (producing 'visible essences') and which parades the *mis*representation that 'characterization' involves by subjecting to irony the falsifying essentialism of 'faithfully presenting a pure woman'. In her excellent essay of 1982, 'Pure Tess: Hardy on Knowing a Woman',[24] Kathleen Blake remarks that the novel 'really scrutinizes the sexual typing that plays havoc with a woman's life', while George Wotton, in his book *Thomas Hardy: Towards a Materialist Criticism*, in suggesting that we recognise 'class and gender conflicts ... as conflicts of perception in the multifarious acts of seeing of the characters who inhabit Wessex', points out that Hardy's 'production (writing) determines consumption (reading) by casting the reader in the role of seer'.[25] In other words, we may say that Hardy's 'moments of vision' disproportion characterization and character so that we can 'see' how they function. Tess as a 'character' is no more than an amalgam – often destructively contradictory – of 'images' of her as perceived by individuals and by 'society': Angel idealizes her, Alec sees her as sex-object, the narrative voice fetishizes her, society regards her as prodigal, the novel 'faithfully presents' her as 'a pure woman' (with all the ironies that phrasing invokes). But Tess *has no character at all*: she is only what others (most especially the author) construct her as; and so she is herself merely a 'series of seemings' or 'impressions'. This, of course, gives the final ironic twist to the notion of her being '(a) pure woman', since there can be no such thing as 'essential character' when a woman is merely the construct of male sociosexual images of her desired form (although my basic point here need not be limited to *gender*-stereotyping). Hardy's novel, then, well ahead of its time, seems to be dismantling the bourgeoishumanist (patriarchal and realist) notion of the unified and unitary human subject, and to be doing so by way of a discourse so selfreflexive and defamiliarizing about representation, so unstable and dialogical, that it deconstructs itself even as it creates. Which is why, I believe, we can justly discover a contemporary postmodern text in *Tess of the d'Urbervilles*.

6

Recasting Hardy the Poet

Hardy's poetry, on the whole, has not had a very satisfactory critical press – which may immediately tell us something about the difficulty of determining the nature of the achievement in his enormous poetic *oeuvre*. At the outset, when Hardy first turned again to poetry after completing his career as a novelist (see Chapter 1, pp. 25–6), the reviewers resented his decision to take up another genre and were often fiercely critical of his work in it. *The Saturday Review*, on the publication of *Wessex Poems*, infamously commented on 'this curious and wearisome volume, these many slovenly, slipshod, uncouth verses, stilted in sentiment, poorly conceived and worse wrought'; rejected some of the ballads there as 'the most amazing balderdash that ever found its way into a book of verse'; and wondered why 'the bulk of the volume was published at all – why he did not himself burn the verse'.[1] E. K. Chambers, also on *WP*, noted that Hardy's 'success in poetry is of a very narrow range'; and, in a view which has become a primary feature of Hardy's critical reception and evaluation as a poet, limited his 'success' to a 'small cluster of really remarkable poems'.[2] On *Poems of the Past and the Present*, *The Academy* judged in 1901: 'there is

The original version of this essay is the 'Critical Commentary' section of my *Thomas Hardy: Selected Poetry and Non-Fictional Prose* (London: Macmillan, 1996). Parts of that, in revised form, reappear in Chapter 5, 'Hardy the Poet', of my *Thomas Hardy* volume for the 'Writers and their Work' series (Plymouth: Northcote House, 1996). Given the place and function of the former (commenting on the selection of poems in the anthology), and the brevity of the latter, the present essay has again been extensively amended and revised in order to make it a coherent, free-standing piece. Nevertheless, the marks of its origin can be detected in the fact that it only refers to poems included in the *Selected Poetry* volume.

more of sheer poetry in his novels'; and *The Athenaeum* that Hardy 'is wholly mistaking his vocation' in switching from fiction to verse.[3] Conversely, in the last quarter of this century, now that 'the essential qualities of his genius',[4] so it seems, can be taken for granted and we know that his 'voice' is 'capable of greatness',[5] Hardy's poetry is the subject of long, painstaking critical monographs full of exegesis, appreciation and interpretation – which nevertheless still leave me, at least, unsure that I am any closer to an understanding of 'the essential qualities of his genius', of what constitutes his 'unique poetic voice'.[6] Trevor Johnson's *A Critical Introduction to the Poems of Thomas Hardy* (1991), for example – devoted and thorough though it is – is too self-assured in tone and judgement to be convincingly illuminating; even Tom Paulin's highly regarded, but by now ageing, *Thomas Hardy: The Poetry of Perception* (1975) raises a question as to the worth of linear critical narratives identifying themes, motifs or tropes in an individual writer's work; and Dennis Taylor's immensely learned two books on Hardy's poetry, despite gestures towards contemporary theoretical initiatives, in fact continue the largely exegetical and descriptive tradition of critical attention paid to his poems.[7] We are – to recast F. E. Smith's classic *mot* – much better informed, but no wiser.

One critical work, however, which stands out from the others – partly because it has been so influential, partly because it is so polemically engaged, and partly because it thus offers a reading of Hardy's poetry which, while contentious, has shaped an illuminating representation of him – is Donald Davie's *Thomas Hardy and British Poetry* (1973). This work sharply focuses what will become a central issue in this chapter. Deeply marked by Davie's experiences during the student 'troubles' at the University of Essex in and around 1968, and written from his newly exiled vantage-point as Professor of English at Stanford University, California in 1972, *Thomas Hardy and British Poetry* is that most unusual example of Anglo-American literary criticism: an engaged *political* work, both in a literary sense and in terms of its ideological animus. In the 'acknowledgement' to his wife, and again in the 'Foreword', Davie states that the book is 'concerned with the temper of political sentiment in modern British society',[8] and he goes on to criticize fiercely the tendency towards political totalitarianism both within the rightist ideology of Anglo-American Modernism, and in the 'irresponsible' perpetual 'oppositionism' of the British 'socialist intelligentsia'

(91–2). Against this, Davie wishes to posit a political tradition and stance which, in relation to Hardy, he defines as 'liberal' and humanist (6–7). This position, it is implied, accepts the political responsibility of the 'social democrat' to challenge and refute – if only in small ways – the authoritarianism which dominates late-20th-century societies either because of passive acceptance or of 'left-wing' refusal to be contaminated by political involvement in state institutions. An analysis of the implications of Davie's own position is out of place here,[9] and the precise *political* connection between Hardy's 'liberal' poetry and anti-authoritarianism is never fully clarified. But suffice to say, Davie promotes Hardy as the major progenitor of an alternative literary and ideological strain in 20th-century British culture to the perceived domination of it by both Anglo-American Modernism and intellectual socialism.

Hardy, Davie argues, 'is the one poetic imagination of the first magnitude in the present century who writes out of, and embodies in his poems, political and social attitudes which a social democrat recognizes as "liberal"'(6). This is defined, in what Davie calls his 'scientific humanism', as Hardy's recognition that, 'cramped and intermittent as that area of freedom may be', 'there is indeed a margin for human choice but the slimmest margin imaginable', and that 'what should motivate our actions within it ... is [in Hardy's own words] "loving-kindness, operating through scientific knowledge"' (7). Such a position sustains Hardy's 'modesty' (40) and 'civility' (36): 'on page after page he bows and retires at just the point where another poet would, for good or ill, advance and take us by the throat' (36), and this, in its turn, helps to account for his 'clumsiness' and 'fallibility' as a technician of verse (25). Davie notes that many critics are discomforted by what Hardy himself called 'cunning irregularity'[10] – the appearance of technical awkwardnesses – but for Davie this is a 'guarantee of integrity', 'for nothing but fidelity to feeling could have caused him to [break the rules]' (26). This 'engaging modesty and decent liberalism' may make Hardy look, to 'the radical', like a 'cop-out' – one who represents 'a crucial selling short of the poetic vocation' – but Davie adds that 'some of his successors in England, and a few out of England, seem to have agreed with him' (40). The trajectory of Davie's project now opens up, for what he really wants to propose is that there is a line of 20th-century British poetry, of similar 'liberalism' and 'modesty', which deviates from – indeed challenges – the relentless 'radicalism' of Modernism: one in which, to short-circuit the argument, Philip Larkin (amongst others, including Davie himself) is Hardy's heir. What characterizes this poetry may seem, especially in America, to be 'an apparent meanness of spirit, a painful modesty of intention, extremely limited objectives' (11), but is, rather, 'an inheritance from Hardy, an attempt to work out problems, especially social and political problems, which Hardy's poetry has posed for the twentieth century' (12). It is, indeed, this modesty, limitation and awkwardness, but also the integrity, which make Hardy the unique 'liberal' in modern poetry. Davie adds, and we come to my central point now: 'it is because we are so unused to liberalism as a consistent attitude in a poet, that we have so much difficulty with the poetry of Hardy' (28).

The 'difficulty' Davie proposes here is precisely that of identifying Hardy's 'greatness' (he notes that, in the conventionally applied sense, 'Hardy is not a great poet at all ... because ... he does not choose to be' (39)), and in particular, of agreeing on those poems which represent the quintessential core of his achievement. In a couple of succinct and perceptive pages, Davie goes to the heart of the crucial critical issue regarding Hardy's poetry – one which, while surfacing regularly and receiving token acknowledgement, is submerged again and again in the mass of myopic critical interpretation and appreciation devoted to it: *which* poems represent the 'true' Hardy? Critic after critic,[11] Davie observes, 'complains that nearly 1000 poems are too much, and asks for a more or less agreed-upon select few, a canon on which Hardy's reputation shall rest' (27). But the problem is no one *can* agree; he quotes Mark Van Doren: '"No poet more stubbornly resists selection. ... There is no core of pieces, no inner set of classic or perfect poems, which would prove his rank. ... It is the whole of him that registers and counts"' (27). Equally, the fact that John Crowe Ransom's selection of Hardy[12] leaves out several of the 'greatest' of the 'Poems of 1912–13' while being neither 'perfunctory' nor 'eccentric', leads Davie to the central conclusion that:

> cast about as one may, and measure one authority against another, one perceives no consensus emerging as to what is centrally significant in Hardy's poetry, still less therefore as to what is the canon of his secure achievements. And if no one can determine where the centre is, no one reading of the corpus can be more eccentric than any other. (27–8)

Unable to discriminate the good from the bad – because of the large number of poems, our inability to date them as early or late or to categorize them securely by genre, and because of Hardy's own 'modesty' in them – 'each reader finds in the poems what he brings to them; what he finds there is his own pattern of preoccupations and preferences. If this is true of every poet to some degree, of Hardy it is exceptionally true' (28–9).

Davie is at once exactly right about the critical problematic of defining what is centrally significant in Hardy's poetry, and – at least by now – rather off the mark about 'the canon of his secure achievements'. As will become clear, making 'Selections' of a writer's work is a fundamentally judgemental and manipulative activity – one reinforced by the writing of 'Introductions' which frame the text. These latter are themselves crucial critical works, and certainly more influential than free-standing scholarly monographs or articles in academic journals. This chapter, therefore, has taken on board Davie's warnings about the absence of consensus in regard to Hardy's 'centrally significant' poetry, and about the necessary 'eccentricity' of all readings of it given only a personal 'pattern of preoccupations and preferences' informing them, and offers a reading of Hardy, for the most part, more by way of a commentary on how editor-critics have selected and introduced him than by offering yet another synoptic critical analysis of the poetry itself. Because of the difficulties in making a selection of Hardy's poems, the metadiscourse of that process reveals those subjective 'preoccupations and preferences' which are so often passed off as an objective representation of 'Hardy the Poet', and tells us rather more about how 'he' is constructed than most ostensibly interpretative criticism does. I will spend a little time, therefore, examining the difficulty editors experience in selecting, organizing and critically introducing Hardy's poetry, before attempting to show that, by now (if not in Davie's 1973), there is indeed a core of 'centrally significant' poems, a Hardy poetic 'canon', which has been created – largely tacitly and cumulatively – by editors and critics. The effects of the processes of selection by which this 'familiar' Hardy is constructed are, subliminally and potently, to throw up a 'true' Hardy comprising poems which Samuel Hynes symptomatically calls 'characteristically Hardyesque',[13] which then closes out the large ruck of 'inferior' work.

Typically, an early influential player in the what-is-the-'great'-Hardy contest was F. R. Leavis. In 1932, in *New Bearings in*

English Poetry, he had firmly characterized Hardy as 'a naive poet of simple attitudes and outlook', of 'naive conservatism', and one whose 'precritical innocence' meant that 'there was little in his technique that could be taken up by younger poets' (Leavis means the Modernists). Importantly, for Leavis Hardy's 'great poems' are only a very small proportion of the huge *oeuvre*: 'his rank as a major poet rests upon a dozen poems. These are lost among a vast bulk of verse interesting only by its oddity and idiosyncrasy'. Leavis characteristically does not say which the 'dozen' great poems are, and compounds the puzzle by adding that 'anthologists choose from his insignificant poems and leave out the great ones',[14] again without specifying which are which. This notion of the 'great' but 'naive' Hardy – represented by only a handful of fortuitous masterpieces surrounded by a vast mass of inferior poems – established something of a line of criticism through the middle years of the century, notably in an influential essay by R. P. Blackmur, and then in the work of Douglas Brown and J. I. M. Stewart.[15]

But the difficulty of identifying the 'essential Hardy' has persisted most apparently in the labours of sympathetic editors of 'Selections' of his poetry right up to the present moment; and the vagaries of, and solutions to, the problem are enlightening. Comparative analysis of the content of such volumes follows below; but it will be helpful, first, to outline the problems perceived by the editors of a number of widely available, more or less contemporary, anthologies, together with some account of the principles of selection and organization on which the poems they include are based, and of the introductory 'frame' by which *their* Hardy is presented. Harry Thomas, for example, in the 'Penguin Classics' *Thomas Hardy: Selected Poems* (1993), notes William Empson, more than 50 years before, remarking that '"a working selection from Hardy's mass of bad poetry is much needed"', and Thomas offers his own, therefore, as just such a 'working selection' of 'the best poems'.[16] David Wright, in a second Penguin edition, *Selected Poems* (in their 'Poetry Library', 1978, but still regularly reprinted) – one of the largest selections with around 380 poems (i.e. between a third and a half of Hardy's total shorter works) – also states that while 'there is no doubt that [he] is one of the major poets of the twentieth century ... it is only difficult to make up one's mind how good, and/or how bad, almost any particular poem of Hardy's is'.[17] (A similar point is tellingly made by Mark Van Doren when he says:

'too many of Hardy's poems ... are not "good" ... but I am always changing my mind as to which ones those are'.[18]) And in his 'Note on the Selection', Wright neatly sums up the 'difficulty' of his task as 'not least because one man's Hardy is often as not another man's bathos' – *his* solution being to print the poems 'more or less thematically, beginning with a handful of the very earliest ones dated by the poet [so that] in this loosely narrative arrangement Hardy's autobiography displays itself'.[19] Eliane Wilson and Howard Shaw in *Thomas Hardy: An Autobiography in Verse* (1984)[20] also expressly select and order their 80 poems, not, of course, in relation to the usually unknown chronology of the poems' composition, but to the personal events of Hardy's life.

Others have solved their problem in similarly factitious ways. A notorious example is Carl J. Weber's *The Love Poems of Thomas Hardy* (1963, but extensively reprinted since), in which he assembles *all* the poems (116 of them) about Hardy's first wife, Emma, 'scattered through' the pages of the *Collected Poems*, and prints them 'segregated and presented as a biographical unit'. Poems, then, from all periods and volumes are organized into ten sections, in order, in effect, to establish a context for 'Poems of 1912–13', which Weber places 'in *some* respects' (his emphasis) first of 'the best three series of love poems in English'.[21] Interestingly, Trevor Johnson, in a recent essay, '"Thoroughfares of Stones": Hardy's "Other" Love Poetry' (1994), takes Weber to task for doing 'his hero a grave disservice' by this strategy: not only do 'Poems of 1912–13' become fetishized, but all the other extensive love poetry Hardy wrote is ignored. This Johnson very properly proposes to correct. It is amusing therefore – if not slightly alarming – to find him organizing some of Hardy's earliest love poetry, while conceding that 'other arrangements are feasible', into a 'schema', 'fictitious or not', which allows us, in 'the remains of Hardy's sequence ... to see *more clearly* how original and daring his overall conception was'.[22] As evidence of the speed with which a 'fictitious schema' becomes a substantive fact, note that 'more clearly'.

Not surprisingly, given 'Wessex' and the Hardy 'industry', there are also illustrated selections of the poems. Peter Porter's *Thomas Hardy* (1981), in the 'Landscape Poets' series (with photographs by John Hedgecoe), arranges its 90 of 'Hardy's best' poems into four sections – the first of which is 'In Wessex: Rural Pictures'. These are based on Porter's critical judgement that Hardy's poetry 'is a hymn to subject-matter, a vindication of the real, the observable and the precise object-in-place'; and that a 'thematic arrangement' is the best way of anthologizing him because 'there is little development in Hardy's verse over the long span of its creation'.[23] Alternatively, the little 'gift-shop' volume, *Thomas Hardy* (1990), edited by Geoffrey Moore for 'The Illustrated Poets' series, represents Hardy's 'greatness' with 23 of his short lyrics, while at the same time reproducing R. P. Blackmur's 1940 judgement that 'Hardy is the great example of a sensibility violated by ideas' (albeit surviving the 'violation'[24]).

T. R. M. Creighton, in the perceptive, if at times perverse, intro-duction to his large anthology (282 items) *Poems of Thomas Hardy: A New Selection* (1974), recognizes the reasons why critics have had 'doubts' about Hardy's 'greatness' – he 'conforms to no academically recognisable type' – and reiterates in passing many of his standard perceived 'flaws' (the apparent 'awkwardnesses' of style, syntax and diction; 'his expressions of gloom ... that make one smile in a way not intended'). Nevertheless, he still posits Hardy's 'greatness', and organizes the selection in such a way as to allow his 'art to reveal itself by reducing its bulk and defining its main kinds and preoccupations, irrespective of his volume divisions: not to present "the best of Hardy" but a cross-section of all he wrote in reduced compass and systematic arrangement'. The vast bulk of the *Collected Poems*, Creighton argues, 'obscure[s] its great-ness'; what he does, therefore – 'the ideal would be the whole *Collected Poems* arranged as I shall now describe' – is to 'rearrange' the poems in categories which reveal Hardy's 'themes "in gradu-ated kinship"'. But it is here that the critical engineering shows most clearly (Creighton's selection has often been criticized for its tendentiousness), largely because of the presuppositions on which the editor announces his volume to be based:

> My broad classifications – Nature, Love, Memory and Reflection, Dramatic and Personative, and Narrative – can claim *almost canoni-cal authority. I have allowed* the poems *to arrange themselves* and have remained *as passive under their guidance as I could. They seemed to require* to begin with the universal themes of nature and love rather than in biographical order with childhood.[25]

There can surely be no clearer example than this of an editor passing off as 'natural' his own critical and ideological interpretative shaping of a writer's work. It is almost with relief that one finds James Reeves and Robert Gittings in their *Selected Poems of Thomas Hardy* (Heinemann, 1981) adopting the logical, if slightly absurd, strategy of organizing their 105 or so poems simply in alphabetical order of title.

Even in those volumes which employ the most straightforward principle of organizing the poems – in the order of Hardy's own published volumes – their actual *selection* remains problematical. As evidence of how a canon 'naturally' forms itself, there are those which contain absolutely *no* explanation of the principles on which the selection has been made. We have no way of knowing, for example, from John Wain's (patronizing) introduction to his *Selected Shorter Poems of Thomas Hardy* (1966, but still in print), how or why his 91 inclusions were picked from the rest ('none of [the latter] quite without interest'[26]) – unless the explanation is that, *à la* Creighton, the best poems pick themselves in a process of un-mediated self-authorization; nor how his larger (*c.*215 poems) *The New Wessex Selection of Thomas Hardy's Poetry* (with Eirian Wain, 1978) differs from it, except in size. In the introduction to that volume, Wain finds 'ten or a dozen' poems equally Hardy's ab-solute 'best', and notes again 'how rarely one comes across a Hardy poem that could fairly be called bad' – even those the editors 'without much regret [and no explanation], screened out of this se-lection'.[27] Even more to the point, Richard Willmott's *Thomas Hardy: Selected Poems* (Oxford University Press, 1992), in the 'Oxford Student Texts' series, again offers no indication as to why the novice Hardy reader (presumably its target market is principally schools) should be reading *these particular* poems – nor, indeed, that the 54 included have been selected in the first place from more than 900 others. It is a very clear case of the way 'primary' texts in secondary and tertiary education, if nowhere else, 'edit' their readers.

Conversely, the high-profile anthology edited by Andrew Motion (the new 'Everyman Library' edition) – which must currently be, together with the Penguin selections by Thomas and Wright above and the two editions by Samuel Hynes for Oxford University Press below, one of the five volumes most likely to be bought by students and general public alike – appears to deal directly with the unman-ageability of Hardy's *oeuvre*. In the introduction to *Thomas Hardy: Selected Poems* (1994; *c.*250 items), Motion once again registers the 'alarm' with which even Hardy's 'most enthusiastic admirers still respond to the enormous bulk' of his *Collected Poems* and the perceived impossibility of making an 'adequate selection ... when no one agreed which were his best poems'. He then proposes to engage with the 'difficulty' announced by Donald Davie (see above, pp. 137–8), but this fizzles out, in fact, with the sentence: 'far from settling the question of what is best, this makes the whole issue even more complex' – an issue which thereafter receives no further direct treatment. Indeed, leaving aside some passing value-judgements – 'whereas in some writers camp is a sign of gravity in Hardy it is a mark of incompetence'; '"Afterwards" says it all' – there is again no explanation of how Motion's selection (of roughly a quarter of the entire *oeuvre*) has been arrived at or of how, finally, he has identified the 'best poems' – unless, that is, we take the presumptive concluding remark that nevertheless '*we* can ... *agree* that his best work fills a fat book'[28] to mean that the 'Everyman Library' anthology is, in itself, its own explanation.

However, perhaps the most revealing example of the tacit evaluative construction of Hardy the Poet are the two paperback selections of his 'Finest' poetry edited by Samuel Hynes for Oxford University Press (he is also editor – the Monopolies Commission take note – of the invaluable Oxford University Press edition of *The Complete Poetical Works of Thomas Hardy*). *Thomas Hardy: A Critical Selection of His Finest Poetry* (1984) in 'The Oxford Authors' series and *Thomas Hardy: A Selection of His Finest Poems* (1994) in the 'Oxford Poetry Library' series are both in print, the covers of both reproduce a verison of the same portrait of Hardy, and the 1984 introduction is reproduced verbatim as the introduction to the 1994 volume (whilst receiving a new '1994' copyright date). This Introduction is entirely silent on the principles of selection used, whilst delivering such question-begging value-judgements of monumental self-assurance as: 'they are not very good poems, and ... are not ... characteristically Hardyesque' (these are the ones that 'do not speak with Hardy's unique poetic voice' – see above, p. 135); others 'are surely "universal", if any poems are'.[29] But such un-'*Critical*' identification of Hardy's 'Finest' poems is all the more worrying when we realize that the 1994 volume contains only just over half (*c.*290 poems) of the poems in the 1984 one (*c.*530 poems); that both are nevertheless entitled Hardy's 'Finest'; and that the poems omitted from the later volume are, by and large,

Chosen Poems (1929), plus James Gibson's 1975 edition of the same, and only two – the earlier Wain and Creighton – of the anthologies I have reviewed above[31]). Taking James Gibson's edition of *The Complete Poems of Thomas Hardy* (1976) as the standard text, and assuming the 947 poems there to be the baseline number for his analysis, Johnson shows that 394 poems (41.6 per cent) are unrepresented in any anthology; 241 in only one, and 130 in only two. At the other end of the scale, while only two ('The Darkling Thrush' and 'The Oxen') appeared in all ten, and two more ('"I Look Into My Glass"' and 'The Convergence of the Twain') in nine of the ten, 104 poems appeared in seven or more anthologies, and 38 in five or more. It is also clear, and a point I will return to later, that a good proportion of these top-ranking poems had also been selected by Hardy himself for *Chosen Poems*. The thrust of Johnson's argument in the light of all this (with which Tim Armstrong seems to concur[32]), is that there has been little unanimity amongst editors of selections, beyond a small core of frequently anthologized poems, about what is the 'essential' Hardy canon, and that a much larger and more diverse proportion of his poetry is regarded as comprising it than Leavis's dozen or so 'great poems'.

That was in 1979. My analysis, now, would propose that the vast majority of poems in Johnson's top seven categories have also been reprinted in most of the larger selections I have reviewed above, and a significant number of them in the smaller or more specialized ones as well; and that these poems have now 'settled' into being Hardy's central achievement. A specimen list of titles of poems which appear in Johnson's seventh category (in only four anthologies or more) or do not appear in his listings at all, but which are now securely in the canon, suggests just how rapidly and uniformly, since 1979, the core of Hardy's achievement has been established. The list would include: 'The Ruined Maid', 'One We Knew', 'Under the Waterfall', 'Your Last Drive', 'Lament', 'At the Word "Farewell"', 'Heredity', 'On a Midsummer Eve', 'Logs on the Hearth', 'Nobody Comes', '"I Am the One"', 'He Resolves to Say No More', 'Thoughts of Phena', 'Nature's Questioning', 'Former Beauties', '"I Found Her Out There"', '"Something Tapped"', 'Transformations', 'The Musical Box', 'The Wind's Prophecy', '"Who's in the Next Room?"', 'Paying Calls', 'Midnight on the Great Western', 'Pround Songsters', 'Christmas: 1924', '"We Are Getting to the End"'. One further measure of the construction and consolidation of this canonic Hardy is represented by even a cursory glance at the BBC Programme Index from the mid-1940s through to the early 1980s,[33] which reveals that Hardy's poems were regularly read on the radio in school broadcasts, 'Interval' and 'Closedown' slots. Only about four of the least well-known ones feature in that period (all, significantly, concerned with sex). But of the most familiar poems, 30 were read – often more than once – with the commonest ones representing a roll-call of those in Johnson's top three or four categories, and certainly those most uncompromisingly favoured since by compilers of selections: 'The Oxen', 'Afterwards', 'The Darkling Thrush', 'Weathers', 'In Time of "The Breaking of Nations"', '"I Look Into My Glass"', 'The Ruined Maid', 'Wessex Heights', 'A Sheep Fair', 'After a Journey', 'At Castle Boterel', 'Midnight on the Great Western', 'Channel Firing', 'During Wind and Rain', 'Throwing a Tree', 'The Convergence of the Twain'.

Some analysis of the possible reasons for this settling process of the canon by which Hardy the Poet is crystallized – his 'characteristic' features and composition, and, thence, the cultural and critical assumptions inscribed in him – is offered below. Suffice to say for now that there is an inner core of perhaps 40 poems without which any notion of 'Hardy's poetry' seems unthinkable; and that these naturalize the 'true', 'essential' character and quality of his achievement. The converse reflex of this, of course, is that there is a large number of poems which are never, seldom, or very variably reprinted in the anthologies and 'Selections' – poems which bring into view some of Hardy's other characteristic, if more disregarded, subjects, stances and practices. To reinsert these less familiar tropes and discourses within the established canon in itself at once defamiliarizes the well-known poems and modifies the received representation of the 'essential Hardy'. It is only proper to note here that this is what the American deconstructionist critic, J. Hillis Miller, has, in his own way, partly done. While himself recognizing the difficulty of dealing with Hardy's huge *oeuvre*, Miller abjures the essentializing tendency described above, and sees the 950-plus individual poems as exemplary for a deconstructive reading. This is because of the 'uniqueness of each moment of experience ... each record[s] in words'; because 'each moment, each text, is incommensurate with all the others'; and because forms of 'discontinuity', 'discord' and 'irrelation' characterize the 'Complete Poems'. Faced with the fact that they are all 'fugitive glimpses, transient readings of life', the critic 'must resist as much as possible the temptation to link poem with poem in some grand scheme'. Miller's own minutely attentive close analyses of 'miscellaneous' poems on either side of the canonic/disregarded divide focuses on their recognition of 'life's incoherence', an incoherence predetermined by the irrational, 'discordant' and unsystematic properties of language.[34] His work has quietly and subtly laid the ground for further readings of Hardy's poetry, across its diverse and undifferentiated entirety, as the kind of heteroglossic, destabilized and destabilizing *text* which conventional constructions of 'Hardy the Poet' preclude, and which that mythical figure sorely needs.

* * * * *

I can now turn to an analysis of the respective character of the 'familiar' and the 'less familiar' Hardy, in terms of (1) some empirical explanation for the development of the former at least, and (2) a rather more speculative examination of their nature – one which attempts to make visible the critical, cultural and ideological premises on which they are founded.

A number of determinants seem to have been at work during Hardy's own lifetime which laid the foundations for the canon. First, as his popularity as a poet overcame the early bafflement and resentment at his change of genre, his poems were increasingly often first published in wide-circulation newspapers and magazines and only later in book form, and it is striking how large a proportion of these (from 'Drummer Hodge' and 'The Darkling Thrush' through 'A Church Romance' and 'Weathers' to 'Proud Songsters', 'Throwing a Tree' and 'Lying Awake') remain central to his 'characteristic' achievement – as though wide early familiarity established their pre-emptive right to continuous later selection. Second, in furtherance of this, some few of the most regularly anthologized poems (e.g. 'The Oxen' and 'In Time of "The Breaking of Nations"') were published by Hardy in the public interest, with no copyright restriction on them, which meant that they could be widely and freely reproduced. Third, in 1916, Hardy published his own volume of *Selected Poems* – the first 'anthology' of his work – which drew, at that point of course, only on his first four books of poetry. In 1927, he revised and rearranged this anthology, which was published posthumously as *Chosen Poems* in 1929. He dropped eight poems from *Selected Poems* and added only three from the earlier books; but he also included 11 from *Moments of Vision*, 15 from *Late Lyrics and Earlier*, and 17 from *Human Shows*. *Winter Words*, of course, was not available for inclusion. As Trevor Johnson points out, however, *Chosen Poems* was only 'a recession [of *Selected Poems*] rather than a complete new start', and therefore retains 'a bias towards his early work'. He also shows, by way of some deft arithmetic, that of the poems Hardy selected, just over two-thirds of those available to him, as an average, commonly appeared in the anthologies Johnson analysed. That figure is a highly significant one, although Johnson's own over-partial interpretation of it is rather less convincing, being an instance of a circular argument proving what it wants to prove: 'a remarkable testimony to Hardy's powers of judgement and self-criticism. ... The poems Hardy picked read like a roll of those chosen for exegesis and praise in the recent past. It looks as if he knew what he was doing, after all.'[35] Indeed they do, and indeed he does – but only in the sense that Hardy also wrote his own 'official' biography (see Chapter 1, pp. 11, 21) and himself put his novels into the categories which helped determine most later critical assessment of his fictional achievement.[36] Apropos of this, it is worth noting that many of the poems in the core canon are also ones that Hardy himself mentions and glosses in *The Life of Thomas Hardy* – as though bringing to our attention the ones preferred in the self-author(iz)ed account of his life's achievement. But surely the point is that *Selected Poems* and *Chosen Poems* between them laid down early, and again with authorial authority, an embryonic canon which is automatically self-perpetuating. (Significantly, Francine Shapiro Puk, in a 1978 edition of *Chosen Poems*, included an appendix of 14 poems not selected by Hardy: 'so as not to deprive the reader of certain additional critical favourites', together with *all* the 'Poems of 1912–13' where Hardy had included only eight[37]). The determinate influence of *Chosen Poems* would also account, in part, for the perceptible weight of the 'familiar Hardy' being on the earlier volumes – an imbalance which Armstrong, for example, explicitly attempts to correct.[38] There is a way in which an editor's anticipation of the reader's expectation of the presence of certain poems in a selection assures that they will indeed be there.

However, empirical reasons only take us part of the way in trying to ascertain the provenance and nature of the canonic Hardy. If we turn back to Creighton's unintentionally self-parodic statement that 'my broad classifications – Nature, Love, Memory and Reflection, Dramatic and Personative, and Narrative – can claim almost canonical authority' (see above, p. 141), then we may move a little further forward. The first four 'classifications' here draw attention to major themes in Hardy's work, and the last three to important modes of writing in it. Certainly, to take the latter aspect first, much of the admiration for Hardy's poetic writing, with some (mainly earlier) cavils at 'awkwardness', 'clumsiness', 'irregularity', etc., has increasingly pointed both to his range, innovativeness and technical skill in prosody – almost every lyric is different in rhythm and rhyme – now praised as the product of extreme professional craft, not of an excellent but untrained ear; and to his style – especially the often clotted syntax and eclectic vocabulary – which is again now seen, not as the flawed primitive poetic discourse of a self-educated rural 'genius', but as evidence of complex control and dedicated precision in the use of language. Equally, there *is* an 'almost canonical' consensus regarding what Hardy's 'finest' poems are about. If we add 'Death and the Dead' to Creighton's list of 'classifications', assume that 'Memory' includes Time, and 'Reflection' religio-philosophical poetry, then most would concur that these themes are indeed what we read Hardy for. John Wain, amongst many others, presents him as 'not prais[ing] the beauty of the countryside, but immers[ing] himself in its slow fruitful rhythms and enjoy[ing] ... the common sights and sounds'; Trevor Johnson sees his love poems as 'constitut[ing] the ultimate touchstone of his poetic genius'; Tim Armstrong notes that 'the dead comprise Hardy's single most important topic'; Samuel Hymes agrees, but also predicts that 'time would be his central subject' – many of the poems expressing his 'sense of the tragic nature of *all* human existence: the failure of hopes, the inevitability of loss, the destructiveness of time', and seeing all these characteristics coming together in 'Poems of 1912–13' – 'a series of elegies that are his finest poems'. In this, he concurs with Andrew Motion (and almost every other modern commentator) when the latter says: 'Hardy's best poems are in their various ways all elegies, and ... the best of these best are the poems to Emma.'[39] Most criticism, too, at greater length and with greater or lesser degrees of sophistication and complexity, also works around these thematic lodestones, and the best-known poems clearly underwrite their prominence.

Grouping the poems by theme is, of course, too exclusive and schematic, as the most characteristic themes interpenetrate widely, but a rough taxonomy would show the following. There are, very obviously, those poems in which Hardy celebrates natural phenomena by way both of sharply precise denotative description and connotative anthropomorphic empathy: e.g. 'An August Midnight', 'At Day-Close in November', 'At Middle-Field Gate in February', 'Weathers', 'Snow in the Suburbs', 'Proud Songsters', 'Throwing a Tree', with 'Afterwards' as the classic text. Linked, are poems like 'She Hears the Storm', 'A Sheep Fair' and 'Shortening Days at the Homestead', which combine vivid rural images with a melancholic recognition of time passing and the transitoriness of living things; and related again are those famous poems which descry a rather more metaphysical significance in the counterpoint of natural and human events: 'Neutral Tones', 'Nature's Questioning', 'The Darkling Thrush', 'In Tenebris I', 'The Convergence of the Twain', 'Wessex Heights', 'In Time of "The Breaking of Nations"'. Then there are the lyrically evocative elegies which memorialize the personal and familial past – again, usually involving a celebratory imagery drawn from natural and homely things: 'Thoughts of Phena', 'The Self-Unseeing', 'The House of Hospitalities', 'Former Beauties', 'A Church Romance', 'The Roman Road', 'One We Knew', 'The Oxen', 'Great Things', 'Old Furniture', 'Logs on the Hearth', 'During Wind and Rain'. Most familiar, too, are the many poems which, in diverse ways, deal with ageing, death and the dead (excepting for the moment the poems obviously about Emma): from the more astringent ones to do with the tensions of becoming old – '"I Look Into My Glass"', 'Shut Out That Moon', 'Reminiscences of a Dancing Man', 'An Ancient to Ancients', 'Nobody Comes', 'He Never Expected Much' – though the variously witty or mournful reflections on a beloved's or his own death – 'In Death Divided', 'On a Midsummer Eve', 'Something Tapped', '"Who's in the Next Room?"', '"I am the One"', 'Lying Awake' – to those most characteristic poems which, in effect, resurrect the known local dead: 'Friends Beyond', 'Transformations', 'Paying Calls', 'Voices from Things Growing in a Churchyard'. There are also three small categories (although these become considerably larger on the reinsertion of the lesser known poetry): first, the poems which centre on female sexuality, occasionally dramatizing the woman's voice: 'She at His Funeral', 'To Lizbie Brown', 'The Ruined Maid', 'A

Trampwoman's Tragedy', 'The Sunshade'; second, poems which display humanistic social observation: for example, 'Midnight on the Great Western' and 'No Buyers'; third, Hardy's much antholo-gized war poems – which, again, display his de-heroicizing human-ism: 'Drummer Hodge', 'The Man He Killed', 'Channel Firing', 'In Time of "The Breaking of Nations"', 'Christmas: 1924'. Finally, there are those poems which seem to lie at the very heart of Hardy's achievement: the poems to and about Emma – all, in one way or another, elegies to a lost love and, as I have suggested in Chapter 1 (pp. 21–2), refashionings of that love in the plangent present dis-course of his poetry: the 'Poems of 1912–13', together with other favoured poems which fall outside the sequence itself: for example, '"When I Set Out for Lyonnesse"', 'Under the Waterfall', 'At the Word "Farewell"', 'The Musical Box', 'The Wind's Prophecy'.

At this point, I should emphatically repeat that I have no inten-tion of trying to disavow the quality of the vast majority of poems catalogued above: individually, many of them are superbly con-trolled lyrical 'inditings' of all those 'hours' – 'too satiate with soul, too ethereal' – which the little-known poem, 'The History of an Hour' (*HS*), invokes, and many of them, as for so many other readers, are personal favourites. It is, indeed, the (apparently) easy control of 'A Darkling Thrush', rather than what it says, which still evokes an awed response from me, as do the upbeat rhythmic drive of 'Reminiscences of a Dancing Man' and the achieved lyric com-pression of 'Former Beauties'. However familiar, the ponderously ironic language and rhythm of 'The Convergence of the Twain' – '"What does this vaingloriousness down here?"' – retain their defa-miliarizing force, just as the painful, slow unfolding of the misery which informs 'Wessex Heights' establishes the experiential authen-ticity of the poem. In 'Old Furniture', there are the delicately ren-dered fading images of the past, but it is the characteristic 'turn' at the opening of the final stanza – 'Well, well. It is best to be up and doing' – which refuses the settling comfort of nostalgia in both poem and reader. Quite how one gets to the position of being able to judge 'During Wind and Rain' one of the 'best poems of the century', as some critics have done,[40] is quite beyond me, but there are surely few readers who do not respond to the biting pathos of its ballad-like refrain, nor to the mordant irony of the repetition of 'Gentleman' in the Yeatsian wittiness of 'An Ancient to Ancients' – especially in the deeply ambiguous compression of its last lines:

downbeat romantic lyricism was looking distinctly *passé*, despite its continued promotion by J. C. Squire in the new *London Mercury* where Hardy published regularly in the 1920s.[42] Because Hardy's earlier poetry (that dating from the heyday of Georgianism) had rapidly become familiar, as we have seen, and remained so in part because of his *Selected* and *Chosen Poems*, it tended to reproduce this notion of the 'Georgian' Hardy in the post-war period when the 'new bearings' of British poetry[43] were being tooled up by the younger generation of Anglo-American Modernists. However, in the context of Modernist cultural despair (the 'Waste-Land' mindset), and perhaps in order to ring-fence the 'great' *modern* Hardy from the now minor Georgians, critics simultaneously also gave greater prominence to some of his bleakest earlier poems (e.g. 'The Darkling Thrush', 'In Tenebris', 'To an Unborn Pauper Child') rather than to those later ones in *HS* and *WW* which, as we shall see, 'uncharacteristically' celebrate ordinary humanity. Be that as it may, it is apparent that it is an amalgam of the 'Georgian' Hardy, leavened with some of the 'gloomy' philosophical poetry and the great elegies to Emma, which becomes, in the course of time, the quintessential Hardy. And it is no surprise, either, that, by and large, it is *this* Hardy which is recuperated by Donald Davie (see above, pp. 136–7) as the anti-totalitarian source of a counter-tradition of modern British poetry – a poetry of liberalism and humanism, of ironic quietism and personal 'integrity' – whose later avatar was Philip Larkin. Words like 'passivity', 'nostalgia', 'determinism', 'guilt', 'remorse', 'resignation' haunt this Hardy – carrying all the potent ideological freight of a strategic disenchantment lying at the heart of what E. P. Thompson has called the 'Natopolis' of post-World-War-II culture and society – a 'discrete ideology of intellectual alienation and of quietism, the apologia for apathy'.[44] Davie may be right – perhaps this *is* Hardy's defining cultural locus; but it still seems to me – and without making any grandiose claims for Hardy's disregarded poems – to predetermine and constrict our reading of him.

* * * * *

As I have indicated earlier, this chapter is more a commentary on the critical shaping of 'Hardy the Poet' than another reading of the poetry itself. But we may now ask in general terms: how is our estimation of his achievement enhanced if we restore to his *oeuvre* poems which by and large fall outside the recognized canon? In answer to my question, some will say: 'it isn't', although a few specific illustrations of how it may be modified will be offered by way of reply. Of course, it is only different *emphases* that we notice rather than a radically 'other' poet. We will not find many examples of strikingly different *kinds* of poetic performance in addition to the extraordinary diversity of the canonic Hardy's prosodical and metrical innovativeness. But the range in the less familiar poetry is equally wide and varied: attention might be drawn, for instance, to the assured handling of the triolet form in the never-anthologized 'The Coquette, and After' (*PPP*); to the long rhythmically controlled and idiomatically inflected lines of the dramatic monologue in 'The Chapel-Organist' (*LLE*; only ever selected by David Wright, who nevertheless dismisses it as an example of Hardy's 'occasional melodramatics'[45]); the lilting song-like measure of the moving *carpe diem* lyric 'Queen Caroline to Her Guests';[46] and the bitterly ironic self-parodying 'jingle' in the never-reprinted 'A Jingle on the Times'.

Equally, while the themes, subjects and tones of the less familiar poems are not markedly different, we may register the changed emphases they bring. This is certainly true of the much enlarged 'humanist' Hardy of social observation and (anti-)war poetry, but especially so of the many poems on women and sexuality which, in their range and diversity, radically transgress the defining frame of the 'great' love poems to Emma. Here is a Hardy writing obsessively and contradictorily about women of all classes, types and degrees of familiarity. This Hardy is wittier, more humorous, satirical and astringent than is normally perceived in the 'characteristic' melancholic or nostalgic quietist; more socially engaged and humanistic than the 'pessimistic' determinist; more erotic and libertarian, more contradictorily positioned – as we would expect of the erstwhile novelist – in relation to female sexuality and male attitudes to it – than the fixated, chaste and remorseful lover of 'Poems of 1912–13' leads us to expect.

A selective sampling of such poems may cause us to wonder what it is that has kept them so comprehensively disregarded. The never-selected 'Tragedian to Tragedienne' (*HS*), for example, despite its dramatic voice, is surely as personal and realized a lyric about death, love and the death of love as many of Hardy's famous poems – as, indeed, is its equally unselected companion-piece (this time in the woman's voice: see also below), 'Circus-Rider to Ringmaster' (*HS*). The late 'Unkept Good Fridays' (*WW*)[47] is a measured, but deeply subversive, affirmation of ordinary human courage and sacrifice which contrasts well with the 'canonic' pessimism, say, of the early 'To an Unborn Pauper Child'; just as the widely ignored elegy (not, however, to Emma) '"Nothing Matters Much"' (*HS*) – with its subtle revision of the first and last lines and its haunting fourth stanza – is surely comparable with the tough, uncompromising late poems in *WW*. Is the seldom-anthologized, but neat, philosophical lyric 'Going and Staying' (*LLE*) any less memorable than the clearly cognate poem '"We Are Getting to the End"', or the seldom-anthologized 'In a Former Resort after Many Years' (*HS*) than its well-known parallel, 'Former Beauties' – although it is doubtless significant that where the latter nostalgically evokes a past(oral) idyll, the other poem forces upon us a grim present reality. Why, one may ask, is the humanistically affirmative 'The Old Workman' (*LLE*) so little-known compared, for example, to the less sanguine 'No Buyers'; why has the bitter anti-war sonnet '"Often When Warring"' (*MV*) – again expressing a mundane humanism – fared so badly[48] *contra* the similarly themed 'The Man He Killed' or the elegiac 'Drummer Hodge'? No doubt less puzzlingly unfamiliar are the neurotically sexual 'The Woman I Met', which at once gives a voice to the prostitute and 'speaks' the male's repressed desire; the strange dramatic monologue, 'The Collector Cleans His Picture' with its overt deconstruction of the masturbatory male gaze; or 'The Chapel-Organist' (all *LLE*) which (positively) counterposes the woman's voluptuous sexuality and large spirit with the mean prurience of the religious culture she is destroyed by. Such poems clearly do not sit easily next to the famous elegiac love poems, to the nostalgic celebratory lyrics like 'To Lizbie Browne', or even to the wry inverted pastoral of 'The Ruined Maid'. Indeed, what they *do* do, when defamiliarizingly juxtapositioned with them, is to set those well-known poems in a rather more complex sexual frame. For example, the fact that the *positive* female eroticism of a number of other poems ('The Dark-Eyed Gentleman', 'Ralph Blossom Soliloquizes', 'Julie-Jane' [all *Time's Laughingstocks*], 'In the Days of Crinoline' [*Satires of Circumstance*]) – often in the women's voice – is offset by the counter-discourse of female sexual tragedy and folly observed and satirized by male 'judgement' (e.g. 'On the Portrait of a Woman about to be

lover, and that 'her' and 'she' in the final stanza must be 'Beauty'
(*not* a female lover) who is 'worshipped' by the female speaker. It is
her courageous affirmation of 'Beauty', then, and *her* acceptance of
its curtailment which is expressed:

> Still, I'd go the world with Beauty,
>   I would laugh with her and sing,
> I would shun divinest duty
>   To resume her worshipping.
> But she'd scorn my brave endeavour,
>   She would not balm the breeze
> By murmuring 'Thine for ever!'
>   As she did upon this leaze.

In almost all cases the woman's voice speaks an honesty and an
openness to life and sexuality which the 'male' poems (despite the
'throbbings of noontide' in '"I Look Into My Glass"') seldom have.
On the contrary, these tend to give utterance to the 'faintheart' who
bemoans his 'lost prizes'.[51] Apropos of this, there has been considerable critical speculation about whether Hardy redeems Emma's voice,
or silences it, in 'Poems of 1912–13'.[52] But the pervasive elegaic voice
of those poems is surely that of Hardy forging a new reality out of a
lost, fading and unfulfilled past. The kind of female voice which
speaks in the less familiar poems glanced at above – positively erotic,
disruptively strong, and sharply aware of the social victimization of
women within patriarchy – could have no place there: Emma must
remain the dim voice of 'the woman calling' ('The Voice'), the 'voice-
less ghost' ('After a Journey'), in the context of Hardy's poetic
remorse and guilt for the 'lost' relationship. The woman's voice, here,
would have destabilized the elegiac love poems which so movingly
express Hardy's attempt to retrieve buried experience – their final
balance and equipoise achieved by its exclusion. But those released
voices in the disregarded poems insistently press us, now, to wonder
what that silenced woman's voice might have said.

Finally – and to bring more clearly into view the unresolved
problematic of what is perceived to constitute 'poetic value', and
how critical discourse does (or does not) define it – I will take three
small groupings of poems, each of which counterpoints a canonic
poem with one or more of the least reprinted or critically considered. 'At Castle Boterel' is one of the most admired of the famous
elegies to Emma in 'Poems of 1912–13':

As I drive to the junction of lane and highway,
     And the drizzle bedrenches the waggonette,
I look behind at the fading byway,
     And see on its slope, now glistening wet,
          Distinctly yet

Myself and a girlish form benighted
     In dry March weather. We climb the road
Beside a chaise. We had just alighted
     To ease the sturdy pony's load
          When he sighed and slowed.

What we did as we climbed, and what we talked of
     Matters not much, nor to what it led, –
Something that life will not be balked of
     Without rude reason till hope is dead,
          And feeling fled.

It filled but a minute. But was there ever
     A time of such quality, since or before,
In that hill's story? To one mind never,
     Though it has been climbed, foot-swift, foot-sore,
          By thousands more.

Primaeval rocks form the road's steep border,
     And much have they faced there, first and last,
Of the transitory in Earth's long order;
     But what they record in colour and cast
          Is – that we two passed.

And to me, though Time's unflinching rigour,
     In mindless rote, has ruled from sight
The substance now, one phantom figure
     Remains on the slope, as when that night
          Saw us alight.

I look and see it there, shrinking, shrinking,
     I look back at it amid the rain
For the very last time; for my sand is sinking,
     And I shall traverse old love's domain
          Never again.

March 1913

It is indeed a fine example of Hardy's low-key revivifying of 'old love's domain' from the poignant stance of one who knows, nevertheless, that it is irredeemably in the past and that even the memory is 'shrinking, shrinking'. If we set next to it the comprehensively ignored poem 'Concerning Agnes' (*WW*),[53] we find another elegy – not this time, however, to Emma, but to Lady Agnes Grove, one of the women Hardy fell in love with in the 1890s and who died in 1926:

> I am stopped from hoping what I have hoped before –
> > Yes, many a time! –
> To dance with that fair woman yet once more
> > As in the prime
> Of August, when the wide-faced moon looked through
> The boughs at the faery lamps of the Larmer Avenue.
>
> I could not, though I should wish, have over again
> > That old romance,
> And sit apart in the shade as we sat then
> > After the dance
> The while I held her hand, and, to the booms
> Of contrabassos, feet still pulsed from the distant rooms.
>
> I could not. And you do not ask me why.
> > Hence you infer
> That what may chance to the fairest under the sky
> > Has chanced to her.
> Yes. She lies white, straight, features marble-keen,
> Unapproachable, mute, in a nook I have never seen.
>
> There she may rest like some vague goddess, shaped
> > As out of snow;
> Say Aphrodite sleeping; or bedraped
> > Like Kalupso;
> Or Amphitrite stretched on the Mid-sea swell,
> Or one of the Nine grown stiff from thought. I cannot tell!

Here, too, is the delicately evoked, but ultimately futile, desire for 'that old romance'; the direct conversational voice ('I could not. And you do not ask me why'); the sense of the frailty of human life and beauty in the unheeding and relentless process of time ('what may chance to the fairest under the sky/Has chanced to her'); but here, also, is the movingly precise image of the 'unapproachable' dead, and the finely controlled classical paean of the last stanza, abruptly humanized by the final admission – 'I cannot tell.' As a hypothetical exercise in the manner of the old Practical Criticism, let us try to envisage these two poems as entirely unfamiliar 'unseen' texts (with the identity, of course, of the woman in each unknown), and consider on what critical criteria of poetic excellence we would judge which one to include in a selection of 'great' poems. We would not be able to say that the obscurity of 'the Larmer Avenue' (a public pleasure-ground at an estate on the Wiltshire/Dorset border with a large dancing area) in l.6 of 'Concerning Agnes' is a problem not present in 'At Castle Boterel', because 'Castle Boterel' itself is just as obscure in that it is Hardy's own name for Boscastle; nor that a word like 'bedraped' in l.21 of the former is awkward and strange, when 'bedrenches and 'benighted' occur in ll.2 and 6 of the latter; nor that the 'booms/Of contrabassos' ('Concerning Agnes' l.12) is any more of a hindrance to understanding than 'In mindless rote' in l.21 of the other poem; nor that the flatly prosaic language and rhythm of ll.5–6 or 13–14 of 'Concerning Agnes' are a blemish, if we cannot convincingly distinguish them from those, say, in ll.7–10 of 'At Castle Boterel'. What *intrinsic* quality is it, then, which makes one of these poems so widely held to be 'great' and the other manifestly not?

A second pair of poems which will bear some comparison are 'Wessex Heights' – to me, as I have indicated earlier, still one of Hardy's most impressive achievements – and 'By Henstridge Cross at the Year's End' (*LLE* – rarely reprinted, and scarcely ever mentioned even among the wide diversity of poems Hardy's critics consider[54]).

Wessex Heights
(1896)

There are some heights in Wessex, shaped as if by a kindly hand
For thinking, dreaming, dying on, and at crises when I stand,
Say, on Ingpen Beacon eastward, or on Wylls-Neck westwardly,
I seem where I was before my birth, and death may be.

In the lowlands I have no comrade, not even the lone man's friend –
Her who suffereth long and is kind; accepts what he is too weak to
    mend:
Down there they are dubious and askance; there nobody thinks as I,
But mind-chains do not clank where one's next neighbour is the sky.

In the towns I am tracked by phantoms having weird detective
    ways –

Shadows of beings who fellowed with myself of earlier days:
They hang about at places, and say harsh heavy things –
Men with a wintry sneer, and women with tart disparagings.

Down there I seem to be false to myself, my simple self that was,
And is not now, and I see him watching, wondering what crass
       cause
Can have merged him into such a strange continuator as this,
Who yet has something in common with himself, my chrysalis.

I cannot go to the great grey Plain; there's a figure against the moon,
Nobody sees it but I, and it makes my breast beat out of tune;
I cannot go to the tall-spired town, being barred by the forms now
       passed
For everybody but me, in whose long vision they stand there fast.

There's a ghost at Yell'ham Bottom chiding loud at the fall of the
       night,
There's a ghost in Froom-side Vale, thin-lipped and vague, in a
       shroud of white,
There's one in the railway train whenever I do not want it near,
I see its profile against the pane, saying what I would not hear.

As for one rare fair woman, I am now but a thought of hers,
I enter her mind and another thought succeeds me that she prefers;
Yet my love for her in its fulness she herself even did not know;
Well, time cures hearts of tenderness, and now I can let her go.

So I am found on Ingpen Beacon, or on Wylls-Neck to the west,
Or else on homely Bulbarrow, or little Pilsdon Crest,
Where men have never cared to haunt, nor women have walked with
       me,
And ghosts then keep their distance; and I know some liberty.

By Henstridge Cross at the Year's End

(From this centuries-old cross-road the highway leads east to London, north
to Bristol and Bath, west to Exeter and the Land's End, and south to the
Channel coast.)

    Why go the east road now?...
That way a youth went on a morrow
After mirth, and he brought back sorrow
      Painted upon his brow:
      Why go the east road now?

Why go the north road now?
Torn, leaf-strewn, as if scoured by foemen,
Once edging fiefs of my forefolk yeomen,
    Fallows fat to the plough:
    Why go the north road now?

Why go the west road now?
Thence to us came she, bosom-burning,
Welcome with joyousness returning....
    She sleeps under the bough:
    Why go the west road now?

Why go the south road now?
That way marched they some are forgetting,
Stark to the moon left, past regretting
    Loves who have falsed their vow....
    Why go the south road now?

Why go any road now?
White stands the handpost for brisk onbearers,
'Halt!' is the word for wan-cheeked farers
    Musing on Whither, and How....
    Why go any road now?

'Yea: we want new feet now,'
Answer the stones. 'Want chit-chat, laughter:
Plenty of such to go hereafter
    By our tracks, we trow!
    We are for new feet now.'

                              During the War.

Both poems are deeply personal meditations at times of crisis in the poet's life (the mid-1890s/'During the War'); both use a geographical mapping device to structure the poem (the four 'heights', plus the 'lowlands', in 'Wessex Heights'/the four 'roads' in 'By Henstridge Cross'); both are complex and knotty in syntax and movement, as the poet struggles to give shape to tortuous significances in the tensions of a personal/public history; both, in different ways, master their informing traumas in the tight control of their versification; both, despite the misery which prompts them, end on a note of hard-won affirmation ('I know some liberty'/'"We are for new feet now"'); both are initially, if not ultimately, obscure at times – especially in terms of their biographical reference

('Wessex Heights', in particular, has been subject to extensive – and unresolved, not to say comic – speculation about the identities of the women referred to in it). And yet, despite all this, 'Wessex Heights' is undeniably at the centre of the Hardy canon and 'By Henstridge Cross' is comprehensively ignored. To my mind, the latter's synoptic charting of formative failure and loss in Hardy's life is equally as resonant as the defiant introversion of 'Wessex Heights': stanza one – whatever it was that happened to him in London in the 1860s; stanza two – the decline of his family's fortunes; stanza three – Emma, then wonderfully 'bosom-burning', now dead; and stanza four – culminating in the vast tragedy of World War I. Furthermore, the fifth stanza – which so typically 'turns' the poem towards its conclusion – encapsulates with astonishing economy the poem's telling double-perspective: the recognition at once of an irresistible dynamic futurity ('brisk onbearers') and of equally insistent doubts about the point of participating in it. Unexpectedly, and against the grain, the language, rhythm and sense of the final liberating stanza all affirm the precedence of the former. Perhaps it is this destablizing of the 'characteristic' 'gloomy' Hardy which keeps a poem, otherwise pressing for an explanation of its neglect, in non-canonic obscurity.

Let us turn, similarly and finally, to 'The Darkling Thrush' (*PPP*), one of – perhaps *the* – most famous of Hardy's poems.

> I leant upon a coppice gate
>   When Frost was spectre-gray,
> And Winter's dregs made desolate
>   The weakening eye of day.
> The tangled bine-stems scored the sky
>   Like strings of broken lyres,
> And all mankind that haunted nigh
>   Had sought their household fires.
>
> The land's sharp features seemed to be
>   The Century's corpse outleant,
> His crypt the cloudy canopy,
>   The wind his death-lament.
> The ancient pulse of germ and birth
>   Was shrunken hard and dry,
> And every spirit upon earth
>   Seemed fervourless as I.

At once a voice arose among
    The bleak twigs overhead
In a full-hearted evensong
    Of joy illimited;
An aged thrush, frail, gaunt, and small,
    In blast-beruffled plume,
Had chosen thus to fling his soul
    Upon the growing gloom.

So little cause for carolings
    Of such ecstatic sound
Was written on terrestrial things
    Afar or nigh around,
That I could think there trembled through
    His happy good-night air
Some blessed Hope, whereof he knew
    And I was unaware.

31 December 1900

In general structure, and certainly in theme, the extensively ne-glected 'Christmastide' (*WW*)[55] compares closely.

The rain-shafts splintered on me
    As despondently I strode;
The twilight gloomed upon me
    And bleared the blank high-road.
Each bush gave forth, when blown on
    By gusts in shower and shower,
A sigh, as it were sown on
    In handfuls by a sower.

A cheerful voice called, nigh me,
    'A merry Christmas, friend!' –
There rose a figure by me,
    Walking with townward trend,
A sodden tramp's, who, breaking
    Into thin song, bore straight
Ahead, direction taking
    Toward the Casuals' gate.

The first stanza contains as precise and chilling a natural landscape as that in the opening of 'The Darkling Thrush' – although it does not anthropomorphize it in the way the latter does, nor does it give it the symbolic resonance achieved by the somewhat forced phrase

'The Century's corpse outleant'. The famous 'frail, gaunt' thrush's 'carolings' are successfully paralleled by the 'sodden tramp's' 'thin song' – surely an image as, if not more, telling of irrepressible hope as the 'full-hearted evensong' of the thrush. In 'Christmastide' Hardy does not extrapolate a moral as he does in the last four lines of the other poem, leaving it implicit in the (to modern readers, now obscure?) irony of the tramp entering 'the Casuals' gate' of the Workhouse. Perhaps this final obscurity is the reason for the disregard given to a finely understated vignette in contrast to the great fame of the designedly 'public' poem. But perhaps, also, the conventionally received 'Hardy' needs 'Nature' (a thrush) rather than a member of the human underclass (a tramp) to point up the egocentricity of an abstract pessimism? But if it is indeed 'Nature' and philosophical extrapolation that is required, another largely neglected poem, 'The Last Chrysanthemum' – which immediately precedes 'The Darkling Thrush' in *PPP* – supplies both. The description of the flower in the first four stanzas seems to me equal to anything else Hardy wrote in this mode, and the irony of the fifth stanza is handled with the spare lyrical economy so often elsewhere admired in his poetry. But if it is the idiosyncratically obscure final two lines of the poem – 'Yet it is but one mask of many worn/By the Great Face behind' – which commit it as a whole to outer darkness, how come we cope elsewhere with 'Doomsters', 'Immanent Will', 'Vast Imbecilities', and so forth (or even with 'The Century's corpse outleant')? Again, as an exercise in explicitly rationalizing our critical discrimination, we should try evaluating the two poems – unranked, unknown, unseen – and then explain their unequal status in Hardy's *oeuvre*.

Finally in the context of 'The Darkling Thrush's apparent preeminence, let me compare with it the once more generally ignored 'On Stinsford Hill at Midnight'.[56]

> I glimpsed a woman's muslined form
>   Sing-songing airily
> Against the moon; and still she sang,
>   And took no heed of me.
>
> Another trice, and I beheld
>   What first I had not scanned,
> That now and then she tapped and shook
>   A timbrel in her hand.

So late the hour, so white her drape,
    So strange the look it lent
To that blank hill, I could not guess
    What phantastry it meant.

Then burst I forth: 'Why such from you?
    Are you so happy now?'
Her voice swam on; nor did she show
    Thought of me anyhow.

I called again: 'Come nearer; much
    That kind of note I need!'
The song kept softening, loudening on,
    In placid calm unheed.

'What home is yours now?' then I said;
    'You seem to have no care.'
But the wild wavering tune went forth
    As if I had not been there.

'This world is dark, and where you are,'
    I said, 'I cannot be!'
But still the happy one sang on,
    And had no heed of me.

Rhythmically not dissimilar to 'The Darkling Thrush', this mysterious poem makes an almost identical statement to it: the 'heedless' happiness of the song of the thrush/woman suggesting some 'blessed Hope' in this 'dark world' which the 'I' of the poem cannot share. Both poems, it should be noted, remain ambiguous – neither clarifies whether it endorses hope or despondency as the proven reality. While 'On Stinsford Hill' clearly does not have the evocative natural description of the opening stanzas of 'The Darkling Thrush' – which certainly may devalue it for inclusion in the 'characteristic' Hardy – it does, nevertheless, have the mystery of its 'event' lyrically defined by the first three eerie stanzas, redolent as they are of Hardy's much-praised expropriations from the ballad tradition. Two factors suggest themselves as to why, once more, we may find ourselves puzzled and unconvinced by the consensual elevation of one poem and the relegation of the other: '*On what grounds?*' must be the insistent question. First, Hardy's explanatory subscript note to 'The Darkling Thrush' gives that poem much of its reverberating resonance. Without it, 'The Century's corpse outleant' would be even more obscure than it already is, and the whole poem could be read only speculatively and with great difficulty as a meditation on the turn of the 19th century. Secondly, I would repeat that the 'characteristic' – i.e. 'great' – Hardy seems to need the presence of a voice from 'Nature' (the thrush), and not from a human being (however ghostly). In effect, the 'heedless' happiness of Nature, in its entire alterity from the human, cannot threaten or challenge the validity of the pessimism of the human mind: it is, simply and ironically, *other*. This, then, legitimizes the continued acceptance of despair as a reasonable – perhaps even exemplary – intellectual posture. If, on the other hand, the agent of an alternative 'happiness' or 'hopefulness' is human, then that absolute otherness breaks down, pessimism becomes only one intellectual option amongst others, and can be challenged for its selfishness and passivity. In other words, it can be shown to be able to be vanquished and transcended by the opposite human capacity: that which embraces happiness, hope, futurity, self-determination – everything, in short, that an ideology of quietistic cultural despair rejects. The canonic Hardy, I am arguing by way of 'The Darkling Thrush', tends to underwrite this critical and ideological stance (see Donald Davie above, amongst others rather less self-aware and explicit), while the neglected poems, at least marginally, problematize it.

My general point, then, is that juxtaposing one kind of poem with another helps to deconstruct the tacit underlying cultural/ideological assumptions and attitudes the 'characteristic' Hardy embodies. It does this, principally and throughout, by the release of sexual affirmation in the women's voice in many poems; by the refusal, in others, to accept despair; by the substitution of human agency for Nature's 'heedlessness' in others again; and by bringing into view the heterogeneity of a body of poetry which is, indeed, an index of Hardy's ironic celebration of the 'incoherence' of the human pursuit of meaning and value – even in a 'new Dark Age'[57] necessarily devoid of 'ontological stability'.[58] As I have already said, to read his poetry thus is not to read it against the grain. The grain is there – clearly visible in so many of the neglected poems, and then also in the familiar ones – once the thickly polished critical patina has been stripped away.

7

Arabella and the Satirical Discourse in *Jude the Obscure*

As Hardy's last novel has recently been doing the rounds at a cinema near you, fronted by those contemporary late-Victorian 'Simpletons',[1] Christopher Ecclestone and Kate Winslet, it seems appropriate to take another look at *Jude the Obscure* the novel before *Jude* the film forever puts a frame round it. (A 'postscript' on the film itself follows this essay for good measure.) And where better to start than with the novel – of all Hardy's fiction – that may well have replicated most closely the mindset informing *Jude*: his famously 'lost', first-written fictional work, which was never published and the manuscript of which at some point destroyed.

The novel was to have been entitled *The Poor Man and the Lady* – 'By the Poor Man' – and the only discrete remnant of it that has survived is the (reworked) long short story, 'An Indiscretion in the Life of an Heiress'. How, then, do we know anything about it? The answer is that in the 1920s, in his eighties and approaching the end of a long and now internationally renowned career as novelist and poet, Hardy devoted several sympathetic pages to it in what is really, in some respects, his last 'fiction', *The Life of Thomas*

This essay has not been published previously elsewhere in its entirety. It began life as a conference paper given at Worcester College of Higher Education in March 1996, and some pages of an earlier draft comprise parts of Chapter 4, 'Hardy the Novelist', of my *Thomas Hardy* volume for the 'Writers and their Work' series (Plymouth: Northcote House, 1996).

Meredith warned Hardy 'not to "nail his colours to the mast" so definitely in a first book, if he wished to do anything practical in literature; for if he printed so pronounced a thing he would be attacked on all sides by the conventional reviewers, and his future injured' – *The Life* adding the pointed observation that, though such a novel might be accepted 'calmly' in the 1920s, 'in genteel mid-Victorian 1869 it would no doubt have incurred ... severe strictures which might have handicapped a young writer for a long time' (62). On Meredith's advice, therefore, Hardy put *The Poor Man and the Lady* to one side and set about constructing 'the eminently "sensational" plot' (63) which was to become *Desperate Remedies*. Nevertheless, the old Hardy pauses to reflect, in the 1920s, that three such eminent Victorian men-of-letters should have seen so much to admire in the work of 'an unknown young man', and that 'such experienced critics' had found it 'aggressive and even dangerous ... (Mr. Macmillan had said it "meant mischief")' (62). Later, writing about the reception of *The Hand of Ethelberta* – 'a Comedy of Society' 'thirty years too soon' for its period – he observes the same of his first novel: 'it had been too soon for a socialist story'. Implicit in this, surely, is Hardy's continuing approbation of it – carefully saying, not that it was 'bad', but that it was ahead of its time: 'too soon for [its] date' (108).

So what happened to the young 'socialistic' novelist? Well, as I noted in Chapter 1, Hardy had to get 'to be considered a good hand at a serial': the tyro novelist had to make his way in the rough world of Victorian Grub Street, and so, in some senses, had to conform. Furthermore, as he got older and more successful, Hardy enjoyed his lionization by High Society, and, as *The Life* makes clear on a number of occasions, saw himself as entirely apolitical – a stance at once typical of, and advantageous to, an insecure meritocrat and *arriviste*. But there is also a sense, I would like to argue, in which that radical young fiction writer goes underground, that he finds an 'acceptable' novelist's guise – the humanist-realist tragedian of Wessex – and then, from within which, both self-subverts his own fiction and destabilizes the wider cultural-ideological positions which make it acceptable in the first place. Hence all those 'flaws' critics have found throughout his *oeuvre*, and especially those disconcerting 'minor novels'. I am suggesting, then, that there is indeed a kind of duplicity even in the Wessex novels, that the latter throw up a screen of signifiers which encourages the more conservative kinds of reading and simultaneously disguises the other textual strategies going on behind it. This is very much what Joe Fisher argues in *The Hidden Hardy* (1992). His general working notion is of a distinction in Hardy's works between his 'traded' texts, 'sold on' to the bourgeois fiction market – in which Wessex is the principal commodity and the 'Novels of Character and Environment' the most obvious cases – and his 'narrated' texts, i.e. the 'Novels of Ingenuity',[4] with their subversive narrative strategies. Fisher sees the 'major' novels as representing 'an inherently conflictual engagement of the two', in which the proficient market 'trader' exploits a gap between the man who sells and the narrator who tells, which at once makes the 'traded object' acceptable and simultaneously 'corrupts' it. The 'Hidden Hardy', then, is a 'self-subversion ... a sustained campaign of deception which runs through all [the] novels, creating hostile and part-visible patterns beneath what might generally be regarded as the "surface" of the text'.[5] The problem with this otherwise convincing reading is that it is over-instrumentalist, leaving Hardy somehow too unequivocally *in charge* of the complex self-subversion of his novels. How far this guerrilla positioning – if so it be – is conscious and intentional on Hardy's part, therefore, remains a moot point and one incapable of conclusive resolution. Let us just work on the principle that an answer lies somewhere between the presence of extensive circumstantial textual evidence that Hardy was extremely self-conscious and self-reflexive in everything he wrote, and a recognition that our contemporary critical optics will 'see' a writer's work in such a way as to bring into view discourses which would not be discerned otherwise.

But, for the moment, let me assess what can be taken from Hardy's comments on *The Poor Man and the Lady*. First, fairly obviously, there is his class animus – the repeated use of the word 'socialistic' implying, I believe, not so much a defined political position as a truculently sensitive stance, especially towards the classes 'above' him: the 'squirearchy and nobility, London society, the vulgarity of the middle class'. Only two pages earlier, *The Life* reproduces one of Hardy's 'Notes of 1866–7', which suggests his already highly nuanced fascination with class relations: 'The defects of a class are more perceptible to the class immediately below it than to itself' (55). Alexander Macmillan criticized the 'class bias' of the novel, and the proposed title – with its pointed use of 'the Lady', plus its sub-title, 'By the Poor Man' – at once indicates its subject and points forward to all those other cross-class sexual relationships at the heart of Hardy's fiction. Secondly, we may consider that the novel which most recognizably reworks this 'socialistic' lost one, even though in a complex and inverted fashion, is *HE* – Hardy's own fictionalized 'Life' (see my reading of that novel in Chapter 3); and it is also significant, as I have already suggested, that his last novel, *Jude*, with *its* 'socialistic' hero, is probably as close in cast of mind to this first one as any of the others intervening. Hardy always strenuously denied – not very convincingly – that *Jude*, too, was autobiographical.[6] Thirdly, there is Hardy's notably irritable sensitivity to the reviewers' dismissal of anything he wrote which was not about 'sheepfolds', and his implicit claim that he is as much a metropolitan as he is a countryman. Perhaps those Wessex 'Novels of Character and Environment' were not so privileged by Hardy as it would seem – he had, after all, cynically commented to Sir Frederick Macmillan in April 1912 that 'the advantage of classifying the novels seems to be that it affords the journalists something to discuss'.[7] Fourthly, we may register Hardy's emphatic self-consciousness about the style of the book, and especially the explicit invocation of Defoe: the phrase 'affected simplicity' surely being a key to Hardy's own sharp sense of the artifice/artificiality of fictional discourse – and especially that claiming to be authentic 'realism'. In two highly self-reflexive passages in that most artificial of fictions, *HE,* the heroine also invokes Defoe while defining herself as a 'professed romancer', and is later described as modelling herself on 'that master of feigning' (Defoe) whose 'talent ... for telling lies' shapes her own ability to make the entirely fictive have 'the one pre-eminent merit of seeming like truth' (see Chapter 3, pp. 56–9). Furthermore, in 1919 (note that he had stopped writing novels over twenty years previously), the 79-year-old Hardy is presented in *The Life* thus:

> A curious question arose in Hardy's mind at this date on whether a *romancer* was morally justified in going to extreme lengths of assurance – after the manner of Defoe – in respect of a tale he knew to be *absolutely false.* ... Had he not long discontinued the writing of romances he would, he said, have put at the beginning of each new one: 'Understand that however true this book may be in essence, in fact it is *utterly untrue*'. (391–2, my emphases)

Hardy's self-consciousness about the art of faking, and his confessed consanguinity with the master illusionist Defoe, cannot be in question. It is also arguable that he *did*, in effect, draw the reader's attention to the fictionality of his fictions – in part in his slyly ironic prefaces to them, but rather more organically in the highly self-reflexive parading, to a greater or lesser extent in all his novels, of the artifice which comprises them. The radical 'underground' Hardy, I would argue, can be read as simultaneously creating illusion and deconstructing it – which makes his novels appear so awkward and uncomfortable to read. Perhaps the 'certain rawness of absurdity' and the 'very excess' of the satire which Macmillan and Morley[8] found in Hardy's 'first' novel were not a beginner's blemishes but a constant and crucial constituent of *all* his fiction: the bedrock of its formal signification.

My fifth and final expropriation from Hardy's comments on *The Poor Man and the Lady* is a central one for the rest of my argument here: Hardy twice uses the word '*satire*' to describe the work. Presumably, in this particular case, he meant the conventional sense of a *social* satire which reveals and excoriates the 'degeneracy of the age' (*The Life*, 62) by way of exaggeration and irony. But in Hardy's work more generally, the notion of satire takes on a wider and more resonant significance: we may think, more or less at random, of an improbable coincidence in *A Laodicean* described as giving 'an added point to the satire' (*Laod.*, 255); of Egdon Heath, at the beginning of *The Return of the Native*, as laying 'a certain vein of satire on human vanity in clothes' (*RN*, 33); of an eventuality in *HE* being referred to as a 'satire of cicumstance' (*HE*, 112); and then of Hardy calling one of his volume of poems *Satires of Circumstance* (1914). In none of these cases is the word used in the sense of the literary genre defined above; it is, rather, a statement about the 'Human Condition', and one in which the farcical absurdity of the human lot in the general scheme of things is made predominant. Satire, in this sense, partakes of both comedy and tragedy, but in itself it is neither. Hardy, of course, uses both these other terms extensively – for example, the sub-title of *HE* is 'A Comedy in Chapters' (although, significantly, in the retrospective 1895 Preface, he questions whether 'comedy' is the right word for it, and by the time of the 1912 'P[ost]S[cript]' suggests that it is 'more accurately, satire'); a short story is entitled 'A Tragedy of Two Ambitions'; a poem, 'A Trampwoman's Tragedy'. But so, too,

* * * * *

I have no intention of wanting to homogenize Hardy's fiction by suggesting that various inflexions of the 'poor-man-and-the-lady' theme everywhere pervade it. Nevertheless, it is difficult to ignore the fact – although many critics have successfully done so – that the plots, and much of the detail, pivot on cross-class relationships between male and female characters or, perhaps more exactly, relationships in which there is significant economic disparity. This is then overdetermined by the vast majority of the main characters, for one reason or another, being displaced from their 'true' class *locus*, being between classes, or being in the wrong place or community for their class type. In a passing phrase in *HE*, Hardy speaks of the 'metamorphic classes of society' (*HE*, 320) – thus exactly summing up the social group he focuses on: classes undergoing, as the dictionary puts it, 'complete transformation'. For most of his protagonists are indeed in transition, are in some way *déclassé* and *déraciné*, are undergoing some structural change in their social positioning. If tragedies (for which read satires) develop, it is not principally because 'Character is Destiny' (for more on this phrase, see below, p. 176) or because a cosmic Fate brings heroic individuals low, it is because the social order is rapidly changing and individuals on the move become involved with others also on the move, neither of whom have any familiar bearings or co-ordinates to navigate by. Such characters may be male or female, but, as an index of Hardy's acute societal intuition in the last half of the 19th century, many of the most 'metamorphic' and destabilizing characters are female: in some sense, he realized that shifts in the traditional class structure of society would be less seismic than upheavals in the patriarchal order.

It is also apparent – without, again, reductively and factitiously transmuting all Hardy's fiction into a 'socialistic' discourse – that the 'satires of circumstance' most of these 'metamorphic' characters find themselves in are the effects – not of Nemesis or of a personal *hamartia* – but of exploitation and dispossession as reflexes of economic (and related, legal) inequities and injustices. *The Mayor of Casterbridge* may, indeed, be 'A Story of a Man of Character', as the sub-title puts it, but Henchard's 'tragedy' is as much the result of social circumstances (poverty, injustice, capitalist economics, *change*) as it is of Fate or any 'fatal flaw' in his 'character'. Indeed, when reading the novel, and despite all the critical claims about it, I always find it difficult – if not impossible – to identify from the text precisely what that defect is supposed to be. Like George Eliot before him, Hardy may write: 'Character is Fate, said Novalis', and cast Henchard as a kind of latter-day Faust, but he makes it emphatically clear, too, that it is the 'trade-antagonism', the 'mortal commercial combat' with Farfrae which determines his 'destiny' (MC, 114–15). All human beings, in some sense, have 'Character', but it is the 'satires of circumstance' which constitute their 'Fate'. Perhaps the full title of Hardy's novel, in its very prosaic flatness – *The Life and Death of the Mayor of Casterbridge: A Story of a Man of Character* – is after all ironic, since Henchard is no more than an ordinary man (of susceptible character, like the rest of humankind) buffeted by the winds of change.

Equally, while the satire of Hardy's fiction may be articulated by 'absurd' instances of chance, coincidence and contingency, these are not its *cause*; rather, they are the telling representation of an ideological artifice which ruins human lives from behind a screen 'realistically' depicting the unjust and predatory current social order as natural, inevitable and sanctified. The event of Tess's happening on the text-writer on her way home after losing her virginity to Alec d'Urberville may well appear 'improbable', but the presence in Hardy's text of the '"Crushing! Killing!"' letters: 'THOU, SHALT, NOT, COMMIT –' (*Tess of the d'Urbervilles*, 96–7) graphically *represents* the 'satire' of her economic and sexual exploitation in a speciously Christian society. Such satirical characteristics, I want to argue, reach their culmination in *Jude* – a recognition of them at once helping to establish a way of reading a text which otherwise appears to demand the placing under erasure of its discordant elements, and to suggest why Hardy, in transgressing the boundaries of the fictional conventions available to him, gave up writing novels thereafter.

* * * * *

As implied earlier – and despite the fact that *Jude* has no 'lady' in it – it seems in several respects to close the circle begun 30 years before with the 'sweeping dramatic satire' and 'socialistic, not to say revolutionary' writing of *The Poor Man and the Lady*. Certainly, *Jude* was a *succès d'exécration* when it was first pub-

lished – fulfilling Meredith's warnings about Hardy's early novel receiving 'severe strictures', being 'attacked on all sides', and doing
the young novelist's career prospects no good at all. There is, therefore, a Hardyan irony in the fact that *Jude*'s reception was a factor
in his decision to give up writing fiction: 'the experience completely
curing me of further interest in novel-writing' (1912 'Postscript' to
the 1895 Preface). Much of the late-Victorian flak was occasioned
by the novel's 'morality', especially in relation to the marriage laws,
but it is a discomforting book to read in all sorts of ways, and my
feeling is that it was the novel's assault on so many cherished tenets
of humanism – and on its handmaiden, realism – which provoked
the antipathy it inspired.

For a start, *Jude* is a 'Wessex novel' only in a pointedly perverse
way, since it abjures rural Dorset, the heart of Wessex, by beginning in 'Marygreen' (Fawley, a village in Berkshire and Jude's
surname) and by locating most of its action in the larger towns and
cities in more peripheral parts of the region – Reading
('Aldbrickham'), Wantage ('Alfredston'), Newbury('Kennetbridge'),
Salisbury ('Melchester'), Oxford ('Christminster'), Bournemouth
('Sandbourne'), Basingstoke ('Stoke-Barehills'), Winchester
('Wintoncester'). Furthermore, even Marygreen is subject to mod-
ernization: 'many of the thatched and dormered dwelling houses
had been pulled down of late years, and many trees felled on the
green', while the ancient church has been 'taken down ... and a tall
new building of modern Gothic design ... erected on a new piece of
ground by a certain obliterator of historic records who had run
down from London and back in a day'.[10] Even more to the point,
the novel's opening line begins: 'The schoolmaster was leaving the
village' (28) – a telling indicator of its fundamental *donnée*, for
everything here is in transition and everyone in transit. In this connection, we should register the preposition in the title of each of
the parts: '*At* Marygreen', '*At* Christminster', '*At* Melchester', '*At*
Shaston', '*At* Aldbrickham and Elsewhere', '*At* Christminster
Again', with its clear implication of *sojourning* rather than
dwelling, of the peripatetic lives of the characters: on the move, un-
settled – *vagrant* in its primary sense. Indeed, one of the difficulties
of comprehending and remembering the novel is our uncertainty as
to where the characters and events are located at any given moment
– an instance, perhaps, of the novel's performative narrative
strategies.

In respect of the main characters, we are left in little doubt as to their 'metamorphic' nature. Phillotson seeks to better himself by becoming 'a university graduate ... then to be ordained' by moving to the 'headquarters' of such aspirations in Christminster (29). Arabella, the daughter of a pig-breeder, having married and deserted the bookish Jude, emigrates to and returns from Australia, marries into the licensed trade (the public house in Lambeth is 'situated in an excellent, densely populated, gin-drinking neighbourhood' [211]), works as a barmaid, and, at the end, is being courted by the (quack) physician, Vilbert. Sue is the daughter of an 'ecclesiastical worker in metal' (54) who passes the Queen's Scholarship examination to enter a teacher-training college at Melchester in order to become a schoolmistress (like Hardy's sister and cousin); she is a religious free-thinker, and is also, the Preface tells us, a 'delineation' of 'the woman who was coming into notice in her thousands every year – the woman of the feminist movement – the slight, pale "bachelor" girl – the intellectualized, emancipated bundle of nerves that modern conditions were producing, mainly in cities as yet': that is, the 'New Woman' of the later 19th century – itself an indicative label. Finally, there is Jude himself: an orphan originating from 'Mellstock' (Hardy's birthplace), of parents whose class position is for once unspecified, autodidact and stonemason, and who is described as 'a species of Dick Whittington' (97) but who signally fails to find the streets of Christminster paved with gold. The rejection letter he receives from Biblioll College contains the following (devastating) 'terribly sensible advice': 'you will have a much better chance of success in life by remaining in your own sphere' (136–7). But the point surely is that Jude – and all the other burgeoning members of the 'metamorphic classes' – *have* no sphere of their own to remain in: their condition is, precisely, to be in transit – therein lies the satire of their circumstance.

And satire, I want to claim, is what the novel most emphatically is. The Preface may speak of 'the *tragedy* of unfulfilled aims', of '*tragedies* in the forced adaptation of human instincts to rusty and irksome moulds', of the marriage laws as supplying 'the *tragic* machinery of the tale', and Sue Bridehead may sense 'a *tragic* doom' hanging over Jude and herself (302, my emphases), but the entire textuality of the novel seems designed to undercut any pretence of tragedy. Not in the eyes of most critics, however, who may find it excessive in its 'unbearable' anguish, its piling of suffering on suffering grotesque and implausible, but who still regard it as the acme of Hardy's tragic writing in fiction. Even R. P. Draper – in an essay whose title, 'Hardy's Comic Tragedy: *Jude the Obscure*', would seem to signal a trajectory along the lines of mine – cannot in the end follow his own logic and discard tragedy as the appropriate generic label for the novel. He notes that it is 'a moot point whether *Jude* ... should be designated as comedy or tragedy', and that its tendency to be simultaneously 'harrowing and ludicrous' renders it impossible 'to pin down the tragic effect ... to one version of tragedy'.[11] But despite making some telling points in this spirit, and adducing many of the same examples from the text as I do below, 'tragedy' the novel remains. Perhaps foregoing the category would be to admit the anti-humanist in Hardy.

At the levels of plot and character alone, however, 'tragic' seems an inappropriate word to describe the book. Jude may have 'noble' aspirations, but these are constantly degraded by a kind of Bakhtinian 'carnival': his recitation of the names of classical writers is punctuated by the pig-girls' '"Ha, ha, ha! Hoity-toity!"' (57); and his grandiloquent idealistic fantasy of the scholarly life – '"Yes, Christminster shall be my Alma Mater; and I'll be her beloved son, in whom she shall be well pleased"' – is shattered by the arrival of the pig's genitals (58). It is also striking that the 'theme' of Jude's high ambition is actually over by the end of Part Second, Chapter Six (i.e. a third of the way through the novel), the rest being largely taken up with his fraught sexual relationships with Sue and Arabella – hardly, then, a 'heroic' story of devoted struggle leading to tragic failure. Nor is Jude notably 'a Man of Character' – except in the sense I suggested Henchard was above; rather, he is a sympathetic man – more than a little *moyen sensuel* – whose susceptibility to women and drink is his direct undoing. What Jude as 'character' *does* do, however, is act as a device for focusing the injustice and inequity of the social institutions which govern his life. Equally, Sue is not built on a tragic scale, but rather, as many recent (feminist and other) critics have pointed out, represents a deadly 'delineation' – whether misogynistic or not – of the 'New Woman': a kind of feminized Angel Clare. But if we turn, finally, to the novel's third protagonist, Arabella, we find a more dynamic and instrumental figure in the satire. No one ever claims that Arabella is tragic, her tarty, dimpled animalism not being the stuff of which tragedy is made; but we should not fail to recognize that it is her continual reappearances throughout the text which centrally drive the plot along, and also, as we shall see, that it is she who concludes it. But if Arabella is Nemesis, 'tragedy' surely becomes 'farce' indeed. What Arabella may *mean* in the totality of this novel demands some serious consideration – which, by and large, criticism has failed to give her.

Almost invariably and right up to the present, most criticism, in its privileging of the 'tragic' Jude/Sue story, has given cursory attention to Arabella – characterizing her simply as an auxiliary 'contrast' in the novel's 'geometric' construction: most particularly, as Sue's binary 'other' in the struggle for possession of Everyman-Jude: 'flesh' (rather than 'spirit'), sensual, streetwise and coarse, what the novel itself refers to as 'a complete and substantial female animal – no more, no less' (59). One very recent rearticulation of this is Timothy Hands's (unregenerate) comment that, in *Jude*, 'Hardy tends to visualise the female sex as offering a choice between brain and the female counterpart of brawn.'[12]

Feminist criticism has, of course, refined things; but it is still surprising that in Margaret Higonnet's well-regarded 1993 collection, *The Sense of Sex: Feminist Perspectives on Hardy*, there are only the briefest passing references to Arabella in the (somewhat myopic) rush to re-read the 'New Woman', Sue. Equally, Marjorie Garson, in her poststructuralist-feminist study, *Hardy's Fables of Integrity: Woman, Body, Text*, still sees Arabella as clearly 'a castrating woman' – 'the last in a long line of wicked temptresses'. However, in this – and as in the case of Sue, too – she sees Hardy 'scapegoating' Arabella for Jude's failure to realize what he 'wants' (desires/lacks) in himself, a textual strategy culminating in her 'disconcerting' and 'implausible' final speech as 'choric commentator', which, Garson says, reaffirms both her and Sue's continuing 'desire' for Jude, and is thus 'borrowed back by Hardy to confirm his male protagonist' at the very end of the novel.[13] As far as I am aware, only Rosemarie Morgan, in *Women and Sexuality in the Novels of Thomas Hardy*, offers an extended *positive* reading of Arabella, but even this is in a chapter entirely focused on Sue, in which Arabella is seen as Hardy's textual auxiliary in the process of 'reading' Sue aright. Nevertheless – despite her being no more than 'Sue's interpreter' and only 'peripheral' to the 'emotional temperature at such a mercurial high' which the novel creates round Jude and Sue – Morgan celebrates the way 'her sexual vitality sharpens, in Hardy's view, her perceptual acuity, her discerning judgment, and her sharp intuition'. As the textual 'reader' of Sue, Arabella is 'consistently reliable', 'wise' and 'truthful', and she represents for Hardy 'the vantage point of woman-perceiving-woman unfettered by sexual ideologies and preconceptions'. Crucially, from within the text, Arabella 'corrects' Jude's own (mis)reading of Sue.[14] While much of this is convincing, by still subordinating her to Sue, Morgan does not need to explain Arabella's discomforting *obtrusiveness* in the novel – at once in presence and in presentation; and this certainly needs to be explained. Here is an example of both in an exchange between Phillotson and Arabella – a passage significantly infrequently quoted – which I would ask the reader also to bear in mind in relation to my subsequent points:

> 'Still – she wanted to go,' he said.
> 'Yes. But you shouldn't have let her. That's the only way with these fanciful women that chaw high – innocent or guilty. She'd have come round in time. We all do! Custom does it! it's all the same in the end! However, I think she's fond of her man still – whatever he med be of her. You were too quick about her. *I* shouldn't have let her go! I should have kept her chained on – her spirit for kicking would have been broke soon enough! There's nothing like bondage and a stone-deaf taskmaster for taming us women. Besides, you've got the laws on your side. Moses knew. Don't you call to mind what he says?'
> 'Not for the moment, ma'am, I regret to say.'
> 'Call yourself a schoolmaster! I used to think o't when they read it in church, and I was carrying on a bit. "Then shall the man be guiltless; but the woman shall bear her iniquity." Damn rough on us women; but we must grin and put up with it! – Haw haw! – Well; she's got her deserts now.'
> 'Yes,' said Phillotson, with biting sadness. 'Cruelty is the law pervading all nature and society; and we can't get out of it if we would!'
> 'Well – don't you forget to try it next time, old man.'
> 'I cannot answer you, madam. I have never known much of womankind.' (338)

This turns out to be a very difficult passage to make sense of: what and whose views does it seem to endorse? Initially, Arabella – 'in character' – appears to be voicing the kind of reactionary 'common-sense' notions we might associate with a woman of her class and type. But as we move down the first paragraph, we have a sneaking suspicion that she is, in fact, voicing stereotypical *male* views about how to treat women, and that she is parodying or caricaturing them. By the time we reach: '"There's nothing like bondage and a stone-deaf taskmaster for taming us women"', the suspicion is becoming a certainty, one confirmed immediately by Arabella's deadly assertion: '"Besides, you've got the laws on your side"' and her unexpectedly knowing reference to Moses. The fact that she is, in effect, mocking the pitiful Phillotson ('"Call yourself a schoolmaster!"'), and indeed the kind of male discourse she is parroting, is reinforced by the explicitly sexist injustice of the quotation from Moses, accompanied by her wonderfully sardonic comment – '"Damn rough on us women; but we must grin and put up with it."' But the crux of this passage is surely Arabella's '"Haw haw!"' which follows it. It is so obtrusive textually that one can see why critics have found failures of realist decorum in this last 'great' novel of Hardy's. But its effect, in fact, is simultaneously to prick the absurd pomposity and pernicious assumptions of patriarchal discourse and, in the Brechtian sense, to 'alienate' the reader from the text in order that they may indeed perceive the speciousness of such discourse. The fact that 'haw haw' sounds like 'whore whore' does nothing to diminish the disruptive force of the phrase. In its aftermath, Phillotson, the representative intellectual and abstract male (remember Angel Clare in *Tess*), becomes even more open to ridicule with his pathetically sonorous axiom about 'Cruelty'; with Arabella's devastatingly sarcastic '"don't you forget it next time, old man"' – where 'old man' cancels out 'next time'; and with his final admission of the defensive ignorance – if not sexual fear – which lies behind the kind of masculinist ideology the passage has initially appeared to endorse: '"I cannot answer you, madam. I have never known much of womankind"' (note the protective abstraction of the generic word 'womankind').

What is especially striking about this passage for my argument here, however, is the way in which Hardy uses *Arabella* – the 'female animal' – at once to caricature patriarchy and to distance the reader from the naturalized 'fiction' of male superiority and power. It makes one wonder whether we should treat Arabella and her utterances elsewhere in the novel with rather more seriousness and respect than we normally do. If she speaks for Hardy, in some sense, here – or at least articulates a subversive counter-discourse to the dominant socio-sexual ones – then does she do the same on other occasions? Does she, indeed, call into question and challenge the novel's own apparent privileging of its dominant 'tragic' story? In this context, we should not miss the fact that Sue is characterized here as one of '"these fanciful women that chaw high"' ('"haw haw"') and that '"she's got her deserts now"'. Does Arabella speak for Hardy here, too; and and if she is 'in character' in this scene, how do we now read her 'character' in the novel as a whole? I shall return to Arabella as the novel's internal and self-deconstructing satiric voice when I consider its final scene in a moment. But first let me indicate that the satire of *Jude* is as much in the fictional discourses themselves as in its characters or themes.

* * * * *

I would not be the first to point to the novel's epigraph as an instruction on how to read what follows. 'The letter killeth' (from 2 Corinthians 3:6) is also quoted in the text by Jude (407), where it points to the destructiveness of abiding by the 'letter' of social law rather than obeying emotional 'spirit'. But the phrase's very 'literariness' (to do with 'letters') suggests another level of reading – concerned with textuality itself. It may imply that 'the letter' of a purported, but necessarily always factitious, 'literal truth' 'killeth' by its (ideological) falsification and misrepresentation; but the 'spirit' of a text – which flouts, subverts and challenges 'lit/letteral' realism – perhaps 'giveth life'. *Jude*, let us remember, is described in the 1895 Preface as giving 'shape and coherence to a series of seemings, or personal impressions, the question of their consistency or their discordance, of their permanence or their transitoriness, being regarded as not of the first moment'. I would argue that the novel's performative anti-realism is centrally directed at the 'killing' fictions fostered by a Christian class society, a central one of which is the misrepresentation that there can be 'literal truth' – a misrepresentation mirrored by realism in art. Hardy stopped writing fiction after *Jude*: perhaps he had taken the genre to the point of auto-deconstruction.

There is plenty of evidence to suggest the degree of Hardy's self-consciousness about what he was up to in *Jude*. The fact that the novel's first title was 'The Simpletons'[15] gives us a clue as to his original conception of the main characters' 'tragic' story, as does a reference to Jude himself, after the book version had been published, in a letter to Edmund Gosse (significantly reprinted in *The Life*), as 'my poor puppet'[16] – where Hardy surely has in mind

Thackeray's Preface to *Vanity Fair*. Equally, in a second letter to Gosse, his invocation of Fielding as the model for 'the "coarse" scenes with Arabella, the battle in the schoolroom, etc.', rather than Zola as the critics had suggested,[17] again points to a comic/satiric modal conception (the specific reference to Arabella is telling here, I think). But a few examples of the novel's own self-advertising fictionality will make the point most effectively.

In respect of the plot – a plot, we learn from the letters to Gosse again, 'almost geometrically constructed' for a novel 'all contrasts' in its 'original conception'[18] – there is the parallel absurdity of the way the main characters remarry each other; the fortuitous 'chance' encounters and re-encounters on which the movement of the novel depends (for example, Arabella's spotting, and then stalking, of Jude and Sue at the Stoke-Barehills agricultural show, Part Fifth, Chapter Five); the grotesque melodrama of Little Father Time and the hanged children – '"Done because we are too menny"' (356). There are the typographical devices in the text: the pointing hand with the inscription 'THITHER J.F.' (94); the Greek 'capital *letters*' (my emphasis) spelling 'The New Testament' – 'like the unclosed eyes of a dead man' (68 – the 'letter killeth' indeed). There are the many *letters* and notes that pass between characters, again reproduced in the text (eg. in Part Fourth, Chapter Three), which often have deadly import for their recipients; there are the endless literary references scattered throughout, but most obtrusively so on Jude's first night in Christminster when 'there were poets abroad, of early date and late' (99). Quotations from these 'spectres' fill much of the rest of the chapter – spectres to whom, in a revealing passage, 'Jude found himself speaking out loud, holding conversations with them as it were, *like an actor in a melodrama* who apostrophizes the audience on the other side of the footlights; till he suddenly ceased with a start at his *absurdity*.' *Whose* 'melodrama', we may ask, is 'apostrophizing the audience', *whose* self-consciousness of 'absurdity' is brought to our attention? It is not without point, either, that the scene is deflated a few lines later by another 'voice [which] reached him out of the shade', that of a policeman – 'a *real and local* voice' (100, my emphases).

Stringing all these obtrusive textual devices together is the insistently ironic, or comically bathetic, narrative voice: the Christminster colleges display 'the rottenness of these historical documents' (102); 'Her Majesty's school-inspector', on a 'surprise visit' to Phillotson's school, is described as 'my gentleman, the king of terrors – to pupil-teachers' (128); a customer at Arabella's bar is 'a chappie with no chin, and a moustache like a lady's eyebrow' (201); Little Father Time is 'Age masquerading as Juvenility, and doing it so badly that his real self showed through crevices' (295); and there is the absurd fracas in Phillotson's schoolroom, which the text itself calls 'a *farcical* yet melancholy event' (my emphasis – one of the 'coarse' scenes picked on by his critics which Hardy saw as an example of 'Fieldingism';[19] see above, p. 184). Here, in what is inescapably self-conscious comic writing, 'a churchwarden was dealt such a topper with the map of Palestine that his head went right through Samaria', and the rector received a bleeding nose 'owing to the zeal of an emancipated chimney-sweep, who took the side of Phillotson's party' (269).

However, it is in the ending of the novel that the satire – 'tragedy as farce' – is most marked:[20] in the arch tones of the narrative voice, in the ironic presentation of the events, and in the undisguised artificiality of the scene's enactment. And it is not without point for my argument here about Hardy's *strategic* decision to close the novel in this mode that in a further letter to Edmund Gosse, again reprinted in *The Life*, he commented: 'in writing Jude my mind was fixed on the ending'.[21] The final chapter opens with an overt narrative intrusion: 'The last pages to which the chronicler of these lives would ask the reader's attention'; Jude, the 'tragic hero', lies dying; Arabella is 'at the looking-glass curling her hair, which operation she performed by *heating an umbrella-stay in the flame of a candle*' (where my emphasis points up the redundant deflationary detail), and is waiting to go out and join a 'festivity' in Christminster that day (422). Leaving Jude sleeping, she departs; Jude wakens, whispers a series of quotations from the Book of Job – four times punctuated typographically by '("Hurrah!")' wafting in on the breeze from the river – and dies. Arabella, invited by some of his workmates to join the festivities, calls in to check on him, discovers he is dead, exclaims, 'in a provoked tone', '"To think he should die just now! Why did he die just now!"', goes out again and reassures the workmen: '"O yes – sleeping quite sound. He won't wake yet"' (425). In the mêlée on the river-bank that follows, while observing 'the gorgeous nosegays of feminine beauty' and 'collegians of all sorts ... watching keenly for "our" boat', the physician Vilbert slips his arm round her waist, whereupon 'an arch expression overspread

Arabella's face' (425–6). Back home, she has Jude's body laid out; and with this done, the narrative comments: 'through the partly opened window the joyous throb of a waltz entered from the ball-room at Cardinal [college]' (427).

The final ending occurs two days later, just before Jude's funeral, and again the scene is framed by sounds coming in through the window – this time from '"the doctors of the *Theatre*, conferring Honorary degrees on the Duke of Hamptonshire and a lot more il-lustrious gents of that sort"' (427, my emphasis). Jude the obscure lies in his coffin; Mrs Edlin and Arabella close the novel; and it is Arabella's voice which has the last word:

> 'Did he forgive her?'
> 'Not as I know.'
> 'Well – poor little thing, 'tis to be believed she's found forgiveness somewhere! She said she had found peace!'
> 'She may swear that on her knees to the holy cross upon her necklace till she's hoarse, but it won't be true!' said Arabella. 'She's never found peace since she left his arms, and never will again till she's as he is now!' (428)

Whether Arabella's 'sudden oracular status' means, as Marjorie Garson contends, that the male discourse of the novel, in finally 'confirming' its hero, requires that Sue and Arabella 'must agree in their desire for [Jude]',[22] or whether it represents, as Rosemarie Morgan would have it, Arabella's 'insight' that Sue is in fact 'a flesh and blood creature with womanly needs and a deeply passionate heart' struggling to free herself from the 'sweet saintly' asceticism that represses her true self,[23] I cannot judge. But however one inter-prets this final utterance – as idealizing Sue and Jude's relationship, say, or merely as Arabella's flatly mundane wisdom – much depends on whether one sees that 'since' in the final sentence as causal (*because* she left him) or temporal (*after* leaving him). Either way, it remains Arabella who ends the novel by calling in question the veracity of the discourse which mediates the tragic protagonists' relationship: 'but it won't be true!'

How are we to read such a concluding chapter? Certainly not, I would suggest, as one of involuntary poor taste; and yet any tragic dignity clinging to Jude is ruthlessly stripped away by the surround-ing business of the scene. In effect, then, the focus is not on Jude as tragic hero, but on the 'satire' of Oxford – of the meretricious

'Theatre' that Christminster represents – and of a working-man's aspiration to become a member of it. But why is the venal Arabella at once an element of 'Carnival' in this final scene *and* its dominant voice? My answer will implicate in the satire Jude and Sue themselves, Christminster, and the reader. Much earlier in the novel, after Jude's rejection by Biblioll College, the narrative, on its hero's behalf, and in a tone unusually sympathetic and unironic, reflects on the two worlds of Christminster:

> He began to see that the town life was a book of humanity infinitely more palpitating, varied, and compendious than the gown life. These struggling men and women before him were *the reality* of Christminster, though they knew little of Christ or Minister. That was one of *the humours of things*. The floating population of students and teachers ... were not Christminster in a local sense at all...
> ... in pursuit of this idea, he went on till he came to a public hall, where a promenade concert was in progress. Jude entered, and found the room full of shop youths and girls, soldiers, apprentices, boys of eleven smoking cigarettes, and light women of the more respectable and amateur class. He had tapped *the real Christminster life*. (137–8, my emphases)

The repetition of the notion that 'reality' and the 'real ... life' of Christminster lie amongst ordinary working people is a significant one (we may recall, too, the 'real and local' voice of the policeman in the spectral poets scene glanced at earlier); and perhaps it is this – in his last novel, as in his first – which Hardy wishes to affirm. Hence, whilst Jude and Sue, in their idealism, modernism and abstraction, are implicated in the absurd and destructive 'Theatre' of a 'gown' Christminster built on bigotry, class privilege and injustice, Arabella is not: she must instead be aligned with the 'light women of the more respectable and amateur class' who comprise the 'real ... life' of 'town' Christminster. That is another 'one of the humours of things'. I do not wish to imply that Hardy makes a sentimental 'salt-of-the-earth' affirmation in Arabella; rather, that this fleshy woman of 'rank passions' (398) and a survivor's cunning and vitality – this 'complete and substantial female animal – no more, no less' – is the ultimate satire on the part of the novel: both *within* it, as the carnivalizing degrader of Jude's idealism and Sue's asceticism, and *from* within it – as a 'heroine' who mocks the effete intellectual self-identification of readers obsessed by the humanist-realist 'tragedy' of Jude's and Sue's story. Arabella 'degrades' us, too.

Postscript: The Film of *Jude*

Whenever I am faced with a film adaptation of a novel I know well, I play an impossible game which involves trying to imagine what someone would make of the film who knows nothing at all of the novel – nor, for good measure, of the author either. So: what would 'someone' have been thinking as they left the cinema after watching Michael Winterbottom's 1996 version of *Jude the Obscure* – the film *Jude*, starring Christopher Ecclestone, Kate Winslet and Rachel Griffiths?

They might have wondered initially – given the ambiguously dated facial appearance and costumes of the characters – in what period the film was set, and then have settled for some time in late-Victorian/Edwardian England. But *where* exactly in England the action was taking place would have produced a more difficult and longer-lasting (perhaps never resolved) puzzlement. The printed section-headers displayed on the screen – 'AT MARYGREEN', 'AT CHRISTMINSTER', 'AT ALDBRICKHAM AND ELSEWHERE', etc. – would not have given any clues to someone who had never seen Hardy's map of 'Wessex'. The rural settings could have been anywhere (or from any recent 'period' dramatization); and while 'Christminster' might have been identified as Oxford – or Cambridge? – the early hazy, distant view that Phillotson and Jude have of it was surely a mock-up from a 19th-century landscape of any medium-sized town/city with some 'gleaming spires'. Furthermore, Jude's accent was sufficiently 'Geordie' – especially if you had faint memories of Ecclestone in *Our Friends from the North* – to scotch any notion that he might have been a country-man from the south-west; Sue's was indelibly Home-Counties – especially if you had faint memories of Winslet in *Sense and Sensibility*; and Arabella's teasingly blended an English country girl's with that of an Irish colleen. What *would* have been clear – this time aided by the section-headers – was that, wherever they were supposed to be, the main characters moved about a lot: that

---

This 'Postscript' was written specially for the present volume. It has not yet appeared elsewhere.

they were in perpetual motion – on foot, in horse-drawn carts and cabs, and especially in railway carriages.

Quite what *class* they come from, however, would have posed more of a problem. Jude, fairly evidently, is of lower-class rural origins, but has (somehow) learnt a trade as a stonemason and has aspirations to 'book learning' and a place at Christminster; Sue, despite claiming that she is still a country girl at heart, seems to be from the urban middle class – educated (she knows Latin), free-thinking and nicely groomed; Arabella starts out as the rural hoyden, daughter of a pig-farmer, goes to Australia, returns to England, becomes a barmaid of easy virtue, and is then left a widow (by the death of her Australian husband), apparently comfortably off and smartly respectable. Even more disconcerting, though, is the impression the film gives that, even when Jude, Sue and the kids are forced to keep moving from job to job and lodging to lodging, they are never in real poverty: Jude always finds work, their clothes, and the furniture and bed-linen in their digs, are clean and of good quality, and money is not in short supply – indeed, immediately before the discovery of the dead children, Jude and Sue are seen skipping through Christminster's shopping centre excitedly anticipating, on the strength of Jude's new job, that they will be able 'buy anything they want'.

But imagine what my 'someone' would be faced with when they came to think: 'what was that all about, then?' They might have been able to say that it was a period drama – for once about people not from the upper classes – in which a working-man's aspirations of becoming highly educated are thwarted at every turn. But would they have been able to identify *what by*? There were some hints of class prejudice keeping Jude down, but surely his susceptibility, and unwise early marriage, to the trickily lubricious Arabella, followed by his obsessive infatuation with the pert but unyielding Sue, were the main cause of his failure to achieve his aim? Apropos of this, were we supposed to see Jude as some kind of 'working-class hero' (but on what substantive evidence in the film?), or as a weak man at the mercy of unreliable women (but then what kind of 'hero' is he?). Is Sue the sympathetic 'modern girl' who isn't quite up to the role of 'New Woman', or is she a silly prude who can't make up her mind? Is Arabella a sexy 'female animal' (the novel calls her that) who simply *wants* Jude – an unprincipled temptress who picks him up and puts him down as the mood takes her – or is she the unhappy penitent who still cares for her lost Jude, as the later parts of the film seem to present her? What are we to make of the long-suffering Phillotson who 'wins' Sue, then relinquishes her to Jude, and later (we are led assume) takes her back again? When first Sue, and then more emphatically Jude, keep reiterating that in living in bigamous sin they are doing 'no wrong', are we to take it that the film is somehow about the imprisoning institution of marriage and the impossibility of divorce for ordinary folks in the late 19th century? But the film never once mentions divorce, and the sinful business of still being married to others only seems to impact on the minds and behaviour of the protagonists when it is peremptory: i.e. it is not the social institutions which persecute them, but their own irregularly functioning consciences.

Furthermore, what are we to make of the second little 'Jude', sent back from Australia, who shockingly kills his siblings and hangs himself – 'because we are too menny'? Is it credible in the context of the film so far? Shouldn't there at least have been an inquest which established why he came to do it? Why does *the film* think he does it? Is it retribution for Jude and Sue's sins (as Sue sees it), or an 'accident' (as Jude calls it)? What does little Jude *mean* in the scheme of things – both in that of the world the film represents, and that of the film itself? Is he some sort of 'modern boy' for whom self-destruction is the only future, or no more than a 'shock-ing' filmic device to provide a climactic resolution for the plot? 'Someone' might finally want to know in this context whether the ending – as endings so often do – reverberates back through the film and reveals what it has been 'about' after all? Well, Arabella has faded out, having told Jude in her final words that 'it wasn't his fault'; Sue, we believe, is on her way back to Phillotson, still loving Jude but broken in spirit; and Jude is left standing in the church-yard as the screen freezes on his lonely figure. Not much to go on there in terms of explaining retrospectively what the *point* of the whole depressing affair has been. And so 'someone' asks – as any good realist viewer would, but as we sophisticates know they are not supposed to do: what happens to them all after the film ends? Does Sue live in non-sexual cohabitation with the worthy Phillotson; does Jude 'keep trying' (the film emphasizes this virtue) to win back his beloved Sue; or do he and Arabella get back to-gether and live a sexually energetic but otherwise empty marriage of convenience? Or does Jude finally get admitted to Biblioll College and later become its Master, throwing open its gates to deserving poor men; does he become an anarchist, and blow up the college instead; or does he emigrate to Australia in his turn? There is, of course, no way of knowing.

In some respects, then, the film might seem rather point*less*. Beautifully filmed and acted it certainly is; it is clearly a period drama about some unstable and peripatetic characters who are nevertheless recognizably 'modern' in their attitudes, psychology and problems; and it is compulsively watchable throughout. But it is also a film, perhaps quite properly, with no discernible coherent 'theme', 'message', or social or philosophical agenda. Its 'point', in other words, seems to lie only in the experiencing of it as a well-made film. But it is at this juncture that the central problematic reveals itself in my trivial pursuit of imagining 'someone' seeing the film who does not know the book. Because the film *is* a version of a written text, and its 'point' must lie – not in how well or badly it reproduces for the cognoscenti the novel's 'themes' or philosophical standpoint, and so establishes its own absent point by referring us to the book's – but precisely in the fact that it *is* a version of the novel *Jude the Obscure*. If we are not in a position to read the intertextual relations between the two, the film may well, indeed, seem 'point'-less; but if we *are* in a position to do so, we may establish the film's point by seeing *what it has had to do to the novel in order to make itself the film it is*. That this work of strategic reproduction and refashioning reveals its affinity with other critical and cultural, social and ideological, processes of our time may not be unexpected.

＊＊＊＊＊

As my disingenuously 'naive' account of the film nevertheless indicates, at first sight *Jude* is, in many respects, 'faithful' to the novel it is based on. Or, to put it more honestly, it seems to correspond with aspects of the novel I emphasize in my reading of it in Chapter 7 above. The film presents a group of characters from the 'metamorphic classes' whose very social instability seems inevitably to court disaster for them; it presents them as continually in transit; and, ironically, it echoes the novel closely in puzzling the audience/reader as to what its own stance to its characters might be; as to what its philosophical standpoint, if any, may be (Hardy always denied his writings were informed by any coherent system of thought); and as to what it is fundamentally 'about'. Many of the film's scenes accurately replicate those in the novel; the plot by and large follows Hardy's – even to the point of making it difficult for us to be certain where the characters are at any given moment; and many of the characters' utterances are more or less verbatim quotations from the book. Having said this, and as might reasonably be expected in any film adaptation of a sizeable novel, there is also quite a lot changed or missing. However, it is not so much in the *fact* of the absences that my main point will subsequently lie, but rather in the *nature* of the pieces left out, for it is there that we can most clearly discern the cultural refashioning of the novel to make it into an acceptable modern film.

First, I may get out of the way the carping – perhaps unfair – cavils that criticism of film adaptations invariably goes in for. We may pick up on details like the film's softening of the sexual force of Jude's first encounter with Arabella by not making the bit of the pig thrown at him more clearly its pizzle; the omission from the Master of Biblioll College's rejection letter to Jude of the sentence saying: 'you will have a much better chance of success in life by remaining in your own *sphere*' (my emphasis), rather than merely saying 'in your kind of work' as the film has it; the changing of 'Little Father Time's' name to Jude or 'Juey'; making the latter, for no perceptible reason, anachronistically watch Sue in childbirth; the unfounded introduction of a socialist orator into an early scene in Christminster, given that working-class politics play no other part in the film. Perhaps more importantly in this context, there is the continual failure to represent the novel's deadly satire on the privilege, prejudice, 'gloom, bigotry, and decay' of 'gown' Christminster – for example, by making it clear that the tiny, bare room in which Little Father Time kills the children and himself is in 'an old intramural cottage' in the brooding shadow of 'Sarcophagus College' (note how Hardy names it). Equally, there is the sympathetic landlady who lets them the same room and then has to ask them to leave, as indeed there is the overly apologetic man who sacks Jude from carving the plaques in the church (in the novel he is carving the Ten Commandments). There is a strong sense, then, that the film at all points *softens* the harshness and injustice of the world of *Jude the Obscure* – let alone the real conditions of the urban poor in the late 19th century.

Perhaps more crucially, there is the question of why Arabella's character is altered in the way that it is: from the novel's rough, cunning, lewd woman of 'rank passions', who nevertheless knows what she needs to survive and how to get it, to the film's sexy but sweet country girl who makes love to Jude with affectionate abandon, carries on curing their pig while he walks away in distaste, 'comforts' him later when he is drunk and miserable, and then turns into a contrite and respectable widow who is nice both to 'Little Father Time' and to Jude in his extremity. Domesticating Arabella is no mean achievement, and I shall return to the reason for it in a moment. In terms of characterization, however, the casting of Kate Winslet as Sue seems to me to be the film's biggest mistake – or, alternatively, its most devious strategy in reprocessing the novel. Physiognomically, Kate Winslet has an inescapably modern face, and all her pert, flirty, self-confident, healthy-young-woman-of-the-1990s mannerisms and expressions seem entirely inappropriate for the intellectually precocious and sexually repressed 'slight, pale ... bundle of nerves' the novel represents Sue Bridehead as being. As a result of the extrovert charm of the actress, then, the disjunction in the film between the carefree and self-confident young woman marching up and down in the pub smoking her cigarette in front of Jude's workmates, and the supposedly uptight virginal girl who marries Phillotson to spite Jude and who abjures sexual relations with either of them until she finally gets jealous that Arabella will give Jude what he wants, is inescapable and strains credibility to breaking-point. *That* young woman, you think, simply could not be the same person as *this* young woman. Her return to the Church, therefore, after the loss of her children – especially with a face, though sad, that is as smooth, bonny and placid as that of the untroubled and cossetted commuter-belt maiden she seems to be – is equally unconvincing. Whether this is no more than the result of miscasting a contemporary cult actress in an unsuitable role, or whether it is a strategic attempt to forge an identification between the problems of a late-19th-century 'New Woman' and those of the (equivocally) emancipated young women of the 1990s, it once again gives the film a nicer and gentler patina than the novel would suggest.

But it is in what the film omits that the nub of my point here lies – as it does also in respect of the preceding chapter on Arabella and the 'satirical discourse' in *Jude the Obscure*. Indeed, in a perverse way the film seems to confirm my argument there. Let me summon up again 'someone', only this time someone who, turned on by the film, has completed a reading of the novel for the first time: 'Bloody hell!', she says, 'Jude dies at the end!' And so indeed is the case – in the novel, but not in the film. It is a fairly significant revision, and, and when I saw it, I simply did not believe the film had ended when it had. What we also miss, immediately preceding this, is Jude's last futile visit to Sue at Phillotson's in pouring rain, which is the immediate cause of the illness which results in his death. Now, we can hypothesize that the scriptwriter and director for some reason did not want the film to end with Jude dead: audience's sensibilities; more in tune with the gentling of the novel I have suggested above; allowing for the possibility that if Jude 'keeps trying' and Phillotson ups and dies one day, there may be the happy ending to the love-story that the film itself can't offer us (but why not, one wonders, having got thus far?). But none of this really washes as an explanation for changing the ending so drastically. What is also missing from the film, however, is the fact that after Sue returns to Phillotson, Arabella effectively tricks Jude into 're-marrying' her in scenes of considerable squalor, drunkenness and chicanery. Jude, in other words, is deeply degraded by the anything-but-respectable Arabella before he makes his final journey to see Sue. Not quite the stuff of which period drama is made, one might think, nor of charismatic cult heroes. Further, on the last page of the novel's penultimate chapter, with Jude ill upstairs, Arabella makes up to the quack physician, Vilbert – a character and scene also omitted from the film. Finally, if we remember that the last chapter of the novel is the grotesquely ironic scene in which Jude dies – while Arabella is out flirting with Vilbert – with the raucous sounds of 'gown' Christminster floating in through the window, and that it is Arabella who has the final words of the novel two days later just before Jude's funeral (see my account of this in Chapter 7), we again wonder what possessed the film-makers to end their film as they did. But we also have a clue here. There is surely no way that a modern director making the kind of 'classic drama' film he *is* making – in association with the BBC – could end his adaptation with a scene in such seemingly absurd bad taste as that which closes *Jude the Obscure*. It would make a mockery of everything that has gone before – of the intense love-story, of its contemporary 'relevance', of the tragedy of these young lives, but most particularly of the 'authentic' realism which the film has so lovingly strived for in acting and setting throughout. It is not without point, either, that other scenes missing from the film – including the farcical battle in Phillotson's schoolroom and Arabella's mocking conversation with him analysed in Chapter 7 – are those which degrade the 'decorum' of tragic realism.

I had no expectations of what the film would be like, only a keen interest in how it would present Arabella, and a fairly predictable sense that it would not promote the satire that I think the novel represents in both content and form. But I was amazed, first, by the neutralizing of Arabella as a fiercely 'carnivalising' presence in the novel – I had anticipated a slightly comic, blowsy trollop as one way of blunting her 'degrading' effect on the 'love-story', but to make her nice and respectable took my breath away; and, second, the changed ending surpassed my wildest dreams. Here, surely, was proof of my thesis that Hardy's anti-humanist, anti-realist satirical fiction can only be granted the status of 'classic' tragic realism precisely when all those elements of his text which make such a reading untenable are stripped out or suppressed. Just as so many literary critics have done in the past to his written fiction, the film *Jude* recasts the novel in drastic fashion in order to be able to make an acceptable film of it at all. And if that means letting the hero live rather than die – in order to avoid a scene the film simply could not handle – then so be it. Ruling cultural ideologies never could abide works of art which reveal – in displaying the factitiousness of their own modes of (mis)representation – that the 'literal truths' claimed by and for those ideologies are no more than self-interested fictions.

Notes

INTRODUCTION

1. See Hardy, Florence Emily (1975), *The Life of Thomas Hardy 1840–1928* (hereafter referred to as *The Life*), pp. 104, 100, 179, 182–3, 286, 291, *passim*.

2. This is Henry James's patronizing phrase.

3. In the 'Acknowledgements' note to Widdowson (1996b).

4. The phrase was commonly deployed in left-wing critical circles in the 1970s and 1980s.

5. See Williams (1970, 1979), Williams and Williams (1980), Goode (1976, 1979), Eagleton (1976, 1981), Jacobus (1975, 1976, 1979), Showalter (1979), Stubbs (1979) and Boumelha (1982).

6. *HE*, p. 320.

7. This is a synoptic version of J. Hillis Miller's view of Hardy the Poet, in Miller (1985), Chapter 6. See also Chapter 6 below for a slightly fuller account of it.

8. Dale Kramer (ed.), Cambridge: Cambridge University Press, forthcoming.

CHAPTER 1: THOMAS HARDY: A PARTIAL PORTRAIT

1. Tim Armstrong makes a similar point in the introduction to Armstrong (ed.) (1993), p. 42.

2. See Gittings (1975, 1978), Millgate (1982), also Martin Seymour-Smith, *Hardy*, London: Bloomsbury, 1994 and James Gibson, *Thomas Hardy: A Literary Life*, Basingstoke: Macmillan, 1996.

3. See also the entry for this volume in the References. I develop this point at greater length in Widdowson (1989), p. 139; the whole of Chapter 4, there, comprises a detailed analysis of *The Life*.

4. A phrase he uses in the 'Apology' which prefaces *LLE*.

5. Hardy, Florence Emily (1975) – hereafter referred to as *The Life* – p. 78. All further references to this work appear as bracketed numbers in the text.

6. Cf. Gittings (1978), p. 100.

7. 17 Sept. and 11 Oct. 1899. Quoted in Millgate (1982), p. 401.

8. Letter to Mrs Henniker, 24 Dec. 1900. Quoted in *ibid.*, p. 403.

9. This poem, together with 'In Time of "The Breaking of Nations"' and 'A Call to National Service' (all in *MV*), were published with notes indicating that they were not in copyright in order to increase their circulation and contribute to the war-effort (cf. Hynes (ed.) (1984a), p. 503).

10. To Sydney Cockerell. Quoted in Hynes (ed.) (1984a), p. 506.

11. Quoted in *ibid*, p. 504.

12. Hardy read, made notes on, and copied extracts from *The Waste Land* into his commonplace book (cf. Johnson (1991), p. 7). For Hardy and *Hugh Selwyn Mauberley*, cf. Millgate (1982), p. 534. Pound recognized his debt to, and admiration for, Hardy on a number of occasions.

13. Cf. *The Life*, p. 98.

14. In her essay, 'The Novels of Thomas Hardy', *The Common Reader*, Second Series, London: The Hogarth Press (1932), 1959, p. 248.

15. Cf. *The Life*, p. 40.

16. Lawrence (1914), pp. 398–516.

17. Cf. *The Life*, p. 430.

18. Williams and Williams (1980), p. 32.

19. Cf. *The Life*, pp. 33–4, 208.

20. Cf. Widdowson (1989), Chapter 4 (especially p. 132), where I have argued this at greater length.

21. *The Life*, p. 55.

22. *The Life*, p. 236.

23. *The Life*, p. 25.

24. Cf. Gittings (1975), Chapter 9.

25. For a discussion – and rebuttal – of this story, cf. *ibid*, 'Appendix: Hardy and Tryphena Sparks', pp. 313–23.

26. In *The Life*, pp. 67–73, Hardy reproduces several pages of Emma's account of this in *Some Reflections*, ed. Evelyn Hardy and Robert Gittings, Oxford: OUP (1961), 1979, pp. 16, 28–37, as representing his own view of it, too.

27. In *Beloved*, New York: Plume Books (1987), 1988, pp. 36, 99, 191.

28. Quoted in Creighton (ed.) (1974), p. 335.

29. *The Life*, p. 50.

30. Gissing's bitter novel of that title is set in the early 1880s.

31. Zeitlow (1974), p. 42, calls it 'a myth of retrospective self-justification'.

32. Armstrong (ed.) (1993), p. 1, cites a further view (Michael Mason, 'The Burning of *Jude the Obscure*', *Notes and Queries*, 233 (1988), 332–4) that Hardy may have found public acclaim for the 'radical' late novels as upsetting as the opprobrium, because he did not wish to be regarded as a 'free-thinker' (cf. my comments on Hardy's rejection of politics, above, pp. 17–18).

33. Hardy's own singularly pre-emptive phrase, in the General Preface to the 'Wessex Edition' of his works (1912), for those novels which have come to be regarded as representing his 'major' achievement (for more on this, see Chapter 2, and Chapter 3, note 8, below). It occurs when he is 'classifying', and, in effect, hierarchically evaluating, his fictional *oeuvre* – with the ones so described clearly privileged. The General Preface is reproduced as an appendix in most modern paperback editions of his novels.

34. The phrase is from an 1887 memorandum about the painter, J. M. W. Turner (cf. *The Life*, p. 185).

35. 'Disproportioning' and '"realism" is not Art' are both phrases from an important memorandum of 1890 (*The Life*, pp. 228–9); '*vérité vraie*' appears in 'The Science of Fiction' (reprinted in Orel (ed.) (1990) and Widdowson (ed.) (1996a)).

36. Cf. Lawrence (1914).

CHAPTER 2: HARDY IN HISTORY: A CASE-STUDY IN THE SOCIOLOGY OF LITERATURE

1. E. H. Carr, *What is History?*, Harmondsworth: Penguin (1961), 1965, p. 11. All further references to this work appear as bracketed numbers in the text.

2. Tony Bennett, 'Text and History', in Peter Widdowson (ed.) *Re-Reading English*, London: Methuen, 1982, pp. 224–5. All further references to this essay appear as bracketed numbers in the text.

3. The ideas which follow here do not, in fact, derive from Terry Eagleton's comments on Hardy in Eagleton (1981), pp. 126–30, which I had not

seen when I was first preparing this essay. I recognize, of course, how similar our notions of the reproduction of 'Thomas Hardy' appear to be.

4. Holly Goulden and John Hartley, '"Nor should such Topics as Homosexuality, Masturbation, Frigidity, Premature Ejaculation or the Menopause be Regarded as Unmentionable"', *LTP* (*Literature Teaching Politics* journal), 1 (1982), p. 6.

5. Cox (ed.) (1970), Introduction, p. xv.

6. See Chapter 1, note 33.

7. Harold Williams, 'The Wessex Novels of Thomas Hardy', *North American Review*, 1914, in Cox (ed.) (1970), p. 429.

8. W. L. Phelps, 'Thomas Hardy', *Atlantic Monthly*, 1910, in Cox (ed.) (1970), p. 398.

9. Edward Wright, 'The Novels of Thomas Hardy', *Quarterly Review*, 1904, in Cox (ed.) (1970), p. 361.

10. Williams, 'The Wessex Novels of Thomas Hardy', p. 433.

11. *ibid.*, pp. 423–4.

12. I am indebted to Charles Swann of Keele University for this quotation. It appeared in an (unpublished?) paper on Hardy first given at the then Thames Polytechnic in the late 1970s.

13. Cecil (1943), p. 153. All further references to this work appear as bracketed numbers in the text.

14. Leavis (1948), p. 140.

15. Richard H. Taylor, 'Thomas Hardy: A Reader's Guide', in Page (ed.) (1980).

16. See Williams (1970, 1979), Williams and Williams (1980), Eagleton (1976, 1981).

17. Respectively, Edward Wright, in Cox (ed.) (1970), p. 356, and Williams, 'The Wessex Novels of Thomas Hardy', p. 429.

18. Baugh (ed.) (1967), p. 1466.

19. Cecil (1943), p. 142.

20. Guerard (1949), p. 51.

21. Williams and Williams (1980).

22. Page (ed.) (1980), Butler (ed.) (1977), Kramer (ed.) (1979).

23. See *HE*, 'Introduction', pp. 15, 18, 21, 27. For more on Gittings and this novel, see also Chapter 3, pp. 63–6, below.

24. It is perhaps significant, too, that a whole book on Hardy's 'Lesser Novels' (Taylor (1982)) appeared the same year as this essay.

25. It has been pointed out to me that *Tess* was on the Roman Catholic Church's *Index* for some considerable time – which might account for the shyness of the Boards in setting it. I do not know when it was taken off.

26. I have become aware – again since writing this essay – of the consonance of some of the ideas here with those expressed in the questions and answers on Hardy in the interviews with Raymond Williams published as *Politics and Letters* (Williams (1979), pp. 222–3, 245–7, 264). It is perhaps worth fleshing out here one point Williams makes about how Leavis's attitude to Hardy changed. In *Mass Civilization and Minority Culture* (1930), Leavis included Hardy in a list of 'major instances' of important writers; when he reprinted this essay in *Education and the University: A Sketch for an 'English School'* (1943), Conrad was substituted for Hardy. (Cf. Iain Wright, 'F. R. Leavis, the *Scrutiny* Movement and the Crisis', in J. Clark *et al.* (eds), *Culture and Crisis in Britain in the '30s*, London: Lawrence and Wishart, 1979, p. 38, note 9.)

27. For a much fuller treatment of this idea, see Catherine Belsey, 'Re-Reading the Great Tradition', in Widdowson (ed.), *Re-Reading English* (see note 2, above).

CHAPTER 3: HARDY AND SOCIAL CLASS: *THE HAND OF ETHELBERTA*

1. *HE*, pp. 307–8. All further references to this novel appear as bracketed numbers in the text.

2. Hardy, Florence Emily (1975) – hereafter referred to as *The Life* – pp. 102–3.

3. Robert Gittings, *HE*, Introduction, p. 15.

4. *The Life*, p. 108.

5. In the *Cornhill* serialization of the novel (from July 1875), the poems were entitled 'Metres by Me'; in the volume version, they became 'Metres by E' (cf. Gittings (1975), p. 290, and his Introduction to *HE*, p. 26).

6. *The Life*, p. 106.

7. The main sources for these are: Björk (ed.) (1985), Orel (ed.) (1990) and Widdowson (ed.) (1996a).

8. 19 Dec. 1863; *The Life*, p. 40.

9. *The Life*, pp. 61, 391–2.

10. Lawrence (1914), p. 413.

11. Leslie Stephen to Hardy *re* the *Cornhill* serialization (1875), quoted in *The Life*, p. 104.

12. Millgate (1971), p. 111, has interesting suggestions to make about Hardy's 'deliberate' reference in this novel to Restoration and 18th-century 'patterns of stage comedy'.

13. *HE*, Introduction, p. 17.

14. Three other sympathetic and perceptive accounts of *HE* are: Millgate (1971), which recognizes it as 'almost ... a parable of social revolution' and as a successful 'experiment' by no means disconnected from the rest of Hardy's work (pp. 107, 115–16); Casagrande (1982), which sees it – in common with many of Hardy's novels – as concerning 'the troubled consciousness of an uprooted native' (p. 119) and as inflecting the author's own such consciousness; and Bayley (1978), which emphasizes how much 'Hardy is here ... completely his own heroine' and is 'wryly envisaging the possible effects on himself of his own social and literary success' (pp. 150, 151). However, none of these critics finally breaks with convention by according the novel, in formal terms, the status of being a sophisticated anti-realist fiction whose discourses 'match' its deracinated social consciousness. [Since this note was written, Penny Boumelha, in Higonnet (ed.) (1993), and Fisher (1992) have also commented instructively on *HE*.]

15. Gittings (1975), p. 289. All further references to this work appear as bracketed numbers in the text.

16. *HE*, Introduction, p. 15. All further references to this essay appear as bracketed numbers in the text.

17. These comments are distributed *passim* throughout Gittings's Introduction.

18. Taylor (1978), pp. 57, 65, 66. All further references to this work appear as bracketed numbers in the text.

19. *HE*, Introduction, p. 19.

20. Gittings (1975), pp. 291–2, indicates how much more obtrusive was the closeness to Hardy's own background in the serial and first editions of the novel compared to the extensively revised 1895 edition, and points out that Neigh's father in the earlier version had married his cook. Hardy's mother had herself been a cook.

21. I am sure keen Hardy watchers will know this, although I have not myself seen it said anywhere: 'Enckworth Court' is almost certainly

based on the house Kingston Lacy in Dorset. Bequeathed to the National Trust on the death of its reclusive owner, Ralph Bankes, in 1982, the house was extensively restored and opened to the public in August 1985. For many years it had been more or less unknown as a significant country house. The house was designed for the Bankes family, after the Restoration, by Sir Roger Pratt – a red-brick building with Portland cornerstones. When William John Bankes succeeded to the estate in 1834, he immediately employed Sir Charles Barry to remodel Kingston Lacy. Pratt's red-brick house was covered with a 'skin' of Chilmark stone and, amongst many other alterations and additions, a 30-foot-wide Carrara marble staircase was installed. Hardy's description of the 'thin freestone slabs' covering the whole brick exterior of Enckworth Court, and of 'the principal staircase, constructed of a freestone so milk-white and delicately moulded as to be easily conceived in the lamplight as of biscuit-ware', suggests that he knew Kingston Lacy quite well. See the opening of Chapter 38 for the full description of the 'false' house, *HE*, pp. 303–5. Hardy apparently visited the house as a guest during the Edwardian period.

22. *HE*, Introduction, pp. 21–2.

CHAPTER 4: HARDY'S 'QUITE WORTHLESS' NOVEL: *A LAODICEAN*

1. Baugh (ed.) (1967), p. 1466. The chapter on 'The 19th Century and After' was by Samuel Chew and R. D. Altick.

2. Respectively: Barbara Hardy, *Laod.*, Introduction, p. 13; Gatewood (ed.) (1991), p. xviii; Bullen (1986), p. 118; Taylor (1982), pp. 96–7.

3. Respectively: Hardy, *Laod.*, Introduction, p. 30 (and c.f. Taylor (1982), p. 4, on the 'lesser novels' generally); Bullen (1986), p. 118.

4. For some of these changes, c.f. Hardy, *Laod.*, Introduction, and Gatewood (ed.) (1991), 'Note on the Text', pp. xx–xxii, and the Appendix (pp. 461ff.) which lists 'significant revisions'. Gatewood makes the interesting point that the novel cannot be seen as representing a 'constant goal' of Hardy's over 32 years – which reached its 'intended form' in the 'Wessex Edition' of 1912 – but that it is 'a different novel' at various points, 'reflecting Hardy's shifting intentions during the book's long history'.

5. The new Penguin edition (edited by John Schad) takes the 1881 version as copy-text.

6. *Laod.*, pp. 362, 365. All further references to this novel appear as bracketed numbers in the text.

7. Cf. those in note 2, *passim*.

8. See also Chapter 1, note 32. In the General Preface, he famously identified what have become his major 'Wessex' novels as 'Novels of Character and Environment'; the second group were classified as 'Romances and Fantasies'; this, the third group, also contained only *DR* and *HE*.

9. In the third chapter of The Revelation of St John the Divine, the Christians of Laodicea are described as 'lukewarm' in their religion – 'neither hot nor cold'. See below, p. 99, for discussion of the title's relevance in the novel.

10. Cf. Taylor (1982), p. 102.

11. From his poem 'The Scholar Gipsy'. Hardy greatly admired Arnold's work.

12. The 'finished writer' mentioned in this passage is Matthew Arnold – here, subject to Hardy's light irony (see note 11, above).

13. *The Life*, p. 147.

14. Bullen (1986), p. 118.

15. In Orel (ed.) (1990), and Widdowson (ed.) (1996a).

16. *The Life*, pp. 110, 179, 182–3; but passing comments of this kind appear throughout.

17. *The Life*, p. 103.

18. 'Thomas Hardy's Novels', *Westminster Review*, April 1883, in Cox (ed.) (1970).

19. Fisher (1992) offers an ingenious reading of Hardy's fiction as 'self-subversive', and also suggests that a novel like *A Laodicean* does not 'cover' its own ingenuity, and is thus 'extremely revealing' (p. 101). For a fuller synopsis of Fisher's thesis, see Chapter 7 on *Jude*, below, p. 171.

20. Cf. *The Life*, p. 61. More on this 'first' novel appears in Chapter 7 on *Jude*, below, pp. 168–70, 171–3.

21. *Laod.*, 'Introduction', pp. 16–23, *passim*.

22. A similar point is made in passing by Gatewood (ed.) (1991), p. xiv.

23. For more on this, see Chapter 5 on *Tess*, below, pp. 132–3.

24. The first four phrases are from Hardy, *HE*, Introduction, *passim*; the next, from Gatewood (ed.) (1991), p. xvii; and the last two from Taylor (1982), p. 99.

25. Taylor (1982), p. 112.

26. *The Life*, p. 52, makes it emphatically clear that as a young man in London in the 1860s, Hardy studied paintings with keen interest. It seems likely, then, that he would at the very least have known about such an infamous contemporary work.

27. Jackson (1985), pp. 91–109, offers a more general consideration of this motif in Hardy's work, including some comments on *Laod.* which echo my own below.

28. *The Life*, pp. 228–9.

29. 'The Profitable Reading of Fiction' (1888), in Orel (ed.) (1990), p. 241, and Widdowson (ed.) (1996a), p. 247.

30. In his introductory essay, 'Le Roman', to his novel *Pierre et Jean*, 1888.

CHAPTER 5: 'MOMENTS OF VISION', ETC.: *TESS OF THE D'URBERVILLES*

1. *Tess*, p. 41. All further references to this novel appear as bracketed numbers in the text.

2. *DR*, pp. 46–7.

3. *Jude*, p. 23.

4. 'Author's Preface to the Fifth and Later Editions' (1892). Hardy, in the same sentence here, also quotes Schiller on 'representation' and 'poetical representations'.

5. See *The Life*, p. 185, for a typical memorandum (Jan. 1887) on this subject during the period of the composition of *Tess*.

6. For extended treatment of this subject, and of Turner in particular, see Bullen (1986), especially Chapter 8, 'Patterns of Light and Dark in *Tess of the d'Urbervilles*'.

7. This 'phase' is perhaps best exemplified by the 1975 edition of Draper (ed.) (1991), and by LaValley (ed.) (1969).

8. For an extended analysis of these by the present author, see Widdowson (1989), especially Chapter 1, 'The Critical Constitution of "Thomas Hardy"'.

9. From the 1912 General Preface – see Chapter 1, note 33, above.

10. See Widdowson (1989), pp. 44–55 especially, for a discussion of the critical treatment of the 'minor novels'; also Chapters 3 and 4 above, *passim*.

11. With those, for example, collected in such volumes as: Bloom (ed.) (1987), Butler (ed.) (1989) and Widdowson (ed.) (1993).

12. Laird (1975), p. 4. For a slightly fuller critique of Laird's stance, see Widdowson (1989), pp. 30–1. There is a further essay by Laird on the textual development of *Tess*, 'New Light on the Evolution of *Tess of the d'Urbervilles*', in *Review of English Studies*, 31: 124 (Winter 1980), 414–35.

13. Thomas Hardy, *Tess of the d'Urbervilles*, ed. Juliet Grindle and Simon Gatrell, Oxford: Clarendon Press, 1983.

14. In the Editor's Preface to Goode (1988), p. vii.

15. For a fuller account and analysis of this, see Wotton (1985), Chapter 13, 'The Production of Meaning: "Hardy's Women" and the Eternal Feminine'.

16. Goode (1976); the following quotations, *passim*, are from pp. 255, 253, 254. Two other influential essays on the textuality/sexuality nexus are: Jacobus (1976) and Hillis Miller's 'Fiction and Repetition: *Tess of the d'Urbervilles*' (1975), reprinted in revised form in Miller (1982). Both essays are also reprinted in Bloom (ed.) (1987).

17. Goode (1979), especially pp. 100, 107–8.

18. Editor's Preface, Goode (1988), p. vii.

19. I have already implied this in note 9 above, regarding Hardy's self-categorization of the novels. But we should also not forget that he effectively author(iz)ed his own life by compiling *The Life* and having it passed off as by his second wife. An account of this characteristically self-protective subterfuge is to be found in Gittings (1975), Chapter 1.

20. See Bullen (1986) for full discussion of this.

21. See note 19, above.

22. *The Life*, p. 114 (see also note 5, above). All further references are given as bracketed numbers in the text.

23. Praxiteles was a 4th-century-BC Greek sculptor whose work celebrated sensuality (for example, by depicting naked gods for the first time).

24. Blake (1982) – also reprinted in Bloom (ed.) (1987).

25. Wotton (1985), p. 4.

CHAPTER 6: RECASTING HARDY THE POET

1. Unsigned review, *The Saturday Review*, 7 Jan. 1899, LXXXVII, 19, in Gibson and Johnson (eds.) (1991), pp. 41–2.

2. Review in *The Athenaeum*, 14 Jan. 1899, in *ibid.*, pp. 45, 44.

3. Unsigned reviews in *The Academy*, 23 Nov. 1901, and *The Athenaeum*, 4 Jan. 1902, in *ibid.*, pp. 46, 52.

4. Hynes (ed.) (1984b, 1994), 'Introduction', p. xxvi/p. xviii. For further comment on these two volumes, see below, pp. 143–4.

5. Motion (ed.) (1994), 'Introduction', p. xxxvi.

6. Hynes (ed.) (1984b, 1994), pp. xxvi, xxii/pp. xviii, xiv (see above, note 4).

7. Taylor (1989; cf., e.g., 'Preface to the Second Edition', p. xxiii), and Taylor (1988). J. Hillis Miller is the principal exception to all this – see below, pp. 146–7.

8. Davie (1973), p.vii. All further references to this work appear as bracketed numbers in the text.

9. A more extended critique of this work is offered in Widdowson (1989), pp. 70–2. I stand by what I said there, while nevertheless acknowledging the sophistication of Davie's book.

10. *The Life*, p. 301.

11. The list would include William Empson, Mark Van Doren, Samuel Hynes and J. Hillis Miller.

12. *Selected Poems of Thomas Hardy*, London: Collier Books (1960), (1966).

13. Hynes (ed.) (1984b, 1994), p. xxi/p. xiii (see above, note 4).

14. Leavis (1932), pp. 52–3, 56.

15. Blackmur (1952), Brown (1954), Stewart (1971).

16. Thomas (ed.) (1993), Preface, pp. xi–xii.

17. Wright (ed.) (1978), Introduction, pp. 15–16.

18. In his *Autobiography*, New York: Harcourt Brace, 1958, pp. 167–8; quoted in Taylor (1989), p. xxiii.

19. Wright (ed.) (1978), p. 29.

20. 'With Calligraphy and Illustrations by Frederick Marns', London: Shepheard-Walwyn, 1984, Introduction, p. 10.

21. 'Papermac' edition, London: Macmillan, 1992, Preface, pp. ix, v–vi. The other two 'series' Weber proposes are Shakespeare's *Sonnets* and Elizabeth Barrett Browning's *Sonnets from the Portuguese*.

22. In Pettit (ed.) (1994), pp. 58, 62–3, my emphasis. This essay is a re-working of Chapter 7 of Johnson (1991).

23. London: Weidenfeld and Nicolson, 1981, Introduction, pp. 16, 10, 16.

24. London: Aurum Press, 1990, Introduction, p. 11. For Blackmur, see note 15 above.

25. Creighton (ed.) (1974), Introduction, pp. xv–xvi, viii, ix, *passim* – my emphases.

26. Wain (ed.) (1975), p. xix.

27. Wain and Wain (eds.) (1978), p. 17.

28. Motion (ed.) (1994), Introduction, pp. xxvi, xxviii, xxxi, xxxvi, *passim* – my emphases.

29. Hynes (ed.) (1984b, 1994), pp. xxi, xxii, xxiv/pp. xiii, xiv, xvii.

30. Armstrong (ed.) (1993), Introduction, p. 43.

31. The others were: G. M. Young, *Selected Poems of Thomas Hardy* (1940); W. E. Williams, *Thomas Hardy: The Penguin Poets* (1960); J. C. Ransom, *Selected Poems of Thomas Hardy* (see note 12); P. N. Furbank, *Selected Poems of Thomas Hardy* (1964); G. Grigson, *A Choice of Hardy's Poetry* (1969); and Johnson's own *Poems by Thomas Hardy* for the Folio Society (1979).

32. Armstrong (ed.) (1993), p. 43.

33. This work was originally undertaken for Widdowson (1989), Chapter 3, and has not been updated.

34. Miller (1985), pp. 270–1, 282, 289, 283, 290, 303–4, *passim*. Five more essays on Hardy's poetry appear in Miller (1990).

35. Johnson (1979), p. 21.

36. In his 1912 General Preface – see Chapter 1, note 33, above.

37. Francine Shapiro Puk (ed.), *Thomas Hardy's Chosen Poems*, New York: Ungar Press, 1978, Appendix I: Critical Additions; Appendix II: Poems of 1912–13; and Introduction, p. xix.

38. Armstrong (ed.) (1993), p. 43.

39. The references, here, are respectively to: Wain (ed.) (1975), p. xv; Johnson (1991), p. 170; Armstrong (ed.) (1993), p. 19; Hynes (ed.)

(1984b, 1994), pp. xxiv, xxix, xxvii/pp. xvi, xxii, xix; Motion (ed.) (1994), p. xxxv.

40. Armstrong (ed.) (1993), p. 228, cites Harold Bloom and Tom Paulin as believing this.

41. Hardy's own phrase in the 'Apology' which prefaces *LLE*.

42. For fuller discussion of Georgianism, see, e.g., James Reeves (ed.), *Georgian Poetry*, Harmondsworth: Penguin, 'The Penguin Poets', 1962, Introduction, p. xvi, where Reeves remarks: 'Undoubtedly Hardy was another father-figure to the Georgians'; V. de Sola Pinto, *Crisis in English Poetry, 1880–1940*, London: Grey Arrow (1951), 1963, Chapter 5; C. K. Stead, *The New Poetic*, Harmondsworth: Penguin (1964), 1967, Chapters 2, 3; Robert H. Ross, *The Georgian Revolt, 1910–1922*, London: Faber (1965), 1967.

43. I am, of course, intentionally invoking here the proselytising spirit of Leavis in *New Bearings in English Poetry* (1932) on behalf of Eliot and Pound in particular.

44. E. P. Thompson, 'Outside the Whale', in Thompson *et al.* (eds.), *Out of Apathy*, London: New Left Books, 1960, p. 153.

45. Wright (ed.) (1978), p. 38.

46. Only reprinted in Creighton (ed.) (1974).

47. Only reprinted in Hynes (ed.) (1984b).

48. Both only reprinted in Wright (ed.) (1978).

49. Taylor (1989), p. 38.

50. Johnson (1991), p. 181, for example, while noting 'a certain ambiguity about the subject of the poem', states: 'it is not quite clear whether Hardy is addressing Love or the woman he once loved'. I would suggest that it is not Hardy who is doing the 'addressing' at all. John Lucas, in an unpublished paper, also insists that the poem represents Hardy remembering a lost love.

51. Cf. the poems 'Faintheart in a Railway Train' (*LLE*) and 'Thoughts of Phena' (*WP*).

52. See Armstrong (ed.) (1993), pp. 23–4, 152, 163.

53. Never once selected by editors to my knowledge – except Widdowson (1996a)!

54. Only reprinted in Hynes (ed.) (1984b, 1994) and Thomas (ed.) (1993), and not referred to, for example, in Paulin (1975), Johnson (1991), or Taylor (1988 and 1989).

55. Only reprinted in Hynes (ed.) (1984b).

56. Only reprinted in Hynes (ed.) (1984b).

57. Cf. note 41.

58. Hillis Miller (1985), pp. 303–4.

CHAPTER 7: ARABELLA AND THE SATIRICAL DISCOURSE IN *JUDE THE OBSCURE*

1. 'The Simpletons' was the title of (the first part of) the novel when it began periodical serialization in *Harper's New Monthly Magazine* in December 1894 (it ran in monthly parts until November 1895). For the second instalment, Hardy changed it to 'Hearts Insurgent'. The first book edition of *Jude the Obscure* was published in November 1895.

2. See above, Chapter 1, p. 11 and note 3 there. In the Introduction to Coleman (ed.) (1976), pp. 5–9, the author adduces two other 'sources' for our knowledge about it: an article by Hardy's close friend, Sir Edmund Gosse, 'Thomas Hardy's Lost Novel', in the *Sunday Times,* 22 Jan. 1928; and a letter of 10 Aug. 1868 from Alexander Macmillan to Hardy (in *The Life and Letters of Alexander Macmillan*, London, 1910) declining publication of this first novel, but praising aspects of it and making detailed comments.

3. *The Life*, p. 56. All further references to this work appear as bracketed numbers in the text.

4. Hardy's phrase in the 1912 General Preface – see Chapter 1, note 33, and Chapter 3, note 8, above.

5. Fisher (1992), Introduction, especially pp. 3, 7. I am grateful to Isobel Armstrong for raising with me in the first place the issue of why 'conservative readings' of Hardy's fiction have persisted for so long.

6. See *The Life*, pp. 252, 274, 392.

7. Purdy and Millgate (eds.) (1978–88), Vol. IV, p. 209.

8. Parts of Morley's comments to Macmillan are quoted in *The Life*, pp. 58–9. A fuller version is in Gittings (1975), p. 154.

9. In Widdowson (1996b), where I have hoped to show that my hypothesis is very evidently applicable to all his other novels, too – as it would be also to his other extensive and important fictional corpus, the short stories: one needs to think only of the titles of two such volumes – *Life's Little Ironies* and *A Group of Noble Dames*.

10. *Jude*, pp. 30–1. All further references to this novel appear as bracketed numbers in the text.

11. Draper (1990), pp. 234, 245–6.

12. Hands (1995), p. 78.

13. Garson (1991), Chapter 6, especially pp. 159, 160, 177–8.

14. Morgan (1988), Chapter 5, especially pp. 140, 143–8, *passim*.

15. See note 1, above.

16. *The Life*, p. 272.

17. *The Life*, p. 273.

18. *The Life*, pp. 272, 271.

19. *The Life*, p. 273.

20. It is not without point that the ending of that most pastoral of 'tragedies', *The Woodlanders*, shows similar features (see Widdowson, 1996b, pp. 56–7).

21. *The Life*, p. 273.

22. Garson (1991), p. 178.

23. Morgan (1988), pp. 153–4, 147.

References

Armstrong, Tim (ed.) (1993), *Thomas Hardy: Selected Poems* (Harlow: Longman).

Baugh, Albert C. (ed.) (1967), *A Literary History of England* (London: Routledge and Kegan Paul; edition referred to: 1970).

Bayley, John (1978), *An Essay on Hardy* (Cambridge: Cambridge University Press).

Björk, Lennart (ed.) (1985), *The Literary Notebooks of Thomas Hardy* (2 vols; London: Macmillan).

Blackmur, R. P. (1952), 'The Shorter Poems of Thomas Hardy' (1940), in R. P. Blackmur, *Language as Gesture* (New York: Brown).

Blake, Kathleen (1982), 'Pure Tess: Hardy on Knowing a Woman' (*Studies in English Literature*, 22:4, Autumn, 689–705).

Bloom, Harold (ed.) (1987), *Modern Critical Interpretations of Thomas Hardy* (New York: Chelsea).

Boumelha, Penny (1982), *Thomas Hardy and Women: Sexual Ideology and Narrative Form* (Brighton: Harvester Press).

Boumelha, Penny (ed.) (1996), *Jude the Obscure* (London: Macmillan, 'New Casebook').

Brooks, Jean (1971), *Thomas Hardy: The Poetic Structure* (London: Elek Books).

Brown, Douglas (1954), *Thomas Hardy* (Harlow: Longman, 1961).

Bullen, J. B. (1986), *The Expressive Eye: Fiction and Perception in the Work of Thomas Hardy* (Oxford: Oxford University Press).

Butler, Lance St John (ed.) (1977), *Thomas Hardy After Fifty Years* (London: Macmillan).

Butler, Lance St John (ed.) (1989), *Alternative Hardy* (London: Macmillan).

Casagrande, Peter (1982), *Unity in Hardy's Novels: 'Repetitive Symmetries'* (London: Macmillan).

Cecil, Lord David (1943), *Hardy the Novelist* (London: Constable).

Coleman, Terry (ed. with intro.) (1976), Thomas Hardy, *An Indiscretion in the Life of an Heiress* (London: Hutchinson).

Creighton, T. R. M. (ed.) (1974), *Poems of Thomas Hardy: A New Selection* (London: Macmillan).

Cox, R. G. (ed.) (1970), *Thomas Hardy: The Critical Heritage* (London: Routledge & Kegan Paul).

Davie, Donald (1972), 'Hardy's Virgilian Purples', *Agenda*, 10 (2–3), 138–56.

Davie, Donald (1973), *Thomas Hardy and British Poetry* (London: Routledge & Kegan Paul).

Draper, R. P. (1990), 'Hardy's Comic Tragedy: *Jude the Obscure*', in Kramer (ed.) (1990) and Draper (ed.) (1991; edition referred to)

Draper, R. P. (ed.) (1975; revised edn 1991) *Thomas Hardy: The Tragic Novels* (London: Macmillan 'Casebook', 1975; 1991).

Eagleton, Terry (1976), *Criticism and Ideology* (LRB, 1976; edition referred to: London: Verso, 1978).

Eagleton, Terry (1981), *Walter Benjamin or Towards a Revolutionary Criticism* (London: Verso).

Ebbatson, Roger (1993), *Hardy: the Margin of the Unexpressed* (Sheffield: Sheffield Academic Press).

Fisher, Joe (1992), *The Hidden Hardy* (London: Macmillan).

Garson, Marjorie (1991), *Hardy's Fables of Integrity: Woman, Body, Text* (Oxford: Clarendon Press).

Gatewood, Jane (ed.) (1991), Introduction to *A Laodicean* (Oxford: Oxford University Press, 'World's Classics' edition).

Gibson, James (ed.) (1976). *Thomas Hardy: The Complete Poems* (London: Macmillan).

Gibson, J. and Johnson, T. (eds.) (1991), *Thomas Hardy: Poems* (London: Macmillan 'Casebook', 1979; 1991).

Gittings, Robert (1975), *Young Thomas Hardy* (edition referred to: Harmondsworth: Penguin, 1978).

Gittings, Robert (1978), *The Older Hardy* (London: Heinemann).

Goode, John (1976), 'Women and the Literary Text', in Juliet Mitchell and Ann Oakley (eds.), *The Rights and Wrongs of Women* (Harmondsworth: Penguin, 1976).

Goode, John (1979), 'Sue Bridehead and the New Woman', in Mary Jacobus (ed.), *Women Writing and Writing about Women* (London Croom Helm, 1979).

Goode, John (1988), *Thomas Hardy: The Offensive Truth*, with 'Editor's Preface' by Terry Eagleton, (Oxford: Blackwell).

Gregor, Ian (1974), *The Great Web: The Form of Hardy's Major Fiction* (London: Faber).

Guerard, Albert, J. (1949), *Thomas Hardy* (revised edition referred to: London: New Directions, 1964).

Hands, Timothy (1995), *Thomas Hardy* (London: Macmillan, 'Writers in their Time').

Hardy, Florence Emily (1975), *The Life of Thomas Hardy, 1840–1928* (London: Macmillan, 1962, 1975) – the one-volume edition of *The Early Life of Thomas Hardy 1840–1891* (London: Macmillan, 1928) and *The Later Years of Thomas Hardy, 1892–1928* (London: Macmillan, 1930) now known to have been largely composed by Hardy himself, with Florence Emily's assistance, during the 1920s. This work has been republished as *The Life and Work of Thomas Hardy* (ed. Michael Millgate, London: Macmillan, 1985) – a theoretically 'restored' version of the 'original', before its editing by Florence Emily and Hardy's other executors.

Higonnet, Margaret R. (ed.) (1993), *The Sense of Sex: Feminist Perpectives on Hardy* (Urbana: University of Illinois Press).

Hynes, Samuel (ed.) (1982, 1984a, 1985, 1995), *The Complete Poetical Works of Thomas Hardy* (5 vols; Oxford: Oxford University Press).

Hynes, Samuel (ed.) (1984b), *Thomas Hardy: A Critical Selection of His Finest Poetry* (Oxford: Oxford University Press, 'The Oxford Authors')

Hynes, Samuel (ed.) (1994), *Thomas Hardy: A Selection of his Finest Poems* (Oxford: Oxford University Press, 'Oxford Poetry Library').

Ingham, Patricia (1989), *Thomas Hardy: A Feminist Reading* (Hemel Hempstead: Harvester Wheatsheaf).

Jackson, Arlene M. (1985), 'Photography as Style and Metaphor in the Art of Thomas Hardy', in Norman Page (ed.), *Thomas Hardy Annual No. 2* (London: Macmillan, 1985, pp. 91–109).

Jacobus, Mary (1975), 'Sue the Obscure' (*Essays in Criticism*, 25, 304–28).

Jacobus, Mary (1976), 'Tess's Purity' (*Essays in Criticism*, 26, 318–38. Reprinted as 'Tess: The Making of a Pure Woman', in Susan Lipshitz (ed.), *Tearing the Veil: Essays on Femininity*, London: Routledge and Kegan Paul, 1978).

Jacobus, Mary (1979) 'Tree and Machine: *The Woodlanders*', in Kramer (ed.) (1979).

Johnson, Trevor (1979), '"Pre-Critical Innocence" and the Anthologist's Hardy', *Victorian Poetry*, 17, 9–24.

Johnson, Trevor (1991), *A Critical Introduction to the Poems of Thomas Hardy* (London: Macmillan).

Kramer, Dale (ed.) (1979), *Critical Approaches to the Fiction of Thomas Hardy* (London: Macmillan).

Kramer, Dale (ed.) (1990), *Critical Essays on Thomas Hardy: The Novels* (New York: G.K. Hall).

Laird, J. T. (1975), *The Shaping of Tess of the d'Urbervilles* (Oxford: Oxford University Press).

Larkin, Philip (1966), 'Wanted: Good Hardy Critic', in *Required Writing: Miscellaneous Pieces, 1955–1982* (London: Faber, 1983).

LaValley, Albert J. (ed.) (1969), *Twentieth-Century Interpretations of Tess of the d'Urbervilles* (Englewood Cliffs, NJ: Prentice Hall).

Lawrence, D. H. (1914), *Study of Thomas Hardy*, in Edward D. McDonald (ed.), *Phoenix* (1936; London: Heinemann, 1970).

Lecercle, Jean-Jacques (1989), 'The Violence of Style in *Tess of the d'Urbervilles*', in Butler (1989); reprinted in part in Widdowson (ed.) (1993).

Leavis, F. R. (1932), *New Bearings in English Poetry* (edition referred to: Harmondsworth: Penguin, 1963).

Leavis, F. R. (1948), *The Great Tradition* (edition referred to: Harmondsworth: Penguin, 1962).

Lucas, John (1986), *Modern English Poetry from Hardy to Hughes* (London: Batsford).

Miller, J. Hillis (1970), *Thomas Hardy: Distance and Desire* (Oxford: Oxford University Press).

Miller, J. Hillis (1982), *Fiction and Repetition: Seven English Novels* (Cambridge, MA: Harvard University Press).

Miller, J. Hillis (1985), *The Linguistic Moment: From Wordsworth to Stevens* (Princeton, NJ: Princeton University Press).

Miller, J. Hillis (1990), *Tropes, Parables, Performatives: Essays on Twentieth-Century Literature* (Hemel Hempstead: Harvester Wheatsheaf).

Millgate, Michael (1971), *Thomas Hardy: His Career as a Novelist* (London: Bodley Head).

Millgate, Michael (1982), *Thomas Hardy: A Biography* (Oxford: Oxford University Press: reissued 1985, 1992).

Morgan, Rosemary (1988), *Women and Sexuality in the Novels of Thomas Hardy* (London: Routledge).

Motion, Andrew (ed.) (1994), *Thomas Hardy: Selected Poems* (London: Orion, 'Everyman').

Orel, Harold (ed.) (1990), *Thomas Hardy's Personal Writings* (London: Macmillan, 1966; 1990).

Orel, Harold (ed.) (1995), *Critical Essays on Thomas Hardy's Poetry* (New York: G. K. Hall).

Page, Norman (ed.) (1980), *Thomas Hardy: The Writer and His Background* (London: Bell and Hyman).

Paulin, Tom (1975), *Thomas Hardy: The Poetry of Perception* (London: Macmillan).

Pettit, Charles, P. C. (ed.) (1994), *New Perspectives on Thomas Hardy* (London: Macmillan).

Pinion, F. B. (1977), *Thomas Hardy: Art and Thought* (London: Macmillan).

Purdy, Richard and Millgate, Michael (eds) (1978–88), *The Collected Letters of Thomas Hardy* (7 vols: Oxford: Oxford University Press). Millgate has also edited *Selected Letters* (Oxford: Oxford University Press, 1990).

Showalter, Elaine (1979), 'The Unmanning of the Mayor of Casterbridge', in Kramer (ed.) (1979) and Draper (ed.) (1991).

Silverman, Kaja (1984), 'History, Figuration and Female Subjectivity in *Tess of the d'Urbervilles*', *Novel*, 18, 5–28. Reprinted in part in Widdowson (ed.) (1993).

Smith, Stan (1982), *Inviolable Voice: History and Twentieth-Century Poetry* (Dublin: Gill and Macmillan).

Southern Review (1940), 'Thomas Hardy Centennial Issue', 6, 1 (Summer 1940).

Stewart, J. I. M. (1971), *Thomas Hardy: A Critical Biography* (Harlow: Longman).

Stubbs, Patricia (1979), *Women and Fiction: Feminism and the Novel, 1880–1920* (edition referred to: London: Methuen, 1981).

Sumner, Rosemary (1981), *Thomas Hardy: Psychological Novelist* (London: Macmillan).

Taylor, Dennis (1989), *Hardy's Poetry, 1860–1928* (London: Macmillan 1981; 1989).

Taylor, Dennis (1988), *Hardy's Metres and Victorian Prosody* (Oxford: Clarendon Press).

Taylor, Richard H. (ed.) (1978), *The Personal Notebooks of Thomas Hardy* (London: Macmillan).

Taylor, Richard H. (1982), *The Neglected Hardy: Thomas Hardy's Lesser Novels* (London: Macmillan).

Thomas, Harry (ed.) (1993), *Thomas Hardy: Selected Poems* (Harmondsworth: Penguin, 'Penguin Classics').

Vigar, Penelope (1974), *The Novels of Thomas Hardy: Illusion and Reality* (London: Athlone Press).

Wain, John (ed.) (1975), *Selected Shorter Poems of Thomas Hardy*, (London: Macmillan, 1966; 1975).

Wain, John and Eirian (eds) (1978), *The New Wessex Selection of Thomas Hardy's Poetry* (London: Macmillan, 'Papermac' edition, 1992).

Widdowson, Peter (1989), *Hardy in History: A Study in Literary Sociology* (London: Routledge).

Widdowson, Peter (ed.) (1993), *Tess of the d'Urbervilles* (London: Macmillan, 'New Casebook').

Widdowson, Peter (ed.) (1996a), *Thomas Hardy: Selected Poetry and Non-Fictional Prose* (London: Macmillan).

Widdowson, Peter (1996b), *Thomas Hardy* (Plymouth: Northcote House, 'Writers and their Work').

Williams, Merryn (1972), *Thomas Hardy and Rural England* (London: Macmillan).

Williams, Raymond (1970), *The English Novel from Dickens to Lawrence* (edition referred to: St Albans: Paladin, 1974); Chapter 4 on Hardy (most of this reappears in *The Country and the City*, Chapter 18).

Williams, Raymond (1979), *Politics and Letters* (London: Verso, 1979; 1981).

Williams, Raymond and Williams, Merryn (1980), 'Hardy and Social Class', in Page (ed.) (1980). Reprinted in part in Widdowson (ed.) (1993).

Wotton, George (1985), *Thomas Hardy: Towards a Materialist Criticism* (Dublin: Gill and Macmillan).

Wright, David (ed.) (1978), *Thomas Hardy: Selected Poems* (Harmondsworth: Penguin, 'The Penguin Poetry Library', 1978, 1986).

Zeitlow, Paul (1974), *Moments of Vision: The Poetry of Thomas Hardy* (Cambridge, MA: Harvard University Press).

Index of Proper Names